MENTAL HEALTH

in
Schools

Engaging Learners, Preventing Problems, and Improving Schools

HOWARD S. ADELMAN   **LINDA TAYLOR**

Skyhorse Publishing

Skyhorse Publishing books may be purchased in bulk at special discounts for sales promotion, corporate gifts, fund-raising, or educational purposes. Special editions can also be created to specifications. For details, contact the Special Sales Department, Skyhorse Publishing, 307 West 36th Street, 11th Floor, New York, NY 10018 or info@skyhorsepublishing.com.

Skyhorse® and Skyhorse Publishing® are registered trademarks of Skyhorse Publishing, Inc.®, a Delaware corporation.

Visit our website at www.skyhorsepublishing.com.

10 9 8 7 6 5 4 3 2

CIP DATA

Library of Congress Cataloging-in-Publication Data

Adelman, Howard S.
  Mental health in schools : engaging learners, preventing problems, and improving schools / Howard S. Adelman, Inda Taylor.
    pages cm
  Includes bibliographical references and index.
  ISBN 978-1-63450-306-8 (pbk. : alk. paper) 1. School children--Mental health services--United States 2. School psychology--United States. I. Taylor, Linda (Linda L.) II. Title.
  LB3430.A34 2015
  371.7'13--dc23
                                    2015024130

Acquisitions Editor: Jessica Allan
Editorial Assistant: Joanna Coelho
Production Editor: Cassandra Margaret Seibel
Copy Editor: Jeannette McCoy
Typesetter: C&M Digitals (P) Ltd.
Proofreader: Taryn Bigelow
Indexer: Jean Casalegno

Cover design by Michael Dubowe

Print ISBN: 978-1-63450-306-8
Ebook ISBN: 978-1-5107-0102-1

Printed in the United States of America

Contents

Preface

This book is about improving schools, preventing problems, and engaging students *by moving in new directions for mental health in schools*. This ambitious agenda requires the attention of all who have a stake in public education. Therefore, our intended audience is quite broad (e.g., leaders, administrators, student support staff, teachers, other practitioners, researchers, those involved in personnel preparation, and policy makers).

Many matters arise when the topic of mental health in schools is discussed. Prominent are questions such as the following:

Why should schools be involved with mental health?
Should the focus of mental health in schools be on

- mental *illness?* mental *health? both?*
- special education students or all students? or
- services or programs or a comprehensive system of supports?

What is the *context* for the work, and who should be *responsible* for its planning, implementation, and evaluation?

We explore all this and much more with a view to moving in new directions.

Over the years, we have pursued the advancement of mental health in schools by focusing on fully integrating the matter into school improvement policy, planning, and practice. Since 1986, our work has been carried out under the auspices of the School Mental Health Project at UCLA, and since 1995, our efforts have been embedded in the Project's national Center for Mental Health in Schools.

One facet of the Center's work is designed to facilitate discussion of issues, write and share policy and practice analyses and recommendations, and develop prototypes for new directions. Another facet provides guides to and resources for practice.

The following is a book-length compilation that pulls together our work over many years. It complements our two books published by Corwin in 2006: (1) *The School Leader's Guide to Student Learning Supports: New Directions for Addressing Barriers to Learning* and (2) *The Implementation Guide to Student Learning Supports in the Classroom and Schoolwide: New Directions for Addressing Barriers to Learning.* Readers who want to drill deeper into the many topics covered in this book can turn to these and to the growing body of resources available at no cost on the UCLA Center's Web site (http://smhp.psych.ucla.edu).

Because of the urgency for creating a school environment that promotes mental health and reduces problems, our primary aim here is to stimulate major systemic transformation. To this end, we stress new directions and resources for systemic change. At the same time, we highlight resources to aid those who currently are striving each day to make lives better for students and school staff.

We begin with a brief reflection on what schools have been and are doing about mental health concerns. Then, we explore major concerns, emerging trends, new directions, policy and systemic change implications, and end with a call to action. While we identify system deficiencies, we have nothing but the highest respect for those professionals who strive each day to ensure that all students have an equal opportunity to succeed at school.

As always, we owe many folks for the contents of this book. We thank everyone for their contribution, and as always, we take full responsibility for any misinterpretations and errors.

Howard Adelman and Linda Taylor

DEDICATION

To those trailblazers who are moving the field forward.

Acknowledgments

N o one will doubt that our work owes much to many. We have benefited from the insights, challenges, and wisdom of so many colleagues and the shared treasure of the accumulated research and writing of scholars over the years.

We are especially indebted to those pioneers who are trailblazing new directions forward.

And we are oh so grateful to Perry Nelson and the host of graduate and undergraduate students at UCLA who contribute so much to our work each day, and we thank the many young people and their families who continue to teach us all.

We also want to acknowledge that partial support for the Center for Mental Health in Schools comes from the Office of Adolescent Health, Maternal and Child Health Bureau (Title V, Social Security Act), Health Resources and Services Administration (Project #U45 MC 00175), U.S. Department of Health and Human Services.

PUBLISHER'S ACKNOWLEDGMENTS

The publisher gratefully acknowledges the following peer reviewers for their editorial insight and guidance:

Pamela Frazier-Anderson, PhD
Program Evaluator (Education
  Programs)
Trained and Nationally Certified School
  Psychologist and Consultant
Norwalk, CT

Lyman Goding
Lecturer, Bridgewater State College
Retired Principal, Plymouth (MA)
  Community Intermediate School
Bridgewater, MA

Diana Joyce, PhD, NCSP
Psychologist
University of Florida
Gainesville, FL

Marian White-Hood
Director of Academics, Accountability,
  and Principal Support
See Forever Foundation
Washington, DC

About the Authors

 **Howard S. Adelman, PhD** is professor of psychology and codirector of the School Mental Health Project and its federally supported national Center for Mental Health in Schools at UCLA. **Linda Taylor, PhD** is codirector of the School Mental Health Project and its federally supported national Center for Mental Health in Schools at UCLA.

The two have worked together for over 30 years with a constant focus on improving how schools and communities address a wide range of psychosocial and educational problems experienced by children and adolescents.

Howard began his professional career as a remedial classroom teacher in 1960. In 1973, he returned to UCLA in the role of professor of psychology and also was the director of the Fernald Laboratory School and Clinic until 1986. In 1986, Linda and he established the School Mental Health Project at UCLA.

In her early career, Linda was involved in community agency work. From 1973 to 1986, she codirected the Fernald Laboratory School and Clinic at UCLA. In 1986, she became codirector of the School Mental Health Project. From 1986 to 2000, she also held a clinical psychologist position in the Los Angeles Unified School District and directed several large-scale projects for the school district.

Over the years, they have worked together on major projects focused on dropout prevention, enhancing the mental health facets of school-based health centers, and developing comprehensive, school-based approaches for students with learning, behavior, and emotional problems. Their work has involved them in schools and communities across the country.

The current focus of their work is on policies, practices, and large-scale systemic reform initiatives to enhance school, community, and family connections to address barriers to learning and promote healthy development. This work includes codirecting the national Center for Mental Health in Schools, which facilitates the *National Initiative: New Directions for Student Support.*

Introduction

Growing numbers of children are suffering needlessly because their emotional, behavioral, and developmental needs are not being met by the very institutions and systems that were created to take care of them.

—U.S. Department of Health and Human Services (2001)

One of those institutions is the school. Indeed, available research suggests that for some youngsters schools already are the main providers of mental health services. As Burns and her colleagues (1995) found, "the major player in the de facto system of care was the education sector—more than three-fourths of children receiving mental health services were seen in the education sector, and for many this was the sole source of care" (p. 152).

WHY MENTAL HEALTH IN SCHOOLS?

In discussing the involvement of schools in mental health, the first question that arises is, "Why should there be a focus on mental health *in schools?*"

While many societal considerations are involved in responding to this question, for the most part the usual answers incorporate either or both of the following points:

- Accessing and meeting the needs of students (and their families) who require mental health services is facilitated at schools
- Addressing psychosocial and mental and physical health concerns is essential to the effective school performance of students

Implied in both answers is the hope of enhancing the nature and scope of mental health interventions to fill gaps, enhance effectiveness, address problems early, reduce stigma, and fully imbue clinical and service efforts with public health, general education, and equity orientations.

Point one typically reflects the perspective and agenda of agencies and advocates whose mission is to improve mental health services. The second point reflects the perspective and agenda of student support professionals and some leaders for school improvement and also provides a supportive rationale for those who want schools to play a greater role related to addressing young people's health concerns.

ADVANCING MENTAL HEALTH IN SCHOOLS

Around the world, many stakeholders are determined to enhance how schools address mental health and psychosocial concerns. And now is a critical period for doing so.

Anyone who has spent time in schools can itemize the multifaceted mental health and psychosocial concerns that warrant attention. For those committed to advancing mental health in schools, the question is,

How should our society's schools address these matters?

The answers put forward tend to reflect different agenda. As a result, efforts to advance the imperative for mental health in schools are confronted with the problem of coalescing agenda and doing so in ways that are responsive to the oft-voiced public concern that schools cannot be responsible for meeting every need of their students.

Education is the mission of schools, and school policy makers are quick to point this out when schools are asked to do more, especially with respect to mental health. They do not disagree with the idea that healthier students learn and perform better. The problem is that prevailing school accountability pressures increasingly have concentrated on instructional practices—to the detriment of all matters not seen as *directly* related to raising achievement test scores.

Those concerned with enhancing mental health in schools must accept the reality that schools are not in the mental health business. Then, they must develop an understanding of what is involved in achieving the mission of schools. After that, they must be ready to clarify how any agenda item for mental health in schools helps accomplish that mission. Of particular importance is how proposed approaches help meet the demand for improving schools, reducing dropout rates, closing the achievement gap, and addressing racial, ethnic, disability, and socioeconomic disparities.

EMBEDDING MENTAL HEALTH
IN THE SCHOOL IMPROVEMENT AGENDA

In 2001, the Policy Leadership Cadre for Mental Health in Schools stressed that advancing mental health in schools is about much more than expanding services and creating full-service schools. The aim is to become part of a comprehensive, multifaceted, systemic approach that strengthens students, families, schools, and neighborhoods and does so in ways that maximizes learning, caring, and well-being.

To this end, policy decision makers and school improvement leaders must transform the education support programs and services that schools own and operate. Such a transformation must draw on well-conceived, broad frameworks and the best available information and scholarship to develop a comprehensive system of supports for addressing problems and enhancing healthy development. Accomplishing this will require weaving together resources from the school, community, and family.

BUILDING ON WHAT HAS GONE BEFORE

Advancing a field requires a perspective on the past and the present. Therefore, Part I offers a brief reflection on what schools have been and are doing about matters related to mental health and then highlights some basic considerations as a foundation for moving forward.

Advancing this field requires a perspective on major concerns and issues that have arisen about the focus on mental health in schools. Part II highlights such matters.

Advancing the enterprise requires a sense of current and emerging opportunities and new strategies for moving forward in developing a comprehensive system that is implemented in the classroom and schoolwide. This is the focus of Part III.

Advancing any field requires rethinking policy and facilitating systemic change. Part IV outlines some major policy and systemic change considerations.

PART I

The Field of Mental Health in Schools

To paraphrase Goethe: Not moving forward is a step backward.

In many schools, the need for enhancing mental health is a common topic. And as recognized by the final report of the President's New Freedom Commission on Mental Health (2003) and *The 2007 Progress Report* on the President's New Freedom Initiative, efforts to enhance interventions for children's mental health must involve schools. Thus, many of those interested in improving education and those concerned about transforming the mental health system in the United States of America and elsewhere are taking a new look at schools (Adelman & Taylor, 2008, 2009; Center for Mental Health in Schools, 2004c; Kutash, Duchnowski, & Lynn, 2006; O'Connell, Boat, & Warner, 2009).

However, while mental health in schools is widely discussed, what's being talked about often differs in fundamental ways. Various agenda are pursued. Divergent policy, practice, research, and training agenda emerge. The result is confusion and conflict. This all adds to the continuing marginalization of efforts to advance mental health in schools (Taylor & Adelman, 2002).

In spite of or perhaps because of the multiple agenda, mental health in schools is an emerging new field. This reality is reflected in federally funded national centers focused on policy and program analyses; published books, reports, and scholarly journals; and university research and training programs. In addition, organizations and centers that have relevance for a school's focus on mental health and psychosocial concerns continue to burgeon. These include a variety of

1

technical assistance, training, and resource centers (see *Gateway to a World of Resources for Enhancing MH in Schools*—available at http://smhp.psych.ucla.edu/gateway/gateway_sites.htm).

As we explore ways to advance the field, a brief overview of its past and present will provide a logical jumping off place and a good foundation for moving forward.

1

Mental Health in Schools

Past and Present

A variety of psychosocial and health problems have long been acknowledged as affecting learning and performance in profound ways. Moreover, behavior, learning, and emotional problems are exacerbated as youngsters internalize the debilitating effects of performing poorly at school and are punished for the misbehavior that is a common correlate of school failure.

Efforts to address mental health concerns in schools are not new. What's new is the emergence of the *field* of mental health in schools. We begin by highlighting some of what has transpired over the last 60 years.

PAST AS PROLOGUE

Because of the obvious need, school policy makers have a lengthy, if somewhat reluctant, history of trying to assist teachers in dealing with problems that interfere with schooling. Prominent examples are seen in the range of health, social service, counseling, and psychological programs schools have provided from the end of the 19th century through today (Baumgartner, 1946; Christner & Mennuti, 2009; Dryfoos, 1994; Flaherty, Weist, & Warner, 1996; Tyack, 1992).

One interesting policy benchmark appeared in the middle of the 20th century when the National Institute of Mental Health (NIMH) increased the focus on mental health in schools by publishing a monograph on the topic (Lambert, Bower, & Caplan, 1964). Since then, many initiatives and a variety of agenda have emerged. Included are efforts to expand clinical services in schools, develop new programs for *at risk* groups, and incorporate programs for the prevention of problems and the promotion of social-emotional development (Adelman & Taylor, 1994; Califano, 1977; Collaboration for Academic, Social, and Emotional Learning, 2003; Dryfoos, 1994; Knitzer, Steinberg, & Fleisch, 1990; Millstein, 1988; Steiner, 1976; Stroul & Friedman, 1986; Weist & Murray, 2007).

Bringing Health and Social Services to Schools

Over the past 20 years, a renewed emphasis in the health and social services sectors on enhancing access to clients led to increased linkages between schools and community service agencies, including colocation of services on school sites (Center for the Future of Children, 1992; Warren, 2005). This *school-linked services* movement added impetus to advocacy for mental health in schools. It promoted school-based health centers, school-based family resource centers, wellness centers, afterschool programs, and other efforts to connect community resources to the schools.

Many advocates for school-linked services coalesced their efforts with those working to enhance initiatives for youth development, community schools, and the preparation of healthy and productive citizens and workers (Blank, Berg, & Melaville, 2006). These coalitions expanded interest in social-emotional learning and protective factors as ways to increase students' assets and resiliency and reduce risk factors (Greenberg et al., 2003; Hawkins, Kosterman, Catalano, Hill, & Abbott, 2008). However, the amount of actual mental health activity in schools generated by these efforts remains relatively circumscribed (Foster et al., 2005; Teich, Robinson, & Weist, 2007).

Federal Support for the *Field* of Mental Health in Schools

In 1995, a direct effort to advance mental health in schools was initiated by the U.S. Department of Health and Human Services through its Health Resources and Services Administration (HRSA), Maternal and Child Health Bureau, Office of Adolescent Health (Anglin, 2003). The purpose of the initiative is to enhance the role schools play in mental health for children and adolescents. Specifically, the emphasis is on increasing the capacity of policy makers, administrators, school personnel, primary care health providers, mental health specialists, agency staff, consumers, and other stakeholders so that they can enhance how schools and their communities address psychosocial and mental health concerns. Particular attention is given to mental health promotion, prevention, and responding early after the onset of problems as critical facets of reducing the prevalence of problems and enhancing well-being.

The core of the work has been embedded in two national centers. The two, which were initially funded in 1995 with a primary emphasis on technical assistance and training, successfully reapplied during the 2000 open competition. A third open competition for a five-year funding cycle was offered in 2005 with an increasing emphasis on policy and program analyses to inform policy, practice, research, and training. Again, the initially funded centers applied and were successful in the process. The two centers are the Center for Mental Health in Schools at UCLA and the Center for School Mental Health at the University of Maryland, Baltimore. (It should be noted from 2000 through 2006, HRSA and the Substance Abuse and Mental Health Services Administration [SAMHSA] braided resources to jointly support the initiative.)

Other federal initiatives promote mental health in schools through a smattering of projects and initiatives. These include (1) programs supported by the U.S. Department of Education's Office of Safe and Drug-Free Schools (including a grants program for the Integration of Schools and Mental Health Systems), its Office of Special Education and Rehabilitative Services, and some of the school improvement initiatives under the No Child Left Behind Act; (2) the Safe Schools/Healthy Students initiative, which is jointly sponsored by SAMHSA and the U.S. Departments of Education and Justice; (3) components of the Centers for Disease Control and Prevention's Coordinated School Health Program; and (4) various projects funded through SAMHSA's Elimination of Barriers Initiative and Mental Health Transformation State Incentive Grant Program. Several other federal agencies support a few projects that fit agenda for mental health in schools. All of the above have helped the field emerge; none of the federal programs are intended to underwrite the field. Government-funded projects are time limited and affected by economic downturns.

In recent years, a growing number of states have funded projects and initiatives, and a few have passed legislation with varying agenda related to mental health in schools. A variety of public and private entities also support projects that contribute to the emerging field.

Other countries are moving forward as well. The growing interest around the world is reflected in the establishment in the early 2000s of the International Alliance for Child and Adolescent Mental Health and Schools, which has members in 30 countries (Weist & Murray, 2007).

Call for Collaboration

Few doubt the need for collaboration. Over the years, those with a stake in mental health in schools frequently have called for joining forces (Center for Mental Health in Schools, 2002; Rappaport, Osher, Garrison, Anderson-Ketchmark, & Dwyer, 2003; Taylor & Adelman, 1996). Building bridges across groups, however, is complex and requires a long-term commitment. We discuss this matter in detail in Chapter 13.

One contemporary effort began in 2000 when the National Association of State Mental Health Program Directors and the Policymaker Partnership at the National Association of State Directors of Special Education (2002) met to explore how the two entities could collaborate to promote closer working relations between state mental health and education agencies, schools and family organizations. A concept paper entitled "Mental Health, Schools and Families Working Together for All Children and Youth: Toward a Shared Agenda" was produced with funds from the Office of Special Education Programs. The paper was designed to encourage state and local family and youth organizations, mental health agencies, education entities, and schools across the nation to enter new relationships to achieve positive social, emotional, and educational outcomes for every child. The vision presented is for schools, families, child-serving agencies, and the broader community to work collaboratively to promote opportunities for and to address barriers to healthy social and emotional development and learning. The aim is to align systems and ensure the promise of a comprehensive, highly effective system for children and youth and their families. In stating the need for agencies and schools to work together, the report stresses the following:

> While sharing many values and overarching goals, each agency has developed its own organizational culture, which includes a way of looking at the world; a complex set of laws, regulations and policies; exclusive jargon; and a confusing list of alphabet-soup acronyms. Funding sources at the federal, state, and local levels have traditionally reinforced this separation into *silos*. The result is that agencies are almost totally isolated entities—each with its own research and technical assistance components and its own service delivery system, even though they are serving many of the same children. The isolation of each agency, combined with its bureaucratic complexity, requires a long-term commitment of all partners to bridge the gaps between them. Collaborative structures must be based on a shared vision and a set of agreed upon functions designed to enable a shared agenda. Legislative, regulatory or policy mandates may help bring agency representatives to the table, but development of true partnerships and the successful accomplishment of goals depends on participants gaining trust in one another as they pursue a shared agenda. (pp. 16–17)

The Policymaker Partnership provided some funds for six states to form state-based Communities of Practice for Education, Mental Health, and Family Organizations. When the funding for the Policymaker Partnership ended, the *Individuals with Disabilities Education Act (IDEA) Partnership* (funded by the U.S. Department of Education's Office of Special Education Programs) has continued to facilitate the Communities of Practice initiative (IDEA Partnership, 2005).

School Professionals Have Led the Way

Historical accounts stress that schools have used their resources to hire a substantial body of student support professionals—variously called support staff, pupil personnel professionals, and specialists. Current status data are available from the *School Health Policies and Program Study* (Brener, Weist, Adelman, Taylor, & Vernon-Smiley, 2007; Centers for Disease Control and Prevention, 2007). This study, conducted by a unit of the Centers for Disease Control and Prevention (CDC), collected data from 51 state departments of education, 538 school districts, and 1,103 schools. Findings indicate that 56% of states and 73% of districts had a policy stating that student assistance programs would be offered to all students, but only 57% of schools offered such programs. Findings for specialist support staff indicate that 78% of schools had a part- or full-time counselor, 61% had a part- or full-time school psychologist, 42% had a part- or full-time social worker, 36% had a full-time school nurse, and an additional 51% had a part-time nurse. Considerable variation, of course, exists state by state.

While the numbers fluctuate, professionals employed by school districts continue to carry out most of the activity related to mental health in schools (Adelman & Taylor, 2006c; Carlson, Paavola, & Talley, 1995; Teich, Robinson, & Weist, 2007). As a result, they are the core around which programs have emerged.

DATA ON NEED

Available data underscore an urgent need. Data cited on diagnosable mental disorders generally suggest that from 12% to 22% of all youngsters under age 18 need services for mental, emotional, or behavioral problems. These figures are cited in the Surgeon General's 1999 mental health report (U.S. Department of Health and Human Services, 1999). Referring to ages 9 to 17, the document states that 21% or "one in five children and adolescents experiences the signs and symptoms of a *DSM-IV* disorder during the course of a year" (p. 123)—with 11% of all children experiencing significant impairment and about 5% experiencing "extreme functional impairment" (p. 124). Similar data are noted in the Centers for Disease Control and Prevention's Youth Risk Behavior Surveys, in a 2004 report from the Annenberg Public Policy Center (see Exhibit 1), and in preliminary data from the 2005 National Health Interview Survey (Simpson, Cohen, Pastor, & Reuben, 2006).

Exhibit 1 Some Data on Students' Mental Health

From April 5, 2004, to May 28, 2004, the Annenberg Public Policy Center surveyed over 1,400 public school professionals as part of the Annenberg Foundation Trust at Sunnylands' Initiative on Adolescent Mental Health. The focus was on how schools provide treatment and counseling for students.

Survey findings indicate that the respondents view high school student depression and use of alcohol and illegal drugs as even more serious problems than various forms of violence, including bullying, fighting, and use of weapons. More than two-thirds (68%) of the high school professionals

(Continued)

(Continued)

surveyed identified depression as a great (14%) or moderate (54%) problem in their schools. Similar overall levels of concern were raised about use of alcohol (71%) and illegal drugs (72%). In contrast, 54% of high school professionals identified bullying as a great (11%) or moderate (43%) problem. Even lower levels of concern were expressed about fighting between students (37%) and weapon carrying (6%) at the high school level. Other concerns cited were anxiety disorders (42%), eating disorders (22%), and various forms of self-harm such as cutting (26%).

Unlike their counterparts in high schools, middle school professionals are more concerned about interpersonal conflict. Although high proportions of middle school professionals identify depression (57%) and use of alcohol (28%) and illegal drugs (37%) as at least moderate problems, bullying is seen as a problem by 82% of professionals and fighting by 57% of professionals in middle schools. Weapon carrying remains a concern among only 5% of professionals.

Although 66% of the high schools indicated having a process for *referring* students with mental health conditions to appropriate providers of care, only 34% reported having a clearly defined and coordinated process for identifying such students. Comparable findings come from the middle schools; however, 42% of professionals reported having a clearly defined process identifying students with mental conditions. Only about 3% of the high schools indicated use of universal screening. An additional 5% claim to screen most of their students.

Asked what percentage of their students in need of counseling or treatment actually receive such services, only 7% of high school professionals said that all do and only 31% said that most do. The majority indicated that only half or fewer received the services they need. When asked the same question about receiving services on site at their school, the percentages were even lower—6% said all do and 22% said most do. Only 24% of school professionals say their high schools have counseling available for students with alcohol or drug dependence problems.

SOURCE: Reported by the Annenberg Public Policy Center. http://www.sunnylandstrust.org/

The picture worsens when one expands the focus beyond the limited perspective on diagnosable mental disorders. Think in terms of all the young people experiencing psychosocial problems and who are "at risk of not maturing into responsible adults" (Dryfoos, 1990, p. 4). Many reports explore the situation from this broader perspective (Centers for Disease Control and Prevention, 2005; Forum on Child and Family Statistics, 2007; Greenberg, Domitrovich, & Bumbarger, 1999; Institute of Medicine, 1994; NIMH, 1993, 1998; also see fact sheets and reports on the Web sites for SAMHSA's Center for Mental Health Services and USDOE's Safe and Drug-Free Schools Program).

Demographic policy estimates suggest that 40% of young people are in bad educational shape and therefore will fail to fulfill their promise (Hodgkinson, 2008). For many large, urban schools, the reality is that well over 50% of their students manifest significant behavior, learning, and emotional problems (Center for Mental Health in Schools, 2003b). For a large proportion of these youngsters, the problems are rooted in the restricted opportunities and difficult living conditions associated with poverty. Almost every current policy discussion stresses the crisis nature of child poverty in terms of future health and economic implications for individuals and society; the consistent call is for fundamental systemic reforms.

UNDERSTANDING THE CONCEPT OF *MENTAL HEALTH* IN SCHOOLS

Mental health is recognized widely as a fundamental and compelling societal concern. The relationship between health and mental health problems is well established. From both the perspective of promoting positive well-being and minimizing the scope of mental health and other health problems, school professionals clearly have an important role to play. The matter is well-underscored when one appreciates the full meaning of the concept of mental *health* and the full range of factors that lead to mental health problems.

Mental *Health* or Mental *Illness?*

The trend toward overusing psychiatric labels reflects the tendency to reduce mental health to mental illness, disorders, or problems. Many people hear the term *mental health,* and they think mental *illness.* When this occurs, mental *health* is defined, de facto, as the absence of problems. This trend ignores the facts: (1) the behavior, learning, and emotional problems experienced by most youngsters stem from sociocultural and economic factors not from psychopathology, and (2) such problems often can be countered through promotion of social and emotional development and preventive interventions.

To address the definitional problem, the following guides are helpful:

- The report of the Surgeon General's Conference on Children's Mental Health (U.S. Department of Health and Human Services, 2001) offers the following vision statement: "Both the promotion of mental health in children and the treatment of mental disorders should be major public health goals." This view is consistent with efforts to define mental health as a positive concept.
- The Institute of Medicine (1994) defines health as a "state of well-being and the capability to function in the face of changing circumstance."
- A similar effort to contrast positive health with problem functioning is seen in SAMHSA's Center for Mental Health Services glossary of children's mental health terms. Mental health is defined as "how a person thinks, feels, and acts when faced with life's situations. . . . This includes handling stress, relating to other people, and making decisions." SAMHSA contrasts this with mental health problems. And the designation *mental disorder* is described as another term used for mental health problems. (They reserve the term *mental illness* for severe mental health problems in adults.)
- Finally, note that the World Health Organization (2004) also stresses that mental health is "a state of well-being in which the individual realizes his or her abilities, can cope with the normal stresses of life, can work productively and fruitfully, and is able to make a contribution to his or her community."

A more recent effort to emphasize mental *health* is found in *Bright Futures in Practice: Mental Health* (National Center for Education in Maternal and Child Health, 2002) that states,

Mentally healthy children and adolescents develop the ability to experience a range of emotions (including joy, connectedness, sadness, and anger) in appropriate and constructive ways; possess positive self-esteem and a respect for others; and harbor a deep sense of security and trust in themselves and the world. Mentally healthy children and adolescents are able to function in developmentally appropriate ways in the contexts of self, family, peers, school, and community. Building on a foundation of personal interaction and support, mentally healthy children and adolescents develop the ability to initiate and maintain meaningful relationships (love) and learn to function productively in the world (work).

Concerns About Differential Diagnosis

Not surprisingly, debates about diagnostically labeling young people are heated. Differential *diagnosis* is a difficult process fraught with complex issues.

Concern arises about the tendency to view "everyday" emotional and behavioral problems as "symptoms," designate them as disorders, and assign them formal psychiatric diagnoses (Adelman, 1995a; Adelman & Taylor, 1994; Dryfoos, 1990). The prevailing comprehensive formal systems used to classify problems in human functioning convey the impression that all behavioral, emotional, or learning problems are instigated by internal pathology. This is well illustrated by the widely used *Diagnostic and Statistical Manual of Mental Disorders, Fourth Edition (DSM-IV)* (American Psychiatric Association, 1994). Some efforts to temper this trend frame pathology as a vulnerability that only becomes evident under stress. Most differential diagnoses of children's problems, however, are made by focusing on identifying one or more disorders (e.g., attention deficit hyperactivity disorder, oppositional defiant disorder, learning disorders, adjustment disorders), rather than first asking, *Is there a disorder?*

Problems experienced by the majority of children and adolescents are sociocultural and economic. This, of course, in no way denies that the primary factor instigating a problem may be an internal disorder. The point simply recognizes that, comparatively, youngsters whose problems stem from person pathology constitute a relatively small group (Center for Mental Health in Schools, 2003a).

Biases in definition that overemphasize person pathology narrow what is done to classify and assess problems. Comprehensive classification systems do not exist for environmentally caused problems or for psychosocial problems (caused by the transaction of internal and environmental factors).

The overemphasis on classifying problems in terms of personal pathology has skewed theory, research, practice, and public policy. The narrow focus has limited discussions of cause, diagnosis, and intervention strategies, especially efforts to prevent and intervene early after onset.

Efforts to address a wider range of variables in labeling problems are illustrated by multifaceted systems. An example is the *Classification of Child and Adolescent Mental Diagnoses in Primary Care: Diagnostic and Statistical Manual for Primary Care (DSM-PC)* published by the American Academy of Pediatrics (Wolraich, Felice, & Drotar, 1996). The work provides a broad template for understanding and categorizing behavior. For each major category, behaviors are described to illustrate what should be considered (1) a developmental variation, (2) a problem, and (3) a disorder. Information also is provided on the environmental situations and stressors that exacerbate the behavior and on commonly confused symptoms. The material is presented in a way that can be shared with families, so that they have a perspective with respect to concerns they or the school identifies.

Available evidence suggests increasing numbers of youngsters manifesting emotional upset, misbehavior, and learning problems routinely are assigned diagnostic labels denoting serious disorders (e.g., attention deficit hyperactivity disorder, depression, learning disabilities). The numbers fly in the face of the reality that the problems of *most* youngsters are not rooted in internal pathology. The likelihood is that many troubling symptoms would not develop under more favorable environmental conditions. Moreover, the trend to label so many diagnosable disorders leads to frequent misdiagnoses and inappropriate and expensive treatments. All this contaminates research and training (Lyon, 2002).

An increasing focus in policy and practice is on reducing misdiagnoses and misprescriptions. One emphasis is on placing mental illness in perspective with respect to psychosocial problems; another aim is to ensure mental health is understood as encompassing the promotion of social and emotional development and learning (Adelman, 1995a; Adelman & Taylor, 1994). Schools are being asked to play a major role in all this through strategies such as assessing "response to intervention" (RtI) prior to diagnosis (discussed in Part III).

Mental Health in Schools: A Broad Concept

Because mental health often is heard as mental *illness,* many people think *mental health in schools* is only about therapy and counseling. However, the reality is that the field is about much more than treating disorders and providing students with clinical services.

Mental health in schools aspires to do the following:

- Provide programs to (a) promote social-emotional development, (b) prevent mental health and psychosocial problems, and (c) enhance resiliency and protective buffers
- Provide programs and services to intervene as early after the onset of behavior, learning, and emotional problems as is feasible
- Enhance the mental health of families and school staff
- Build the capacity of all school staff to address barriers to learning and promote healthy development
- Address systemic matters at schools that affect mental health, such as high stakes testing, including exit exams, and other practices that engender bullying, alienation, and student disengagement from classroom learning
- Develop a comprehensive, multifaceted, and cohesive continuum of school-community interventions to address barriers to learning and promote healthy development

CURRENT STATE OF AFFAIRS

The current state of affairs related to mental health in schools is discussed mostly in terms of services and programs. For example, Exhibit 2 provides a summary of findings excerpted from the first national survey of school mental health services (Foster et al., 2005). The sample was representative of public schools across the United States, and the data amplify and support previous findings, including those discussed above.

Exhibit 2   Some Baseline Data on School Mental Health Services

As reported in *School Mental Health Services in the United States, 2002–2003* (Foster et al., 2005), the survey topics included types of mental health problems encountered in school settings; types of mental health services that schools are delivering; numbers and qualifications of school staff providing mental health services; types of arrangements for delivering mental health services in schools, including collaboration with community-based providers; and major sources of funding for school MH services.

Key Findings as Reported in the Executive Summary

- Nearly three-quarters (73%) of the schools reported that "social, interpersonal, or family problems" were the most frequent mental health problems for both male and female students.
- For males, aggression or disruptive behavior and behavior problems associated with neurological disorders were the second and third most frequent problems.
- For females, anxiety and adjustment issues were the second and third most frequent problems.
- All students, not just those in special education, were eligible to receive mental health services in the vast majority of schools (87%).
- One-fifth of students on average received some type of school-supported mental health services in the school year prior to the study.
- Virtually all schools reported having at least one staff member whose responsibilities included providing mental health services to students.
- The most common types of school mental health providers were school counselors followed by nurses, school psychologists, and social workers. School nurses spent approximately a third of their time providing mental health services.
- More than 80% of schools provided assessment for mental health problems, behavior management consultation, and crisis intervention, as well as referrals to specialized programs.
- A majority also provided individual and group counseling and case management.
- Financial constraints of families and inadequate school mental health resources were the most frequently cited barriers to providing mental health services.
- Almost half of school districts (49%) used contracts or other formal agreements with community-based individuals and/or organizations to provide mental health services to students. The most frequently reported community-based provider type was county mental health agencies.
- Districts reported that the most common funding sources for mental health services or interventions were the Individuals with Disabilities Education Act (IDEA), state special education funds, and local funds. In 28% of districts, Medicaid was among the top five funding sources for mental health services.

(Continued)

(Continued)

- One-third of districts reported that funding for mental health services had decreased since the beginning of the 2000–2001 school year, while over two-thirds of districts reported that the need for mental health services increased.
- Sixty percent of districts reported that since the previous year, referrals to community-based providers had increased. One-third reported that the availability of outside providers to deliver services to students had decreased.

While survey findings indicate that schools are responding to the mental health needs of their students, they also suggest increasing needs for mental health services and the multiple challenges faced by schools in addressing these needs. Furthermore, more research is needed to explore issues identified by this study, including training of school staff delivering mental health services, adequacy of funding, and effectiveness of specific services delivered in the school setting.

SOURCE: Foster et al., 2005, pp. 1–2.

Another example comes from a national survey by the Substance Abuse and Mental Health Services Administration (SAMHSA, 2008). The report indicates that for youth 12 to 17 years of age, the combined 2005 and 2006 data show an annual average of 3.0 million youths (12.0%) received services for emotional or behavioral problems in a school-based setting. In contrast, 3.3 million youths (13.3%) received services for emotional or behavioral problems in a specialty mental health setting and around 752,000 (3.0%) received such services in a general medical setting. Females were more likely than their male counterparts to receive services in a specialty mental health or educational setting.

Cataloging services and their use certainly is necessary. However, a deeper understanding requires appreciation of the diverse agenda stakeholders bring to the field, the funding situation, and current policy and practice.

Diverse Agenda for Mental Health in Schools

Different stakeholders are pursing different and sometimes conflicting agenda. Analyses of the contrasting enterprises pursued under the banner of mental health in schools find seven different agenda concerned in varying degrees with policy, practice, research, and/or training. In Exhibit 3, the agenda are grouped and subdivided in terms of the *primary* vested interests of various parties. While some agenda are complementary, some are not.

Exhibit 3 Diverse Agenda for Mental Health in Schools

1. Efforts to use schools to increase *access* to kids and their families for purposes of

   a. conducting research related to mental health concerns
   b. providing services related to mental health

2. Efforts to increase *availability* of mental health interventions

   a. through expanded use of school resources
   b. through colocating community resources on school campuses
   c. through finding ways to combine school and community resources

3. Efforts to get schools to adopt and/or enhance specific programs and approaches

   a. for treating specific individuals
   b. for addressing specific types of problems in targeted ways
   c. for addressing problems through schoolwide, *universal* interventions
   d. for promoting healthy social and emotional development

4. Efforts to *improve specific processes and interventions* related to mental health in schools (e.g., improve systems for identifying and referring problems and for case management, enhancing *prereferral* and early intervention programs)

5. Efforts to enhance the *economic interests* of various entities (e.g., specific disciplines, guilds, contractors, businesses, organizations) that are

   a. already part of school budgets
   b. seeking to be part of school budgets

6. *Efforts to change how student supports are conceived* at schools (e.g., rethink, reframe, reform, restructure) through

   a. enhanced focus on multidisciplinary teamwork (e.g. among school staff, with community professionals)
   b. enhanced coordination of interventions (e.g., among school programs and services, with community programs and services)
   c. appropriate integration of interventions (e.g., that schools own, that communities base or link with schools)
   d. modifying the roles and functions of various student support staff
   e. developing a comprehensive, multifaceted, and cohesive component for systematically addressing barriers to student learning at every school

7. Efforts to *reduce school involvement* in mental health programs and services (e.g., to maximize the focus on instruction, to use the resources for youth development, to keep the school out of areas where family values are involved)

Given the diverse agenda, competing interests often come into conflict with each other. For example, those concerned with nurturing positive youth development and mental health and those focusing on the treatment of mental and behavioral disorders often find themselves in counter-productive competition for sparse school time and resources. This contributes to the low priority and the backlash to efforts to enhance policy and practice for mental health in schools.

Over the years, our center at UCLA has pursued a broad agenda for advancing mental health in schools. We emphasize (1) embedding the work into every school's need to address barriers to learning and teaching and promote healthy development and (2) fully integrating the agenda into school improvement policy and practice. We stress that the agenda encompasses enhancing greater family and community involvement in education. And it requires a fundamental shift in thinking about what motivates students, staff, and other school stakeholders.

In the absence of a broad agenda, mental health in schools commonly is viewed as concerned mainly with providing interventions for a relatively few of the many students who need some form of help. Efforts to promote social and emotional health and prevent problems are sparse. Diverse agenda have created counter-productive competition for sparse funds. Ad hoc policy and categorical funding have created a fragmented and piecemeal enterprise.

Funding

Inadequate data are available on how much schools spend to address behavior, emotional, and learning problems. Exhibit 4 provides a bit of a perspective.

Exhibit 4   What Is Spent in Schools?

As reported by the National Center for Educational Statistics (2008), data for fiscal year (FY) 2006 indicate that approximately $520.6 billion was collected in revenues for public elementary and secondary education in the 50 states and the District of Columbia. "The greatest percentage of revenues came from state and local governments, which together provided $473.1 billion, or 90.9% of all revenues; the federal government's contribution was $47.6 billion, or 9.1% of all revenues."

"Current expenditures" totaled $449.6 billion. These include those for "day-to-day operation of schools and school districts (salaries, benefits, supplies, and purchased services) for public elementary and secondary education." They exclude expenditures for construction, equipment, property, debt services, and programs outside of public elementary and secondary education such as adult education and community services.

Current expenditures per pupil for public elementary and secondary education were $9,154. Adjusting for inflation, current expenditures per pupil have grown 25.1% since FY 1995 ($7,315) and 51.0% since FY 1985 ($6,062). In FY 2006, $274.2 billion was spent on instruction. This includes spending on salaries and benefits for teachers and teacher aides, classroom supplies and services, and extracurricular and cocurricular activities.

Looking at per pupil current expenditures for public elementary and secondary education, instruction expenditures ranged from $10,109 in New York to $3,453 in Utah. Instruction accounted for 61.0% of all current expenditures for public elementary and secondary education. Total support services accounted for 34.9%, food services accounted for 3.8%, and enterprise operations made up 0.2% of total current expenditures.

Breaking all this down to clarify what goes for regular student and learning supports and special education is not easy.

In 1997, Monk, Pijanowski, and Hussain reported that 6.7% of school spending is used for student support services such as counseling, psychological services, speech therapy, health services, and diagnostic and related special services for students with disabilities. The amount specifically devoted to learning, behavior, and emotional problems is unclear.

But note that these figures do not include costs related to time spent on such matters by other school staff such as teachers and administrators. Also not included are expenditures related to initiatives such as safe and drug-free school programs and arrangements such as alternative and continuation schools and funding for school-based health, family, and parent centers, and much more.

Federal government figures indicate that total spending to educate all students with disabilities found eligible for special education programs was $78.3 billion (U.S. Department of Education, 2005). About $50 billion was spent on special education services; another $27.3 billion was expended on regular education services for students with disabilities eligible for special education; and an additional $1 billion was spent on other special needs programs (e.g., Title I, English language learners, or gifted and talented education). Estimates in many school districts indicate that about 20% of the budget is consumed by special education. How much is used directly for efforts to address learning, behavior, and emotional problems is unknown, but remember that over 50% of those in special education are diagnosed as learning disabled and over 8% are labeled emotionally and/or behaviorally disturbed.

Focusing only on pupil service personnel salaries in calculating how much schools spend on addressing behavior, emotional, and learning problems probably is misleading and a major underestimation. This is particularly so for schools receiving special funding. Research needs to clarify the entire gamut of resources school sites devote to student problems. Budgets must be broken apart in ways that allow tallying all resources allocated from general funds, support provided for compensatory and special education, and underwriting related to programs for dropout prevention and recovery, safe and drug-free schools, pregnancy prevention, teen parents, health services, family literacy, homeless students, and more. In some schools receiving funds from multiple categorical funding streams, school administrators tell us that as much as 25% to 30% of the budget may be expended on problem prevention and correction.

As stressed by the Policy Leadership Cadre for Mental Health in Schools (2001):

> To date there has been no comprehensive mapping and no overall analysis of the amount of resources used for efforts relevant to mental health in schools or of how they are expended. Without such a *big picture* analysis, policy makers and practitioners are deprived of information that is essential to determining equity and enhancing system effectiveness.

Whatever the expenditures, few schools come close to having enough resources to deal with a large number of students with behavior, emotional, and learning problems. Moreover, the contexts for intervention often are limited and makeshift because of how current resources are allocated and used. A relatively small proportion of space at schools is earmarked specifically for programs that address student problems. Many special programs and related efforts to promote health and positive behavior are assigned space on an ad hoc basis. Support service personnel often must rotate among schools as *itinerant* staff. These conditions contribute to the tendency for such personnel to operate in relative isolation of each other and other stakeholders. To make matters worse, little systematic inservice development is provided for new *support* staff when they arrive from their preservice programs. Obviously, all this is not conducive to effective practice and is wasteful of sparse resources.

Clearly, diverse school and community resources are attempting to address complex and overlapping psychosocial and mental health concerns. The need is great. The current response is insufficient.

Nature of Current Practice and Policy

Data on schools, districts, and students in public schools are in a constant state of flux. Available data indicate over 90,000 public schools in about 15,000 districts enroll about 49 million students. Over the years, most—but obviously not all—schools have instituted policies and programs designed with a range of mental health and psychosocial concerns in mind.

Policies are in place to support school counseling, psychological, and social service programs and personnel and to connect community programs and personnel with schools. As a result, most schools have some interventions to address a range of mental health and psychosocial concerns, such as school adjustment and attendance problems, substance abuse, emotional problems, relationship difficulties, violence, physical and sexual abuse, delinquency, and dropouts. A large body of research supports the promise of much of this activity.[1]

Practices. School-based interventions relevant to mental health encompass a wide variety of practices, an array of resources, and many issues. However, as we have noted, addressing psychosocial and mental health concerns in schools typically is not assigned a high priority. Such matters gain stature for a while whenever a high visibility event occurs—a shooting on campus, a student suicide, an increase in bullying. Because of their usual humble status, efforts continue to be developed in an ad hoc, piecemeal, and highly marginalized way.

School-based and school-linked programs have been developed for purposes of early intervention, crisis intervention and prevention, treatment, and promotion of positive social and emotional development. Some programs are provided throughout a district, others are carried out at or linked to targeted schools. The interventions may be offered to all students in a school, to those in specified grades, or to those identified as *at risk*. The activities may be implemented in regular or special education classrooms or as out of classroom programs and may be designed for an entire class, groups, or individuals. A focus may also be on primary prevention and enhancement of healthy development through use of health education, health services, guidance, and so forth—though relatively few resources usually are allocated for such activity.

Exhibit 5 highlights the five major *delivery mechanisms and formats* used in schools to pursue the various agenda for mental health.

Exhibit 5   Delivery Mechanisms and Formats for Mental Health in Schools

The five mechanisms and related formats are as follows:

1. *School-Financed Student Support Services*—Most school districts employ pupil services professionals such as school psychologists, counselors, school nurses, and social workers to perform services related to mental health and psychosocial problems—including related services designated for special education students. The format for this delivery mechanism usually is a combination of centrally based and school-based services.

2. *School-District Mental Health Unit*—A few districts operate specific mental health units with clinics and school services and consultation. Some have started to finance their own school-based health centers with mental health services as a major element. The format for this mechanism has been a centralized unit with the capability for outreach to schools.

3. *Formal Connections With Community Mental Health Services*—Increasingly, schools have connected with community agencies, often as the result of the school-based health center movement, school-linked services initiatives (e.g., full-service schools, family resource centers), and efforts to develop systems of care (*wrap-around* services for those in special education). Four formats and combinations predominate:

   - Colocation of community agency personnel and services at schools—sometimes in the context of school-based health centers partly financed by community health organizations
   - Formal linkages with agencies to enhance access and service coordination for students and families at the agency, at a nearby satellite clinic, or in a school-based or linked family resource center
   - Formal partnerships between a school district and community agencies to establish or expand school-based or linked facilities that include provision of MH services
   - Contracts with community providers to provide needed student services

4. *Classroom-Based Curriculum and Special Out of Classroom Interventions*—Most schools include a focus on enhancing social and emotional functioning in some facet of their curriculum. Specific instructional activities may be designed to promote healthy social and emotional development and/or prevent psychosocial problems such as behavior and emotional problems, school violence, and drug abuse. And, of course, special education classrooms always are supposed to have a constant focus on mental health concerns. Three formats are as follows:

   - Integrated instruction as part of the regular classroom content and processes
   - Specific curriculum or special intervention implemented by personnel specially trained to carry out the processes
   - Curriculum implemented as part of a multifaceted set of interventions designed to enhance positive development and prevent problems

(Continued)

(Continued)

5. *Comprehensive, Multifaceted, and Integrated Approaches*—A few school districts have begun to reconceptualize piecemeal and fragmented approaches to addressing barriers that interfere with students having an equal opportunity to succeed at school. The intent is to develop a comprehensive system of student and learning supports and integrate it with instructional efforts that affect healthy development. The process involves restructuring student support services and weaving them together with community resources. Minimally, the focus is on establishing a full continuum of programs and services to promote positive development, prevent problems, respond as early after onset as is feasible, and offer treatment regimens. Mental health and psychosocial concerns are a major focus of the continuum of interventions, as reflected in initiatives designated as expanded school mental health. Efforts to move toward comprehensive, multifaceted approaches are reflected in initiatives to integrate schools more fully into systems of care and the growing movement to create community schools. Three formats are emerging:

- Mechanisms to coordinate and integrate school and community services
- Initiatives to restructure student support programs/services and integrate them into school reform agenda
- Community schools

Personnel. As already noted, school districts employ personnel such as psychologists, counselors, social workers, psychiatrists, nurses, special educators, and a variety of others whose focus encompasses mental health and psychosocial concerns. Federal and state mandates tend to determine how many pupil services professionals are employed, and states regulate compliance with mandates. Governance of their work usually is centralized at the district level. In large districts, counselors, psychologists, social workers, and other specialists may be organized into separate units, overlapping regular, compensatory, and special education.

Specialists tend to focus mainly on students causing problems or having problems. The many *functions* of such professionals can be grouped into the following: (1) direct services and instruction; (2) coordination, development, and leadership related to programs, services, resources, and systems; and (3) enhancement of connections with community resources. Some of this involves linking and collaborating with community agencies and programs to enhance resources and improve access, availability, and outcomes.

Prevailing direct intervention approaches encompass responding to crises; identifying the needs of targeted individuals; prescribing one or more interventions; offering brief consultation; and providing referrals for assessment, corrective services, triage, diagnosis, and various gatekeeping functions. In some situations, however, resources are so limited that specialists can do little more than assess for special education eligibility, offer brief consultations, and make referrals to special education and/or community resources.

Because the need is so great, other personnel often are called on to play a role in addressing problems of youth and their families. These include instructional professionals (health educators, other classroom teachers, special education staff, resource staff), administrative staff (principals, assistant principals), students (including trained peer counselors), family members, and almost everyone else involved with a school (aides, clerical and cafeteria staff, custodians, bus drivers, paraprofessionals, recreation personnel, volunteers, and professionals in training). As noted, districts are connecting with specialists employed by other public and private agencies, such as health departments, hospitals, social service agencies, and community-based organizations, to provide services to students, their families, and school staff (Atkins, Graczyk, Frazier, & Abdul-Adil, 2003; Romer & McIntosh, 2005).

In summation, most districts provide schools with some personnel to address a range of mental health and psychosocial concerns, such as school adjustment and attendance problems, dropouts, physical and sexual abuse, substance abuse, relationship difficulties, emotional upset, delinquency, and violence. Some are funded by the district or through extramural grants; others are the result of linkages with community service and youth development agencies.

But It Is All Marginalized. While a range of mental health and psychosocial problems are addressed, no one should think that mental health is a high priority in school policy and practice (Adelman & Taylor, 2006d; Taylor & Adelman, 2000). Schools and districts treat student and learning supports as desirable but not an imperative. Since the activity is not seen as essential, the programs and staff are pushed to the margins. Planning of programs, services, and delivery systems is done on an ad hoc basis; interventions are referred to as *auxiliary* or *support* services, and student support personnel almost never are a prominent part of a school's organizational structure. Such staff usually are among those deemed dispensable as budgets tighten.

Because student supports are so marginalized, they are developed in a piecemeal manner. The marginalization spills over to how schools pursue special education mandates and policies related to inclusion. The low policy status shapes how they work with community agencies and initiatives for systems of care, wrap-around services, school-linked services, and other school-community collaborations. And all this negatively affects adoption and implementation of evidence-based practices.

Evidence of the marginalization is found in school improvement plans. Analyses of such planning indicate that schools give sparse attention to mental health and psychosocial concerns (Center for Mental Health in Schools, 2005a, 2005b, 2005d).

CONCLUDING COMMENTS

Anyone who has worked in a school knows how hard school professionals toil. Anecdotes about great programs and outcomes are legion.

Our discussion in this chapter and the rest of the book underscores that exceptional talent and effort has brought the field of mental health in schools to this stage in its development. At the same time, we stress that too little is being done in most schools and significant work lies ahead.

Current practices have been generated and function in relative isolation of each other. Intervention planning and implementation are widely characterized as fragmented and piecemeal. This, of course, is an ineffective way for schools to deal with the complex sets of problems confronting teachers and other staff.

Organizationally, policy makers tend to mandate and planners and developers focus on specific services and programs with too little thought or time given to mechanisms for program development and collaboration. The work rarely is envisioned in the context of a comprehensive approach to addressing behavior, emotional, and learning problems and promoting healthy development.

Functionally, most practitioners spend their time applying specialized interventions to targeted problems, usually involving individual or small groups of students. Consequently, programs to address behavior, emotional, learning, and physical problems rarely are coordinated with each other or with educational programs.

The above state of affairs is not meant as a criticism of those who are doing their best to help students in need. Our intent is to underscore a fundamental policy weakness, namely: *Efforts to address barriers to learning and teaching are marginalized in current education policy.* This maintains an unsatisfactory status quo related to how schools address learning, behavior, and emotional problems. Analyses indicate that school policy is currently dominated by a two-component systemic model (Adelman, 1995b, 1996a, 1996b; Adelman & Taylor, 1994, 1997b, 1998, 2006c; Center for Mental Health in Schools, 1996, 1997). That is, the primary thrust is on improving instruction and school management. While these two facets obviously are essential, ending the marginalization of efforts to effectively address barriers to learning, development, and teaching requires establishing a third component as a fundamental facet of transforming the educational system. We amplify on this matter in the next chapter and throughout the book.

NOTE

1. In addition to the references included in this book, an online list of relevant references is regularly updated and available from the national Center for Mental Health in Schools at UCLA at http://smhp.psych.ucla.edu/qf/references.htm. Also see Chapter 14 for an annotated listing of sources for identifying evidence-based strategies for strengthening student supports; the list also is online with direct links at http://smhp.psych.ucla.edu/pdfdocs/aboutmh/annotatedlist.pdf.

2

About Moving Toward a Comprehensive Approach

We can't solve problems by using the same kind of thinking we used when we created them.

—Albert Einstein

The problems students bring to school are multifaceted and complex. Moreover, in many schools, the number of students experiencing problems is extensive. It is well-known that a student who has a learning problem is likely to have behavior problems and vice versa. Moreover, students with learning and behavior problems usually develop an overlay of emotional problems. Of course, emotional problems can lead to and exacerbate behavior and/or learning problems. Schools find that a student who abuses drugs often also has poor grades, is truant, at risk of dropping out, and more.

When students are not doing well, teachers often refer them directly for assessment in hopes of referral for special assistance, perhaps even assignment to special education. In some schools and classrooms, the number of referrals is dramatic. Where special teams exist to review students for whom help is requested, the list grows as the year proceeds. The longer the list, the longer the lag time for review—often to the point that, by the end of the school year, only a few have been processed. *And, no matter how many are reviewed, there are always more referrals than can be served.* In many schools, the numbers of students experiencing problems is staggering.

NEEDED: A COMPREHENSIVE APPROACH

The fragmentation of programs and services described in Chapter 1 and illustrated graphically in Figure 2.1 reflects the tendency for policy makers to mandate and planners and developers to focus on specific problems and categorical programs. As a result, most practitioners spend their time working on targeted problems and give little thought or time to developing comprehensive and cohesive approaches.

Moreover, the need to label students in order to obtain special, categorical funding further skews practices toward narrow and unintegrated intervention

Figure 2.1   Talk About Fragmented!

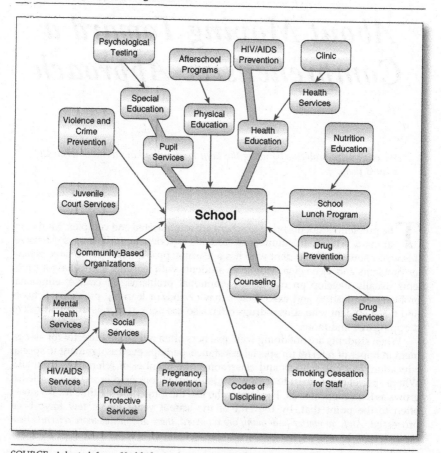

SOURCE: Adapted from *Health Is Academic: A Guide to Coordinated School Health Programs,* by E. Marx and S. Wooley with D. Northrop (Eds.), 1998, New York: Teachers College Press. Copyright 1998 by Teachers College Press. Adapted with permission.

approaches. One result is that a student identified as having multiple problems may be involved in programs with several professionals working independently of each other. Similarly, a youngster identified and helped in elementary school may cease to receive needed help upon entering middle school. Pursuit of grant money often further diverts attention from one problem to another. Exhibit 6 highlights concerns that arise about categorical and other funding as related to development of a comprehensive and cohesive system for addressing barriers to learning and teaching.

Exhibit 6 Concerns About Categorical and Other Sources of Funding

Are the ways that schools underwrite student and learning supports undermining creation of an effective system for addressing overlapping psychosocial and mental health problems?

School budgets always are tight. So schools seek all forms of extra funding from public and private sectors to help underwrite student and learning supports. Tight budgets lead schools to embrace categorical funding and a range of other sources to underwrite programs and services. This contributes to the use of narrow, targeted initiatives focused on discrete problems such as bullying, suicide screening, substance abuse prevention, and on and on. Moreover, the sporadic and cyclical way policy attends to such matters leads to *flavor of the month* strategies.

Categorical approaches, however, conflict with the science-base that indicates many student problems overlap. Evidence also indicates that categorical approaches don't produce major changes in mobilizing large numbers of students to reengage in learning.

We find that certain types of funding distort, distract, and undermine efforts to develop a comprehensive student support system. Major examples include funding for *Supplemental Services* under Title I (which has focused only on tutoring and has limited and skewed after-school programming), Medicaid funding for school-based services that ends up redefining the roles of some school support staff (by turning them mainly into providers of fee-based clinical services), and extramural project funding for relatively small projects that end up redirecting staff attention away from system building and cause mission drift (dubbed *projectitis*).

Tight budgets also lead to recommendations to do away with programs and the personnel who staff them. Policy makers are contracting out services provided by personnel such as school psychologists, social workers, counselors, nurses, and others who deal with psychosocial and mental health matters. A related concern is the degree to which managed care and changes in Medicaid and health insurance influence such decisions. Such matters have the impact of reducing rather than increasing the total amount of resources available in schools for dealing with psychosocial and mental health concerns. And they work against redeploying resources to develop a comprehensive system of *learning supports* as a critical step for making durable progress in raising test scores and closing the achievement gap.

The solution is not found in efforts to convince policy makers to fund more special programs and services at schools. Even if the policy climate favored more special programs, such interventions alone are insufficient. More services to treat problems certainly are needed. But so are programs for prevention and early after problem onset that can reduce the numbers that teachers send to review teams.

The fact is that *multifaceted problems usually require comprehensive, integrated solutions applied concurrently and over time.* The field must move beyond the type of categorical thinking that dominates current policy and practice (Maser et al., 2009).

HOW CLOSE ARE SCHOOLS TO HAVING A COMPREHENSIVE APPROACH?

As highlighted in Chapter 1, analyses consistently find major gaps and a high degree of fragmentation and marginalization related to school and community efforts to address barriers to learning. Few collaborative initiatives braid resources and establish effective mechanisms for sustainability. Little horizontal and vertical integration is found for programs and services within and between jurisdictions (e.g., among departments, divisions, units, schools, clusters of schools, districts, community agencies, public and private sectors). Such integration is needed to counter tendencies to develop separate programs for every observed problem.

For the most part, schools are not developing the type of support systems that *enable* all students to benefit from higher standards and improved instruction. In particular, schools do relatively little to prevent or intervene early after the onset of a student's learning, behavior, or emotional problem. As budgets have tightened, they are doing less and less to provide students with social supports and recreational and enrichment opportunities. Even as educators call for greater home involvement, proactive outreach to help family members overcome barriers to involvement remains sparse (e.g., improving family literacy, facilitating social support networks).

WHAT'S HOLDING THINGS BACK?

Let's look at school reform and improvement through the lens of learning, behavior, and emotional problems and the need for a comprehensive system to address such problems. Doing so, we find school improvement policies and planning mostly give short shrift to these matters. The exceptions proving the point are a few pioneering initiatives demonstrating how schools and communities can meet the challenge.

Our analysis of prevailing policies for improving schools indicates that the primary focus is on two components: (1) enhancing instruction and curriculum and (2) restructuring school management. Implementation of such efforts is shaped by demands for every school to adopt high standards and expectations and be more accountable for results, as measured by standardized achievement tests. Toward these ends, the calls are to enhance direct academic support and move away from a *deficit* model by adopting a strength- or resilience-oriented paradigm. All this is reflected in federal guidelines and the emphasis on tutoring as the main *supplemental service.*

At the same time, barriers that cannot be ignored—school violence, drugs on campus, dropouts, teen pregnancy, delinquency, and so forth—are funded and pursued as *categorical* initiatives. Analyses consistently underscore the fragmented and marginalized way in which policy makers attend to these multifaceted barriers that interfere with students learning and performing well at school.

> Marginalization is seen in the sparse attention consolidated school improvement plans and certification reviews pay to addressing barriers to learning and teaching. It also is seen in the lack of mapping, analysis, and rethinking related to allocating resources for addressing barriers. A prime example is the fact that educational reformers virtually ignore the need to reframe the work of pupil services professionals and other student support staff. All this seriously hampers efforts to provide the help teachers and students so desperately need.

NEEDED: A POLICY SHIFT

Some policy makers appreciate that limited intervention efficacy is related to programs operating in isolation of each other. Thus, we hear calls for enhancing program coordination. Initiatives for improving coordination, however, fail to come to grips with the underlying *marginalization* that leads to piecemeal approaches and maintains fragmentation.

Present policies designed to enhance support for teachers, students, and families are seriously flawed. An agenda to enhance academics is unlikely to succeed in the absence of concerted attention to ending the marginalized status of efforts to address barriers to learning and teaching. As long as the whole enterprise of addressing barriers is treated as supplementary in policy and practice, little attention will be given to integrating it fully into school improvement planning.

Increased awareness of policy deficiencies has stimulated analyses that indicate current education policy is dominated by a two-component model of school improvement. That is, the primary policy focus is on improving instruction and school management. While these two facets obviously are necessary, our analyses emphasize that a third well-designed component—one to enable students to learn and teachers to teach—is missing in policy (see the top part of Exhibit 7).

Exhibit 7 Current Two-Component Model for Reform and Restructuring

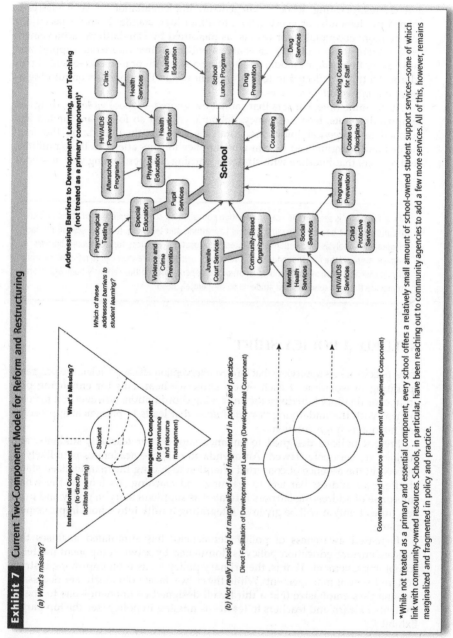

(a) What's missing?

Instructional Component (to directly facilitate learning)

What's Missing?

Student

Management Component (for governance and resource management)

Which of these addresses barriers to student learning?

Addressing Barriers to Development, Learning, and Teaching (not treated as a primary component)*

Clinic

Health Services

Nutrition Education

School Lunch Program

HIV/AIDS Prevention

Health Education

Drug Prevention

Drug Services

Afterschool Programs

Physical Education

Smoking Cessation for Staff

Psychological Testing

Special Education

Pupil Services

School

Counseling

Codes of Discipline

Violence and Crime Prevention

Juvenile Court Services

Community-Based Organizations

Pregnancy Prevention

Social Services

Child Protective Services

Mental Health Services

HIV/AIDS Services

(b) Not really missing but marginalized and fragmented in policy and practice

Direct Facilitation of Development and Learning (Developmental Component)

Governance and Resource Management (Management Component)

*While not treated as a primary and essential component, every school offers a relatively small amount of school-owned student support services—some of which link with community-owned resources. Schools, in particular, have been reaching out to community agencies to add a few more services. All of this, however, remains marginalized and fragmented in policy and practice.

Used as a proxy for the missing component are all the marginalized and fragmented activity that goes on as school after school struggles to address the many factors interfering with student learning and performance (see the bottom section of Exhibit 7). Various states and localities are moving in the direction of pulling all these resources together into a primary and essential third component for *school improvement*. (Some of the pioneering efforts are highlighted on our center's Web site—see *Where's It Happening?* online at http://smhp.psych.ucla.edu/summit2002/wheresithappening.htm.) In each case, there is recognition at a policy level that schools must do much more to enable *all* students to learn and *all* teachers to teach effectively. In effect, the intent, over time, is for schools to play a major role in establishing a full continuum of school-community interventions.

Overlapping what schools offer are initiatives from the *community* to link resources to schools (e.g., school-linked services, full-service schools, community and school partnerships, community schools). Some of these efforts braid resources together; however, others contribute to further fragmentation, counterproductive competition, and marginalization of student support.

A third set of initiatives is designed to promote coordination and collaboration among *governmental* departments and their service agencies. For instance, establishment of local, state, and federal intra-agency and interagency councils is meant to facilitate coordinated planning and organizational change. On a local level, some school boards are rethinking their committee structures. The intent is to foster integrated approaches. Some of this emphasizes greater local control, increased involvement of parents, and locating services at schools when feasible.

Although federal and state government agencies offer various forms of support to promote coordination and collaboration, few school districts have pursued the opportunity in ways that have resulted in comprehensive and multifaceted approaches for addressing barriers to learning. The various initiatives do help *some* students who are not succeeding at school. However, they come nowhere near addressing the scope of need. Indeed, their limited potency further highlights the degree to which efforts to address barriers to learning are marginalized in policy and practice.

A THREE-COMPONENT POLICY FRAMEWORK FOR SCHOOL IMPROVEMENT

The limited impact of current policy points to the need to rethink school reform and improvement. Our analyses indicate that the dominating two-component model is inadequate for significantly improving the role of schools in helping prevent and correct learning, behavior, and emotional problems.

Prevailing approaches to school improvement do not address the factors leading to and maintaining students' problems, especially in schools where large proportions of students are not doing well. Despite this, in their rush to raise test scores, school leaders usually pursue instruction as if this was sufficient to ensure that every student will succeed. That is, the emphasis is mostly on intensifying and narrowing the agenda for school improvement to discussions of curriculum, instruction, and classroom discipline. (See almost any school improvement planning guide.) This ignores the need to restructure fundamentally school and community resources for *enabling learning*.

No one denies improved instruction is necessary. For too many youngsters, however, improved instruction is insufficient. Students who arrive at school lacking motivational readiness and/or certain abilities need more. We suggest that what they need is best conceived as a major component to address barriers to learning. Adoption of a three-component framework elevates addressing barriers to the level of a fundamental and primary facet of school improvement.

> Movement to a three-component model is necessary so schools can do better in enabling all young people to have an equal opportunity to succeed at school.

CONCLUDING COMMENTS

How often have you been asked the following?

Why don't schools do a better job in addressing students' problems?

We answer the question by stressing that *efforts to address such problems are marginalized in school policy and daily practice.* We emphasize that most programs, services, and special projects providing learning supports at a school and districtwide are treated as nonessentials. The following may happen as a result:

- Planning and implementation often are done on an ad hoc basis.
- Staff tend to function in relative isolation of each other and other stakeholders, with a great deal of the work oriented to discrete problems and with an overreliance on specialized services for individuals and small groups.
- In some schools, the deficiencies of current policies give rise to such aberrant practices as assigning a student identified as at risk for grade retention, dropout, and substance abuse to three counseling programs operating independently of each other. This fragmentation not only is costly, it works against cohesiveness and maximizing results.

We note that the fragmentation is compounded by most school-linked services initiatives. This happens because such initiatives focus primarily on coordinating *community* services and *linking* them to schools using a colocation model rather than integrating such services with the ongoing efforts of school staff. Reformers often offer the notions of *Family Resource Centers* and *Full-Service Schools* to link community resources to schools and coordinate services. Clearly, much more fundamental changes are needed.

We also stress that reforms often focus only on fragmentation, which is a symptom not a cause of the poor impact of student support programs. The result is an overreliance on enhancing coordination as a solution. Better coordination is a good idea. But this one-factor solution ignores the ongoing marginalization of school-owned student supports. And it does little to enhance the involvement of a full range of community resources.

The marginalized status and associated fragmentation of efforts to address student problems are long-standing and ongoing. The situation is unlikely to change as long as reforms continue to ignore the need to rethink the work of student support professionals. Most school improvement plans do not focus on using such staff to develop a comprehensive, multifaceted, and integrated approach for addressing the many overlapping barriers to learning, development, and teaching.

Also, mediating against developing schoolwide approaches to address factors interfering with learning and teaching is the way in which these matters are handled in providing on-the-job education. Little or none of a teacher's inservice training focuses on improving classroom and schoolwide approaches for dealing effectively with mild to moderate behavior, learning, and emotional problems. Paraprofessionals, aides, and volunteers working in classrooms or with special school projects and services receive little training and/or supervision before or after they are assigned duties. Plus, little or no attention is paid to inservice for student support staff.

The time has come to change all this. New directions for student and learning supports must become a fundamental agenda item for school improvements. From an educational and a public health perspective, the need is for a full continuum of interventions and organized content conceived as an integrated system that braids together the resources of schools and communities.

As a colleague of ours often says, "All children want to be successful—let's give them a fighting chance." This requires *enabling* every student to have an equal opportunity to succeed at school and in life.

Our work has led us to understand that moving toward a comprehensive approach that fully embeds mental health and psychosocial concerns begins with an expanded policy for addressing barriers to learning and teaching. Then, school decision makers and planners must confront three other fundamental and interrelated matters—namely the following:

- Student-learning supports must be reframed into a unifying, comprehensive system of intervention.
- The organizational and operational infrastructure for schools, feeder patterns, districts, and school-community collaboration must be reworked to facilitate the development of a comprehensive system.
- New approaches must be adopted for planning necessary system changes and for sustaining and replicating them to scale.

Each of these will be discussed later in this book as we explore new directions and strategies for mental health in schools—strategies that create a school environment that promotes mental health and reduces learning, behavior, and emotional problems.

For more on this topic, see the following policy reports from the Center:

School Improvement Planning: What's Missing?
http://smhp.psych.ucla.edu/whatsmissing.htm

Addressing What's Missing in School Improvement Planning: Expanding Standards and Accountability to Encompass an Enabling or Learning Supports Component
http://smhp.psych.ucla.edu/pdfdocs/enabling/standards.pdf

Another Initiative? Where Does It Fit? A Unifying Framework and an Integrated Infrastructure for Schools to Address Barriers to Learning and Promote Healthy Development
http://smhp.psych.ucla.edu/pdfdocs/infrastructure/anotherinitiative-exec.pdf

Also see *The School Leader's Guide to Student Learning Supports: New Directions for Addressing Barriers to Learning* (2006d) by Howard Adelman and Linda Taylor (published by Corwin).

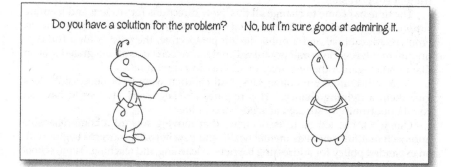

PART II

Three Major Issues Confronting the Field

In the last analysis, we see only what we are ready to see. We eliminate and ignore everything that is not part of our prejudices.

—Jean-Martin Charcot (1857)

Not long ago a group in Virginia called for the removal of counselors from their elementary schools. The group argued the following: (1) school counselors introduce matters to their children that are inappropriate, such as child abuse, death, and opposite-sex relationships, and (2) schools should not be centers for mental health and should focus solely on academics.

In response, teachers and counselors launched a counter campaign. They stressed the need for support services in schools by noting the many problems students experience that must be addressed in order to succeed.

The incident underscores that mental health in schools remains highly controversial in some places and that certain practices may be controversial almost anywhere. Those who support mental health in schools must understand the issues and problems and be prepared to help schools make decisions about how to address them.

In this section, we explore three fundamental matters that highlight why the field is controversial. These matters permeate the field and represent ongoing challenges in moving forward.

3. Labeling, Screening, and Over-Pathologizing

4. Evidence-Based Practices in Schools: Concerns About Fit and Implementation

5. Social Control Versus Engagement in Learning: A Mental Health Perspective

3

Labeling, Screening, and Over-Pathologizing

Normality and exceptionality (or deviance) are not absolutes; both are culturally defined by particular societies at particular times for particular purposes.

—Ruth Benedict (1934)

Consider the American penchant for ignoring the structural causes of problems. We prefer the simplicity and satisfaction of holding individuals responsible for whatever happens: crime, poverty, school failure, what have you. Thus, even when one high school crisis is followed by another, we concentrate on the particular people involved—their values, their character, their personal failings—rather than asking whether something about the system in which these students find themselves might also need to be addressed.

—Alfie Kohn (1999)

What's in a name? Strong images are associated with diagnostic labels, and people act upon these images. Sometimes, the images are useful generalizations; sometimes, they are harmful stereotypes. Sometimes, they guide practitioners toward good ways to help; sometimes, they contribute to *blaming the victim*—making young people the focus of intervention rather than pursuing system deficiencies that are causing the problem in the first place. In all cases, diagnostic labels can profoundly shape a person's future.

Youngsters manifesting emotional upset, misbehavior, and learning problems commonly are assigned psychiatric labels that were created to categorize internal disorders. Thus, terms such as *attention deficit hyperactivity disorder* (ADHD), *depression,* and *learning disabilities* (LD) are used increasingly. This happens despite the fact that the problems of most youngsters are not rooted in internal pathology. Indeed, many of their troubling symptoms would not have developed if their environmental circumstances had differed in appropriate ways.

Concern

Misdiagnosis

Of particular concern for schools is the widespread *misuse of the terms ADHD and LD.* This includes nonprofessional applications of these labels and the reality of misdiagnoses. Almost 50% of those assigned a special education diagnosis are identified as having learning disabilities. This has contributed to the backlash to LD seen in the move toward response to intervention that emerged from the last reauthorization of the Individuals with Disabilities Education Act (retitled the Individuals with Disabilities Education Improvement Act but still widely referred to as IDEA). Concern also is on the rise about the number of youngsters who manifest *garden-variety* misbehavior who may be misdiagnosed as ADHD. Reports appear rather regularly that suggest a growing backlash, especially as related to the increasing use of medication to treat children. For example, research from the Eastern Virginia Medical School reports significant overdiagnosis; this led to hearings and community forums and a bill by the legislature prohibiting school personnel from recommending psychotropic medications for students.

DIAGNOSING BEHAVIORAL, EMOTIONAL, AND LEARNING PROBLEMS

As we stressed in Part I, prevailing formal systems used to classify problems in human functioning convey the impression that all behavioral, emotional, or learning problems are instigated by internal pathology. Some efforts to temper this notion see the pathology as a vulnerability that only becomes evident under stress. However, most differential diagnoses of children's problems still are made by focusing on identifying specific disorders (e.g., oppositional defiant disorder, ADHD, or adjustment disorders), rather than first asking, *Is there a disorder?*

Bias toward labeling problems in terms of personal rather than social causation is bolstered by factors such as (1) attributional bias—a tendency for observers to perceive others' problems as rooted in stable personal dispositions and (2) economic and political influences—whereby society's current priorities and other extrinsic forces shape professional practice.

Overemphasis on classifying problems in terms of personal pathology skews theory, research, practice, and public policy. For instance, comprehensive classification systems do not exist for environmentally caused problems or for psychosocial problems (caused by the transaction of internal and environmental factors). As a result, these matters often are de-emphasized in assessing cause.

The irony is that so many practitioners who use prevailing diagnostic labels understand that most problems in human functioning result from the interplay of person and environment. To counter nature versus nurture biases in thinking about problems, it helps to approach diagnostic classification guided by a broad perspective of what determines human behavior.

THE DEBATE ABOUT THE ROLE OF SCHOOLS IN SCREENING

Reasonable concern for the well-being of children and adolescents and the need to address barriers to learning and teaching has led schools to deploy resources to deal with a variety of health and psychosocial matters (e.g., bullying, depression, suicide, ADHD, LD, obesity). Some of the activity is helpful; some is not; some has unintended negative consequences. And concerns arise.

> Are schools colluding with practices that sensationalize and pathologically label young people's behavior?

> Should schools be involved in universal, first-level screening for behavior and emotional problems?

We all have experienced the tendency to generalize from extreme and rare incidents. While one school shooting is too many, fortunately few students ever act out in this way. One suicide is too many; fortunately, few students take their own life. Some young people commit violent crimes, but the numbers are far fewer than news media convey, and the trajectory is downward.

No one is likely to argue against the value of preventing violence, suicide, and other mental heath and psychosocial concerns. In recent years, schools have been increasingly vigilant about potential violent incidents on campus. Even so, policy makers conflict over whether schools should play an institutionalized role in screening for mental health problems. Issues arise around the following:

> Is such monitoring an appropriate role for schools to play?

> If so, what procedures are appropriate, and who should do it?

> If so, how will schools avoid doing more harm than good in the process?

In discussing these issues, concerns are raised about (1) the lack of evidence supporting the ability to predict who will and won't be violent or commit suicide; (2) what will be done to those identified as *threats* or *at risk*, including a host of due process considerations; (3) whether the procedures are antithetical to the schools education mission; and (4) the negative impact on the school environment of additional procedures that are more oriented to policing and monitoring than to creating school environments that foster caring and a sense of community.

Concerns also arise about parental consent, privacy and confidentiality protections, staff qualifications, involvement of peers, negative consequences of monitoring (especially for students who are false positive identifications), and access and availability of appropriate assistance.

Examples of often heard pro and con positions are as follows:

- School personnel are well situated to keep an eye on kids who are *risky* or *at risk*.
- Teachers can't take on another task and aren't qualified to monitor such students.
- Such monitoring can be done by qualified student support staff.
- Monitoring infringes on the rights of families and students.
- It's irresponsible not to monitor anyone who is *risky* or *at risk*.
- It's inappropriate to encourage kids to *spy* on each other.
- Monitoring is needed so that steps can be taken to help quickly.
- Monitoring has too many negative effects.

Concern

Screening and Profiling

With growing interest in expanding preschool education programs comes an increasing reemphasis on *early-age screening for behavioral, emotional, and learning disabilities,* (e.g., enhancing Early Periodic Screening, Diagnosis, and Treatment [EPSDT]) and screening programs in Head Start and kindergarten.

- *Drug testing at school has long been advocated as a way to deter drug use.*
- *Student-threat profiling is proposed as a way to prevent school violence.*
- *Schools are called on to screen for suicide risk.*

On a regular basis, legislators at federal and state levels express concern about some facet of the agenda for mental health in schools. An ongoing debate focuses on the role of public schools in screening for mental health and psychosocial problems.

Advocates for primary and secondary prevention want to predict and identify problems early. Large-scale screening programs, however, can produce many false positives, lead to premature prescription of *deep end* interventions, focus mainly on the role of factors residing in the child and thus collude with tendencies to *blame victims,* and so forth. As with most debates, those in favor emphasize benefits (e.g., "Screening lets us identify problems early, and can help prevent problems such as suicide."). Those against stress costs. For example, one state legislator is quoted as saying, "We want all of our citizens to have access to mental health services, but the idea that we are going to run everyone through some screening system with who knows what kind of values applied to them is unacceptable."

(Continued)

(Continued)

With respect to drug testing at school, in an article from the New York Times Online, Lloyd Johnston and colleagues at the University of Michigan have reported the first major study (76,000 students nationwide) on the impact of drug testing in schools. They conclude such testing does not deter student drug use any more than doing no screening at all. Based on the study's findings, Dr. Johnston states, "It's the kind of intervention that doesn't win the hearts and minds of children. I don't think it brings about any constructive changes in their attitudes about drugs or their belief in the dangers associated with using them" (Winter, 2003). At the same time, he stresses, "One could imagine situations where drug testing could be effective, if you impose it in a sufficiently draconian manner—that is, testing most kids and doing it frequently. We're not in a position to say that wouldn't work" (Winter, 2003). Graham Boyd, director of the ACLU Drug Policy Litigation Project who argued against drug testing before the Supreme Court last year, said, "In light of these findings, schools should be hard-pressed to implement or continue a policy that is intrusive and even insulting for their students" (Winter, 2003). But other researchers contend that the urinalysis conducted by schools is so faulty, the supervision so lax, and the opportunities for cheating so plentiful that the study may prove only that schools do a poor job of testing. Also noted is that the Michigan study does not differentiate between schools that do intensive, regular, random screening and those that test only occasionally. As a result, the findings do not rule out the possibility that the most vigilant schools do a better job of curbing drug use.

Those arguing that schools should screen emphasize the need to monitor anyone at risk or who is a risk to others in order to intervene quickly. They state that school personnel are well situated to screen students and with training can screen effectively using appropriate safeguards for privacy and confidentiality. Moreover, proponents believe that positive benefits outweigh any negative effects.

A central argument against screening students to identify threats and risks is that the practice infringes on the rights of families and students. Other arguments stress the following: teachers should not be distracted from teaching; teachers and other nonclinically trained school staff are ill equipped to monitor and make such identifications; existing monitoring practices are primarily effective in following those who have already attempted suicide or have acted violently and that monitoring others has too many negative effects (e.g., costs can outweigh potential benefits).

For more on all this, see the Center's Online Clearinghouse Quick Find topics:

Assessment and Screening—http://smhp.psych.ucla.edu/qf/p1405_01.htm

Stigma Reduction—http://smhp.psych.ucla.edu/qf/stigma.htm

NEEDED: A BROADER CLASSIFICATION FRAMEWORK

The need to address a wider range of variables in labeling problems is seen in efforts to develop multifaceted systems. The multiaxial classification system developed by the American Psychiatric Association in its recent editions of the *Diagnostic and Statistical Manual of Mental Disorders* (*DSM*) represents the dominant approach. This system does include a dimension acknowledging *psychosocial stressors*. However, this dimension is used mostly to deal with the environment as a contributing factor rather than as a primary cause.

The conceptual example illustrated in Exhibit 8 is a broad framework that offers a useful starting place for classifying behavioral, emotional, and learning problems in ways that avoid overdiagnosing internal pathology. As outlined in the exhibit, such problems can be differentiated along a continuum that separates those caused by internal factors, environmental variables, or a combination of both.

Exhibit 8   A Continuum of Problems Based on a Broad Understanding of Cause*

PRIMARY SOURCE OF CAUSE

Problems caused by factors in the environment (E)	*Problems caused equally by environment and person*	*Problems caused by factors in the person (P)*
E (E⇔p)	E⇔P (e⇔P)	P

|—————————————————|—————————————————|—————————————————|

Type I Problems	*Type II Problems*	*Type III Problems (e.g., LD, ADHD, other disorders)*
• Caused primarily by environments and systems that are deficient and/or hostile	• Caused primarily by a significant *mismatch* between individual differences and vulnerabilities and the nature of that person's environment (not by a person's pathology)	• Caused primarily by personal factors of a pathological nature
• Problems are mild to moderately severe and narrow to moderately pervasive	• Problems are mild to moderately severe and pervasive	• Problems are moderate to profoundly severe and moderate to broadly pervasive

*Using a transactional view, the continuum emphasizes the *primary source* of the problem and in each case is concerned with problems that are beyond the early stage of onset.

Problems caused by the environment are placed at one end of the continuum and referred to as Type I problems. At the other end are problems caused primarily by pathology within the person; these are designated as Type III problems. In the middle are problems stemming from a relatively equal contribution of environmental and person sources, labeled Type II problems.

To be more specific, in this scheme, diagnostic labels meant to identify *extremely* dysfunctional problems *caused by pathological conditions within a person* are reserved for individuals who fit the Type III category. Obviously, some problems caused by pathological conditions within a person are not manifested in severe, pervasive ways, and there are persons without such pathology whose problems do become severe and pervasive. The intent is not to ignore these individuals. As a first categorization step, however, they must not be confused with those seen as having Type III problems.

At the other end of the continuum are individuals with problems arising from factors outside the person (i.e., Type I problems). Many people grow up in impoverished and hostile environmental circumstances. Such conditions should be considered first in hypothesizing what *initially* caused the individual's behavioral, emotional, and learning problems. (After environmental causes are ruled out, hypotheses about internal pathology become more viable.)

To provide a reference point in the middle of the continuum, a Type II category is used. This group consists of persons who do not function well in situations where their individual differences and minor vulnerabilities are poorly accommodated or are responded to hostilely. The problems of an individual in this group are a relatively equal product of personal characteristics and failure of the environment to accommodate that individual.

Of course, variations occur along the continuum that do not precisely fit a category. That is, at each point between the extreme ends, environment-person transactions are the cause, but the degree to which each contributes to the problem varies.

Clearly, a simple continuum cannot do justice to the complexities associated with labeling and differentiating problems. Furthermore, some problems are not easily assessed or do not fall readily into a group due to data limitations and individuals who have more than one problem (i.e., comorbidity). However, the above scheme shows the value of starting with a broad model of cause. In particular, the continuum helps counter the tendency to jump prematurely to the conclusion that a problem is caused by deficiencies or pathology within the individual. This can help combat tendencies toward blaming the victim. It also helps highlight the notion that improving the way the environment accommodates individual differences often may be a sufficient intervention strategy.

Using Response to Intervention to Minimize False Identification

By now, most people working in and with schools have heard about response to intervention (RtI). The process is proposed as a corrective to misdiagnosis and first-level screening. However, considerable differences arise in how the concept is discussed by school policy makers and practitioners. With respect to operationalizing the process, two extremes can be identified. One mainly stresses the introduction of better (i.e., evidence-based) instruction and using the intervention to clarify whether the problem stems from a teaching deficit or if a referral is needed for disability assessment. At the other extreme, the emphasis is on proceeding in stages beginning with personalized instruction designed to enhance a better match with the learner's current motivation and capabilities and as necessary, sequencing in a hierarchical way to (1) develop missing learning and performance prerequisites and/or (2) provide needed specialized interventions that can address other existing barriers to learning (both external and internal barriers).

ADDRESSING THE FULL RANGE OF PROBLEMS AND POTENTIAL BARRIERS TO HEALTHY DEVELOPMENT AND LEARNING

Amelioration of the full continuum of problems requires a comprehensive continuum of interventions. The continuum ranges from programs for primary prevention, including the promotion of mental health, and early-age intervention—through those for addressing problems soon after onset—to treatments for severe and chronic problems. The range of programs highlights that many problems must be addressed developmentally and with a wide spectrum of programs—some focused on individuals and some on environmental systems, some focused on mental health and some on physical health, education, and social services. With respect to concerns about integrating programs, the continuum underscores the need for concurrent inter-program linkages and for linkages over extended periods of time.

The continuum also recognizes the full nature and scope of factors that can lead to problems. In particular, care is taken not to lose sight of research findings indicating that the primary causes for most youngsters' behavior, learning, and emotional problems are external factors related to neighborhood, family, school, and/or peers. Problems stemming from individual disorders and differences affect only a few. An appreciation of the research on the role played by external and internal factors makes a focus on such matters a major part of any effort to address the needs of all students.

Examples of Risk-Producing Conditions That Can Become Barriers to Healthy Development and Learning

Environmental Conditions*			Personal Factors*
Neighborhood	Family	School and Peers	Individual
• Extreme economic deprivation	• Chronic poverty	• Poor quality school	• Medical problems
	• Conflict, disruptions, violence	• Negative encounters with teachers	• Low birth weight/ neurodevelopmental delay
• Community disorganization, including high levels of mobility	• Substance abuse		• Psychophysiological problems
	• Models problem behavior	• Negative encounters with peers and/or inappropriate peer models	• Difficult temperament & adjustment problems
• Violence, drugs, and so on	• Abusive caretaking		
• Minority and/or immigrant status	• Inadequate provision for quality child care		• Inadequate nutrition

*A reciprocal determinist view of behavior recognizes the interplay of environment and personal variables.

CONCLUDING COMMENTS

Strong images are associated with diagnostic labels, and people act upon these notions. Sometimes, the images are useful generalizations, but often they are harmful stereotypes. Sometimes, they guide practitioners toward good ways to help. But often, they contribute to *blaming the victim* by making young people the focus of intervention rather than pursuing system deficiencies that are causing the problem. In all cases, diagnostic labels can profoundly shape a person's future.

A large number of young people are unhappy and emotionally upset; only a small percentage are clinically depressed. A large number of youngsters behave in ways that distress others; only a small percentage have ADHD or a conduct disorder. In some schools, the majority of students have garden-variety learning problems; only a few have learning disabilities. Thankfully, those suffering from true internal pathology (those referred to above as Type III problems) represent a relatively small segment of the population. Society must never stop providing the best services it can for such individuals, and doing so means taking great care not to misdiagnose others whose *symptoms* may be similar but are caused to a signif-icant degree by factors other than internal pathology (those referred to above as Type I and II problems).

As community agencies and schools struggle to find ways to finance pro-grams for troubled and troubling youth, they continue to tap into resources that require assigning youngsters labels conveying severe pathology. Reimbursement for mental health and special education interventions is tied to such diagnoses. The situation dramatically illustrates how social policy shapes decisions about who receives assistance and the ways in which problems are addressed. Labeling young people also represents a major ethical dilemma for practitioners. That dilemma is not whether to use labels but rather how to resist the pressure to inappropriately use labels that yield reimbursement from third-party payers.

Misdiagnoses lead to policies and practices that exhaust available resources and serve a relatively small percentage of those in need. That is one reason why resources are sparse for addressing the barriers interfering with the education and healthy development of so many youngsters who are seen as troubled and troubling.

For these and other reasons, considerable criticism exists about some diagnostic labels, especially those applied to young children. Nevertheless, sound reasons underlie the desire to differentially label problems. One reason is that if properly identified, some can be prevented; another is that proper identification can enhance correction.

However, the labeling process remains difficult. Severity has been the most common factor used to distinguish many student problems (e.g., ADHD and LD) from the many commonplace behavior, learning, and emotional problems that permeate schools. Besides severity, concern exists about how pervasive the problem is (e.g., how far behind an individual lags in academic and social skills). Specific criteria for judging severity and pervasiveness depend on prevailing age, gender, subculture, and social status expectations. Also important is how long the problem has persisted.

Because of the dramatic increase in misdiagnoses over the last 20 years, *response to intervention* is offered as a precursor and aid in differentiating commonplace problems from individual pathology. As we suggest in a subsequent chapter, however, mobilizing unmotivated students remains a core difficulty in using this process to rule out whether a student has a true disability or disorder. Schools must do even more to counter inappropriate labeling (see Exhibit 9).

Exhibit 9   Are Schools Doing Enough to Counter Inappropriate Labeling of Students?

1. Are student support staff doing the following?

   - Providing general information about the wide range of *normal* behavior and individual differences and the importance of not over-pathologizing (e.g., distributing information and fact sheets, offering information as part of a school's inservice program)
     - See *Bias in Psychiatric Diagnosis* (2004) by P. J. Caplan & L. Cosgrove (Eds.)

(Continued)

(Continued)

- Offering specific feedback on specific incidents and students (e.g., using staff concerns and specific referrals as opportunities to educate them about what is and is not pathological and what should be done in each instance)
  - See *Guidebook on Common Psychosocial Problems of School Aged Youth: Developmental Variations, Problems, Disorders and Perspectives for Prevention and Treatment*—http://smhp.psych.ucla.edu/pdfdocs/psysocial/entirepacket.pdf
  - See *Revisiting Learning & Behavior Problems: Moving Schools Forward*—http://smhp.psych.ucla.edu/pdfdocs/contedu/revisitinglearning.pdf

- Resisting the pull of special funding (One of the hardest things to do is avoid using the need for funds and other resources as justification for interpreting a student's actions as *pathological.*)
  - See *The Impact of Fiscal Incentives on Student Disability Rates* (1999) by Julie Berry Cullen, National Bureau of Economic Research, Working Paper 7173—http://www.nber.org/papers/w7173
  - See *Effects of Funding Incentives on Special Education Enrollment* (2002) by J. P. Greene, & G. Forster, Manhattan Institute for Policy Research—http://www.manhattan-institute.org/html/cr_32.htm

- Using the least intervention appropriate when students require special assistance
  - See *Least Intervention Needed: Toward Appropriate Inclusion of Students With Special Needs*—http://smhp.psych.ucla.edu/pdfdocs/leastint/leastint.pdf

2. Is there a focus in the professional development of teachers to ensure they have the knowledge and skills to do the following?

- Engage all students in learning
- Reengage students who have become disengaged from classroom learning
- Accommodate a wider range of individual differences when teaching
- Use classroom assessments that better inform teaching
  - See *Reengaging Students in Learning* (Quick Training Aid)—http://smhp.psych.ucla.edu/pdfdocs/quicktraining/reengagingstudents.pdf
  - See *Reengaging Students in Learning at School* (article)—http://smhp.psych.ucla.edu/pdfdocs/Newsletter/winter02.pdf
  - See *Enhancing Classroom Approaches for Addressing Barriers to Learning: Classroom-Focused Enabling* (Continuing Education Modules)—http://smhp.psych.ucla.edu/pdfdocs/contedu/cfe.pdf

As Nicholas Hobbs (1975) stressed many years ago, "Society defines what is exceptional or deviant, and appropriate treatments are designed quite as much to protect society as they are to help the child. . . . To take care of them can and should be read with two meanings: to give children help and to exclude them from the community" (pp. 20–21). Clearly, the trend to over-pathologize students contributes more to the latter than to the former.

4

Evidence-Based Practices in Schools

Concerns About Fit and Implementation

Effective practices typically evolve over a long period in high-functioning, fully engaged systems.

—Tom Vander Ark (2002)

Another project, another program, another initiative to address students' behavior, learning, and emotional problems, make school safe, and promote healthy development. The following are two questions that the field must answer:

What's the evidence that it works?

How does it all fit together?

These are pressing matters for efforts to improve schools. And they are fraught with controversy.

Increasingly, proposals for adding another program, project, or initiative have been met with the demand that schools adopt practices that are evidence based.

As a result, terms such as *science based* or *empirically supported* are assigned to almost any intervention identified with data generated in ways that meet *scientific standards* and that demonstrate a level of *efficacy* deemed worthy of application (see Exhibit 10).

Exhibit 10	Finding Information About Evidence-Based Practices

Information about evidence-based programs for prevention, early intervention, and treatment are available from the Center's Quick Find Online Clearinghouse and from our Resource Packets (free online) at http://smhp.psych.ucla.edu/.

Examples of Topics:

Program/Process Concerns

- Violence Prevention and Safe Schools
- Screening and Assessing Students: Indicators and Tools
- Responding to Crisis at a School
- Behavioral Initiatives in Broad Perspective
- Least Intervention Needed: Toward Appropriate Inclusion of Students With Special Needs
- Parent and Home Involvement in Schools
- Assessing to Address Barriers to Learning
- Cultural Concerns in Addressing Barriers to Learning
- Early Development and Learning from the Perspective of Addressing Barriers
- Transitions: Turning Risks Into Opportunities for Student Support
- School-Based Client Consultation, Referral, and Management of Care
- School-Based Mutual Support Groups (for Parents, Staff, Older Students)
- Volunteers to Help Teachers and School Address Barriers to Learning
- Welcoming and Involving New Students and Families
- After-School Programs and Addressing Barriers to Learning
- Resource Mapping and Management to Address Barriers to Learning: An Intervention for Systemic Change
- Evaluation and Accountability Related to Mental Health in Schools

Psychosocial Concerns

- Attention Problems: Intervention and Resources
- Affect and Mood Problems Related to School-Aged Youth
- Anxiety, Fears, Phobias, and Related Problems: Intervention and Resources for School-Aged Youth
- Autism Spectrum Disorders and Schools
- Conduct and Behavior Problems in School-Aged Youth
- Dropout Prevention
- Learning Problems and Learning Disabilities

(Continued)

(Continued)

- Protective Factors (Resiliency)
- Preventing Youth Suicide
- Teen Pregnancy Prevention and Support
- Social and Interpersonal Problems Related to School-Aged Youth
- Substance Abuse
- Sexual Minority Students

Also see Chapter 14 for an annotated listing of compilations of empirically supported and evidence-based interventions for school-aged children and adolescents; also online at http://smhp .psych.ucla.edu/pdfdocs/aboutmh/annotatedlist.pdf

A somewhat higher standard is used for the subgroup of practices referred to as evidence-based *treatments*. This designation usually is reserved for interventions tested in more than one rigorous study (multiple case studies, randomized control trials) and consistently found better than a placebo or no treatment.

Currently, most evidence-based practices are discrete interventions designed to meet specified needs. A few are complex sets of interventions intended to meet multifaceted needs, and these usually are referred to as programs. Most evidence-based practices are applied using a detailed guide or manual and are time limited.

CONCERNS AND CONTROVERSIES

No one argues against using the best science available to improve professional expertise. However, the evidence-based practices movement is reshaping mental health in schools in ways that raise concerns. For example, as suggested in the previous chapter, there is a skewed emphasis on gathering evidence for practices that focus on individual pathology.

From a school perspective, a central concern is that practices developed under highly controlled laboratory conditions are pushed prematurely into widespread application based on unwarranted assumptions. This concern is especially salient when the evidence base comes from short-term studies and has not included samples representing major subgroups with which the practice is to be used.

Until researchers demonstrate a prototype is effective under *real world* conditions, it can only be considered a promising and not a proven practice. Even then, best practice determination must be made.

With respect to the designation of *best*, remember that best simply denotes that a practice is better than whatever else is currently available. How *good* the practice is depends on complex analyses related to costs and benefits.

As the evidence-based movement gains momentum, an increasing concern is that certain interventions are officially prescribed and others are proscribed by policy makers and funders. This breeds fear that only those practitioners who adhere to official lists are sanctioned and rewarded.

For purposes of our discussion here, we start with the assumption that evidence exists that a practice is good, and advocates want schools to adopt it. In such cases, the question for decision makers is, "How well does it *fit* into efforts to improve schools?" If the answer is positive, the problem becomes how to *implement* the practice in an optimal way.

Policy and practice analyses conducted by our center have explored concerns about fit and implementation. We briefly highlight some major points here.

Controversy

Can Schools Wait for Empirical Support?

Given the need to address psychosocial and mental health concerns, can schools afford to wait for research support? Should they drop activity where not enough sound research is available (e.g., approaches that address problems in noncategorical ways; schoolwide approaches; comprehensive, multifaceted approaches)? In general, the potential *tyranny* of evidence-based practices is a growing concern, and the possibility that overemphasizing such programs can inadvertently undermine rather than enhance schoolwide reform efforts. Virtually no evidence exists that evidence-based practices contribute to overall school effectiveness, and ironically, little data on the matter are gathered.

ANOTHER INTERVENTION—WHERE AND HOW DOES IT FIT?

In isolation, evidence-based interventions are viewed only in terms of advancing the state of the art. From a systemic and public policy perspective, however, introducing any new practice into an organization such as a school requires justification in terms of how well it fits into and can advance the organization's mission.

For schools trying to improve how they address barriers to learning and teaching, we suggest that a proposed practice should contribute to *developing* a comprehensive system of student supports. From this perspective, school decision makers must consider whether the practice is designed to do the following:

- Replace a necessary, but ineffective practice
- Fill a high-priority gap in a school's efforts to meet its mission
- Integrate into school improvement efforts
- Promote healthy development, prevent problems, respond early after problem onset, or treat chronic problems
- Help many not just a few students
- Integrate into a comprehensive continuum of interventions rather than become another fragmented approach

To appreciate the importance of these matters, review the discussion of the current state of the art in Part I. In doing so, note that dealing with behavior, learning, and emotional problems in schools involves two major considerations: (1) helping students address these barriers to performing well at school *and* (2) engaging and reengaging them in classroom instruction. Interventions that do not accomplish the second consideration generally are insufficient in sustaining student involvement, good behavior, effective learning at school, and general well-being.

Just adding evidence-based practices, then, does not meet a school's needs. For schools, the fundamental concern is, *Does a practice contribute to development of a comprehensive system for addressing barriers to learning and teaching?*

In a practice guide for dropout prevention from the federal *What Works Clearinghouse*, the authors stress that while individual strategies clearly can help a few students, "the greatest success in reducing dropout rates will be achieved where multiple approaches are adopted as part of a comprehensive strategy to increase student engagement" (Dynarski et al., 2008, p. 5). They stress that "while dropping out typically occurs during high school, the disengagement process may begin much earlier and include academic, social, and behavioral components. The trajectory of a young person progressing in school begins in elementary grades, where students establish an interest in school and the academic and behavioral skills necessary to successfully proceed.

During the middle school years, students' interest in school and academic skills may begin to lag, so that by... high school, students... may need intensive individual support or other supports to reengage them.... Educators and policymakers need to consider how to implement intermediate strategies aimed at increasing student engagement." (Dynarski et al., 2008, p. 4)

The guide offers six recommendations in the context of the following three categories:

- Diagnostic processes for identifying student level and schoolwide dropout problems
- Targeted interventions for a subset of middle and high school students who are identified as at risk of dropping out
- Schoolwide reforms designed to enhance engagement for all students and prevent dropout more generally

This brings us to the implementation problem.

THE IMPLEMENTATION PROBLEM

When the decision is made to add any practice, implementation plans must be formulated for how best to integrate it into the organization. For schools, this should involve fully integrating the practice into school improvement plans for reframing student-learning supports and weaving together school, community, and home resources. For school districts, additional concerns arise around planning for sustainability and equitable replication in all schools.

Implementing new practices requires careful planning based on sound intervention fundamentals. Key facets of the work include social marketing, articulation of a shared vision for the work, ensuring policy commitments, negotiating agreements among stakeholders, ensuring effective leadership, enhancing and developing an infrastructure (e.g., mechanisms for governance and priority setting, steering, operations, resource mapping, and coordination), redeploying resources and establishing new ones, building capacity (especially personnel development), establishing strategies for coping with the mobility of staff and other stakeholders, developing standards, and establishing formative and summative evaluation processes and accountability procedures.

Clearly, moving efficacious prototypes into the real world is complex. Unfortunately, for the most part, the complexities have not been well addressed.

As the National Implementation Research Network (2009) has stressed,

> . . . very little is known about the processes required to effectively implement evidence-based programs on a national scale. Research to support the implementation activities that are being used is even scarcer.

Early research on the implementation problem is directed at matters such as dissemination, readiness, fidelity and quality of implementation, generalizability, adaptation, sustainability, and replication to scale. All of these matters obviously are important.

However, for the most part, the implementation problem is studied with too limited a procedural framework and with too little attention to context. This results in skipping by fundamental considerations involved in moving evidence-based practices into common use.

Controversy

Fidelity of Implementation or Meaningful Adaptation?

Frequently reported failure to transfer empirically supported interventions into widespread daily school practice has increased focus on the *implementation* problem (sometimes discussed as the fidelity of replication problem). An emerging issue is whether it makes sense to frame the problem in such a manner. Critics suggest that expecting schools to adopt a program without adapting it to fit the specific setting is unrealistic and inappropriate (e.g., the need is to match the motivation and capacities of staff who will do the implementation). As Richard Price states, "Effective implementation depends not on exclusive and narrow adherence to researcher definitions of fidelity but also on mutual adaptation between the efficacious program features and needs and competencies of the host organization" (Price, 1997, p. 176).

The deficiencies of many implementation efforts become apparent when the process is conceived in terms of the complexities of (1) *diffusing innovations* and (2) doing so in the context of *organized systems* that have well-established institutional cultures and infrastructures. This calls for viewing the implementation problem from the vantage point of the growing bodies of literature on diffusion of innovations and systemic change. These two overlapping arenas provide the broad perspective necessary for advancing research associated with moving evidence-based practices into the real world. This broad perspective helps reframe the implementation problem as *a process of diffusing innovation through major systemic change.* Such a process encompasses the complexities of facilitating systemic changes for appropriate and effective adoption and adaptation at a particular site, as well as the added complexities of replication to scale (see Exhibit 11).

Exhibit 11   Resistance, Reluctance, or Relevant Concerns?

The following matters are often heard in schools when efforts are made to introduce some evidence-based practices:

"I don't believe their *evidence-based* intervention is better than what I do; they need to do the research on what I do before they claim theirs is better."

"That intervention is too narrow and specific to fit the problems I have to deal with."

"We wanted to use the grant money to enhance the work we already are doing, but we've been told we have to use it to buy evidence-based programs that we think don't really fit our needs."

"How do we know that if the school adopts this evidence-based program we will get the results they got in their research?"

"We have so many things we have to do now; when are we going to have time to learn these new practices?"

"They make it sound as if I am doing bad things. Soon, they will be suggesting that we are incompetent and need to be fired."

"I've heard that some of the highly touted science-based programs have been found not to work well when they are tried throughout a school district."

"I'm not taking the risk of giving up what I believe works until they prove their laboratory model does better than me out here in the real world."

Beyond these off-the-cuff remarks, more sophisticated concerns about the demand for adoption of evidence-based practices in schools come from policy makers and practitioners who are enmeshed

(Continued)

(Continued)

in transforming public education. In reacting to such concerns, researchers must be careful not to dismiss them as antiscientific and mindless resistance.

It is a truism that not everyone is ready for major changes in their lives. At the same time, not all concerns raised about proposed changes are simply resistance. The motivation for each of the above statements may simply reflect a desire not to change, or it may stem from a deep commitment to the best interests of schools and the students and families they serve. Still, such rhetoric has influenced interpretations about why achieving prototype fidelity in schools (and clinics) is so difficult.

Whatever the motivation, the controversies and concerns about what practices are appropriate and viable are major contextual variables affecting implementation. Their impact must be addressed as part of the process of implementation, especially in settings that have well-established institutional cultures and organizational and operational infrastructures.

Researchers need to avoid the blame game and appreciate the complexities of diffusing innovations and making major systemic changes. From such a vantage point, the focus shifts from "I'm right, and they're wrong" to "What haven't I done to promote readiness for change?"

SOME KEY FACETS OF CHANGE

Michael Fullan (2005) stresses that effective change requires leadership that "motivates people to take on the complexities and anxieties of difficult change" (p. 104). We would add that such leadership also must develop a refined understanding of how to facilitate change.

Major elements involved in implementing empirically supported innovative practices in an institutional setting are logically connected to considerations about systemic change. That is, the same elements can frame key intervention concerns related to implementing the practice and making systemic changes, and each is intimately linked to the other.

At any given time, an organization may be involved in introducing one or more innovations at one or more sites; it may also be involved in replicating one or more prototypes on a large scale. The nature and scope of the activity and the priorities assigned by policy and decision makers are major factors influencing implementation. For example, the broader the scope, the higher the costs; the narrower the scope, the less the innovation may be important to an organization's overall mission. Both high costs and low valuing obviously can work against implementation and sustainability.

Critical to implementation, sustainability, and replication to scale is a well-designed and developed organizational and operational infrastructure. This includes *administrative leadership* and *infrastructure mechanisms* to facilitate changes (e.g., well-trained change agents). Usually, existing infrastructure mechanisms must be modified to guarantee new practices are effectively operationalized.

A well-designed organizational and operational infrastructure ensures local ownership of innovations and a critical mass of committed stakeholders. Mechanisms pursue processes that overcome barriers to stakeholders working productively together and use strategies that mobilize and maintain proactive effort so that changes are implemented and renewed over time.

Whether the intent is to establish a prototype at one site or replicate it at many, systemic change involves four overlapping phases: (1) *creating readiness*—increasing a climate and culture for change through enhancing both the motivation and the capability of a critical mass of stakeholders, (2) *initial implementation*—change is phased in using a well-designed infrastructure for providing guidance and support and building capacity, (3) *institutionalization*—accomplished by an established infrastructure for maintaining and enhancing productive changes, and (4) *ongoing evolution and creative renewal*—through use of mechanisms to improve quality and provide continuing support in ways that enable stakeholders to become a community of learners who creatively pursue renewal.

Unsuccessful implementation and failure to sustain are associated with infrastructure deficits that are not addressed in ways that ensure major tasks related to these four phases are accomplished effectively. We discuss systemic change in more detail in Chapter 15.

ABOUT READINESS FOR CHANGE

One of the most flagrant systemic change errors is failing to give sufficient attention and time to creating readiness. Effective systemic change begins with activity designed to create readiness in terms of both motivation and capability among a critical mass of key stakeholders.

Organization researchers in schools, corporations, and community agencies clarify factors for creating an effective climate for institutional change. In reviewing this literature, the following points are highly relevant to enhancing readiness for change:

- A high level of policy commitment that is translated into appropriate resources, including leadership, space, budget, and time
- Incentives for change, such as intrinsically valued outcomes, expectations for success, recognition, and rewards
- Procedural options from which those expected to implement change can select those they see as workable
- A willingness to establish mechanisms and processes that facilitate change efforts, such as a governance mechanism that adopts ways to improve organizational health
- Use of change agents who are perceived as pragmatic—maintaining ideals while embracing practical solutions

- Accomplishing change in stages and with realistic timelines
- Providing progress feedback
- Institutionalizing mechanisms to maintain and evolve changes and to generate periodic renewal

Enhancing readiness for and sustaining change involves ongoing attention to daily experiences. Stakeholders must perceive systemic changes in ways that make them feel they are valued and contributing to a collective identity, destiny, and vision. From the perspective of intrinsic motivation theory as outlined by Ed Deci and Richard Ryan (1985, 2002), both individual and collective work must be facilitated in ways that enhance feelings of competence, self-determination, and connectedness with and commitment to others and must minimize conditions that produce psychological reactance. From the perspective of theories about enhancing a sense of community and fostering empowerment, there is growing emphasis on understanding that empowerment is a multi-faceted concept. In this context, Stephanie Riger (1993) distinguishes *power over* from *power to* and *power from*. Power over involves explicit or implicit dominance over others and events; power to is seen as increased opportunities to act; power from implies ability to resist the power of others.

CONCLUDING COMMENTS

Those who set out to implement evidence-based practices in schools are confronted with a complex set of tasks related to demonstrating *fit* and implementing systemic change. This is especially so because "the current evidence base . . . consists almost entirely of ['efficacy' studies] and very little 'effectiveness' research" (Green & Glasgow, 2006, p. 127).

A myriad of political and bureaucratic difficulties are involved in making institutional changes, especially with limited financial resources. The process rarely is straightforward, sequential, or linear. A high degree of commitment, relentlessness of effort, and realistic time frames are required.

Our intent at this point is only to foster greater appreciation for and more attention to concerns about fit and implementation as related to evidence-based practices. A more sophisticated approach is necessary to improve schools in general and address barriers to learning and teaching in particular. Chapter 15 amplifies the matter.

5

Social Control Versus Engagement in Learning

A Mental Health Perspective

A SmartBrief sent out by the Association for Supervision and Curriculum Development (ASCD) states the following: Southern schools increasingly are requiring students to take "character" classes as part of an effort to combat disrespectful behavior. Louisiana lawmakers, for instance, recently passed "courtesy conduct" legislation that requires elementary students to address their teachers as "ma'am" and "sir."

—Association for Supervision and Curriculum Development (2000)

Misbehavior disrupts. In some forms, such as bullying and intimidating others, it is hurtful. And observing such behavior may disinhibit others.

When a student misbehaves, a natural reaction is to want that youngster to experience and other students to see the consequences of misbehaving. One hope is that public awareness of consequences will deter subsequent problems. As a result, a considerable amount of time at schools is devoted to discipline; a common concern for teachers is *classroom management*.

In their efforts to deal with deviant and devious behavior and to create safe environments, the degree to which schools rely on social control strategies becomes a significant issue. For example, concerns have been raised that such practices model behavior that can foster rather than counter development of negative values and often produces other forms of undesired behavior. The tactics often make schools look and feel more like prisons than community treasures.

To move schools beyond overreliance on punishment and control strategies, advocates suggest social skills training, positive behavior support, new agendas for emotional intelligence training, asset development, and character education, and a renewed focus on school climate. Related calls are for greater home involvement, with emphasis on enhanced parent responsibility for their children's behavior and learning. More comprehensively, some reformers want to transform schools in ways that create an atmosphere of *caring, cooperative learning, and a sense of community.* Such advocates usually argue for schools that are holistically oriented and family centered. They want curricula to enhance values and character, including responsibility (social and moral), integrity, self-regulation (self-discipline), identification with academics, and a work ethic. They also want schools to foster intrinsic motivation, self-efficacy, self-esteem, diverse talents, and emotional well-being.

In general, teaching involves the ability to apply strategies for teaching content and acquiring knowledge and skills—with some degree of attention given to the process of engaging students. All this works fine in schools where most students come each day ready and able to deal with what the teacher is ready and able to teach. Indeed, teachers are fortunate when they have a classroom where the majority of students show up and are receptive to the planned lessons. In schools that are the greatest focus of public criticism, this is not the case. Teachers in such settings usually are confronted with an entirely different teaching situation. They encounter many students who not only frequently misbehave but who are also not easily intimidated by *authority* figures. Efforts to correct this state of affairs often escalate into an overemphasis on social control tactics. At the same time, little attention may be paid to reengaging students who are disengaged and often resistant to the prevailing teaching practices. Indeed, strategies for reengaging students in *learning* rarely are a prominent part of preservice or inservice preparation and seldom are the focus of interventions pursued by professionals whose role is to support teachers and students.

Concern

Pushouts

Can public education be saved while maintaining the commitment to universal education?

Dropouts or *pushouts?* Increasing pressures for school improvements seem to have the negative consequence of creating policies and practices that in effect cleanse the rolls of troubled and troubling students and anyone else who may *compromise* the progress of other students and keep achievement score averages from rising. Examples are seen in zero tolerance policies, the end of social promotion, and the backlash to *special* education and to equity of opportunity.

The following excerpt from a resolution by the National Coalition of Advocates for Students (2000) highlights basic concerns: " . . . the current national trend toward zero tolerance policies requires predetermined, harsh, and immediate consequences for a growing list of infractions resulting in long-term or permanent exclusion from public school, regardless of the circumstances, and often without due process. . . . Such policies are more likely to result in increased dropout rates and long-term negative consequences for children and communities. . . . Such policies have a disparate impact on children of color and do not result in safe schools and communities. . . . Alternatives to such policies could more effectively reduce the incidence of violence and disruption in our schools, including but not limited to the following: (1) creating positive, engaging school environments; (2) provision of positive behavioral supports to students; (3) appropriate preservice and inservice development for teachers; and (4) incorporating social problem-solving skills into the curriculum for all students."

DISENGAGED STUDENTS AND SOCIAL CONTROL

Among the most pressing problems confronting schools is that of engaging and reengaging students in classroom learning. The degree of concern about student engagement varies with school population.

Students not engaged or who have become actively disengaged from classroom instruction are among the most frequent discipline and learning problems. And behavior and learning problems may eventually lead to dropout and mental health problems.

Teachers know something about engaging students; many indicate, however, they would appreciate help to learn how to reengage disengaged students. For school personnel striving to enhance their understanding of and planning for student engagement, the review by Fredricks, Blumenfeld, and Paris (2004) is helpful (see Exhibit 12). The work differentiates three types of engagement (i.e., behavioral, emotional, and cognitive); identifies school, classroom, and individual factors that affect engagement; and outlines the focus for measuring engagement. The authors conclude, "Engagement is associated with positive academic outcomes, including achievement and persistence in school; and it is higher in classrooms with supportive teachers and peers, challenging and authentic tasks, opportunities for choice, and sufficient structure" (p. 87).

When students are not engaged in the lessons at hand, they tend to pursue other activity. As teachers and other staff try to cope with disruptive students, concern often shifts from instruction to *classroom management*. At one time, a heavy dose of punishment was the dominant approach. Currently, the stress

Exhibit 12 Engagement in Learning

The review by Fredricks et al. (2004) notes the following:

Engagement is defined in three ways in the research literature:

- *Behavioral engagement* draws on the idea of participation; it includes involvement in academic and social or extracurricular activities and is considered crucial for achieving positive academic outcomes and preventing dropping out.

- *Emotional engagement* encompasses positive and negative reactions to teachers, classmates, academics, and school and is presumed to create ties to an institution and influences willingness to do the work.

- *Cognitive engagement* draws on the idea of investment; it incorporates thoughtfulness and willingness to exert the effort necessary to comprehend complex ideas and master difficult skills.

Antecedents of engagement can be organized into the following:

- *School-Level Factors:* voluntary choice, clear and consistent goals, small size, student participation in school policy and management, opportunities for staff and students to be involved in cooperative endeavors, and academic work that allows for the development of products

- *Classroom Context:* Teacher support, peers, classroom structure, autonomy support, task characteristics

- *Individual Needs:* Need for relatedness, need for autonomy, need for competence

Engagement can be measured as follows:

- *Behavioral Engagement:* conduct, work involvement, participation, persistence (e.g., completing homework, complying with school rules, absent and/or tardy, off task)

- *Emotional Engagement:* self-report related to feelings of frustration, boredom, interest, anger, satisfaction; student-teacher relations; work orientation

- *Cognitive Engagement:* investment in learning, flexible problem solving, independent work styles, coping with perceived failure, preference for challenge and independent mastery, commitment to understanding the work

is on developing more positive practices designed to provide *behavior support* in and out of the classroom. For the most part, however, the practices aim directly at reducing disruptive behavior through *social control* strategies. An often stated assumption is that stopping misbehavior will make the student amenable to teaching. In a few cases, this may be so. However, the assumption ignores all the work on understanding *psychological reactance* and the need for individuals to restore their sense of self-determination. Moreover, it belies two painful realities: the number of students who continue to manifest poor academic achievement and the staggering dropout rate in too many schools.

The argument sometimes is made that the reason students continue to misbehave is because the socialization practices used are the wrong ones or are incorrectly implemented. In this context, the move from punishment to positive approaches is widely praised.

However, few behavioral initiatives adequately focus on a basic system failure that must be addressed so that improved behavior is maintained. That is, most of the approaches pay too little attention to helping teachers deal with (1) enhancing student engagement in classroom learning *and* (2) *reengaging* students who have disengaged. As long as a student is disengaged, misbehavior is likely to occur and reoccur. As long as the emphasis is, first and foremost, on implementing social control techniques, too little attention focuses on motivation for classroom learning.

A perspective on all this comes from appreciating distinctions between helping and socialization interventions.

WHEN HELPING CONFLICTS WITH SOCIALIZATION: THE CHALLENGE FOR MENTAL HEALTH IN SCHOOLS

When interveners focus on deviant behavior, the following question arises: Is the agenda to help, socialize, or both? The key to differentiating helping from formal socialization interventions is to determine whose interests are served (see Exhibit 13). Helping interventions are defined in terms of a primary intention to serve the client's interests; socialization interventions primarily seek to serve the interests of the society.

How does one know whose interests are served? Criteria include the nature of the consent and ongoing decision-making processes. That is, using these criteria, the interests of individuals are served when they consent to intervention without coercion and have control over major intervention decisions. In contrast, socialization agenda usually are implemented under a form of *social contract* that allows society's agents to decide on certain interventions for individuals without asking for consent; and during intervention, society maintains control over major intervention decisions.

In schools, helping and socializing agenda often come into conflict. For instance, socialization versus helping conflicts often occur when decisions are made about dealing with behavior the majority of stakeholders finds disruptive or views as inappropriate. Think about how decisions are made with respect to dealing with children who misbehave at school.

One major reason for *compulsory* education is that society wants schools to act as socializing agencies. When a youngster misbehaves at school, one facet of

Exhibit 13 Helping and Socialization Interventions

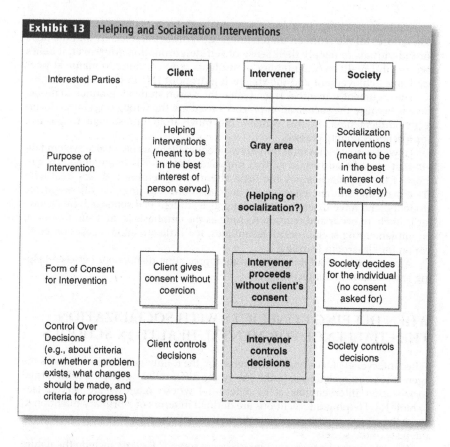

responding involves bringing the deviant and devious behavior under control. Interventions usually are designed mainly to convince students they should conform to the proscribed limits of the social setting. Parents tend to value a school's socializing agenda but also want schools to provide special help when behavior, learning, and emotional problems arise. Students for the most part do not appreciate efforts to control their behavior, especially since many of their actions are intended to enable them to escape such control. Under the circumstances, not only is conflict likely among the involved parties, the intervention efforts are likely to cause students to experience negative emotional and behavior reactions.

Practitioners commonly are confronted with situations where socialization and helping agenda are in conflict. Some resolve the conflict by clearly defining themselves as socializing agents and in that role pursue socialization goals. In such a context, helping is not the primary concern. Others resolve the conflict by viewing individuals as *clients* and pursuing helping interventions. In such cases, the goal is to work with the consenting individual to resolve problems, including efforts designed to make environments more accommodative of individual differences. Some practitioners are unclear about their agenda or are forced by circumstances to try to pursue helping and socialization simultaneously; this often adds confusion to an already difficult situation.

Situations arise when the intent is to serve the individual's interest but eliciting truly informed consent or ensuring the individual has control is not feasible. Interveners, then, are forced to operate in a gray area. This is likely to arise with young children and those with severe and profound behavior and emotional problems. Interveners also work in a gray area when intervening at the request of a surrogate who sees the intervention as in a person's best interests despite an individual's protests.

The problem of conflicting agenda is particularly acute for those who work in *institutional* settings such as schools and residential *treatment* centers. In such settings, the tasks confronting the practitioner often include both helping individuals overcome underlying problems and controlling misbehavior to maintain social order. At times, the two are incompatible. Although all interventions in the setting may be designated as *remediation* or *treatment*, the need for social control can overshadow the concern for helping. Moreover, the need to control individuals in such settings can result in coercive and repressive actions. Ultimately, every practitioner must personally come to grips with what is morally proper in balancing the respective rights of the various parties when interests conflict.

Concern

Concentrated Grouping of Aggressive Students

Researchers are reporting (and school personnel have long recognized) levels of deviancy increase with concentrated groupings of aggressive students. As Dishion and Dodge (2005) note, "The influence of deviant peers on youth behavior is of growing concern, both in naturally occurring peer interactions and in interventions that might inadvertently exacerbate deviant development" (p. 395).

Such a contagion effect has relevance for student groupings resulting from grade retention and zero tolerance policies, alternative school assignments, special education diagnoses and placements, and more. Concerns are raised that the resulting student groupings exacerbate negative outcomes such as increased misbehavior at school, neighborhood delinquency, substance abuse, and dropping out of school.

For more on these matters, see the Center's Quick Find Online Clearinghouse topic: "Behavior Problems and Conduct Disorders" http://smhp.psych.ucla.edu/qf/p3022_01.htm

INTRINSIC MOTIVATION IS FUNDAMENTAL TO ENGAGEMENT

Efforts to engage and reengage students in learning draw on what is known about human motivation. What many of us are taught about dealing with student misbehavior and learning problems runs counter to what we intuitively understand about human motivation. Teachers and parents, in particular, often learn to overdepend on reinforcement theory despite the appreciation they have about the importance of intrinsic motivation.

A broad understanding of motivation clarifies the importance of avoiding processes that limit options, make students feel controlled and coerced, and focus mostly on *remedying* problems. From an intrinsic motivational perspective, such processes are seen as likely to produce avoidance reactions in the classroom and to school and thus, reduce opportunities for positive learning and for development of positive attitudes. This leads to students' disengagement from classroom learning. Reengagement involves interventions that minimize conditions that negatively affect motivation and maximize conditions that have a positive motivational effect.

Teachers, parents, and support staff, of course, cannot control all factors affecting motivation. Indeed, when any of us address behavior and learning concerns, we directly control a relatively small segment of the physical and social environment. We try to maximize the likelihood that opportunities to learn are a good fit with the current *capabilities* of a given youngster. With learning engagement in mind, we try to match individual differences in *motivation*. Effective school interventions match individual differences in *both* capabilities and motivation and recognize that for some students, motivation is the primary factor that must be addressed.

Matching individual differences in *motivation* means attending to such matters as the following:

• *Motivation as a readiness concern.* Optimal performance and learning require motivational readiness. The absence of such readiness can cause and/or maintain problems. If a student is not motivationally ready, strategies must be pursued to develop such readiness (often including a focus on reducing avoidance motivation). Readiness should not be viewed in the old sense of waiting until an individual is interested. Promoting readiness involves establishing environments that students perceive as caring, supportive places and offering stimulating activities that are valued, challenging, and doable.

• *Motivation as a key ongoing process concern.* Many students get caught up in the novelty of a new activity, but after a few sessions, interest wanes. Some students are motivated by the idea of obtaining a given outcome but may not be motivated to pursue certain processes and so may not pay attention or may try to avoid them. For example, some are motivated initially to work on overcoming their problems but may not maintain that motivation. Strategies must elicit, enhance, and maintain motivation so that a youngster stays mobilized.

• *Minimizing negative motivation and avoidance reactions as process and outcome concerns.* Those working at a school and those at home not only must try to increase motivation—especially intrinsic motivation—but also must avoid or at least minimize conditions that decrease motivation or produce negative motivation. This involves, for example, not overrelying on extrinsics to entice and reward because doing so may decrease intrinsic motivation. At times, school is seen as unchallenging, uninteresting, overdemanding, overwhelming, overcontrolling, nonsupportive, or even hostile. When this happens, a student may develop negative attitudes and avoidance about a given situation and over time, about school and all it represents.

• *Enhancing intrinsic motivation as a basic outcome concern.* A critical outcome is to enhance motivation for pursuing a given area (e.g., good behavior, reading). The aim of good intervention is to develop a positive, intrinsic attitude that mobilizes learning and behaving outside school. Achieving such an outcome involves use of strategies that do not overrely on extrinsic rewards and that do enable youngsters to play a meaningful role in making decisions about valued options. In effect, enhancing intrinsic motivation is a fundamental *protective factor* and is the key to developing *resiliency.*

Students who are intrinsically motivated at school seek out opportunities and challenges and go beyond requirements. In doing so, they behave, perform, and learn more and learn more deeply than do classmates who are extrinsically motivated. Facilitating the engagement of such students is a fairly straightforward matter and fits well with school improvements that primarily emphasize enhancing instructional practices. The focus is on helping establish ways for students who are motivationally ready and able to achieve and of course, to maintain and enhance their motivation. The process involves knowing when, how, and what to teach and also knowing when and how to structure the situation so they can learn on their own.

In contrast, students who manifest behavior, learning, and emotional problems usually have extremely negative perceptions of teachers and programs. They are not likely to be open to people and activities that look like *the same old thing.* If the youngster is to perceive the situation is different, major changes in approach are required. Minimally, exceptional efforts must be made so they (1) view the teacher and other interveners as supportive (rather than controlling and indifferent) and (2) perceive content, outcomes, and activity options as personally valuable and obtainable. Thus, any effort to reengage disengaged students begins by addressing negative perceptions. School support staff and teachers must work together to reverse conditions that led to such perceptions.

Increasing intrinsic motivation involves affecting a student's thoughts, feelings, and decisions. In general, the intent is to use procedures that can potentially reduce negative and increase positive feelings, thoughts, and coping strategies with respect to learning. For learning and behavior problems in particular, this means identifying and minimizing experiences that maintain or may increase avoidance motivation.

For more on this topic, see the Center's Quick Find Online Clearinghouse topic: "Motivation" http://smhp.psych.ucla.edu/qf/motiv.htm

Also, note that the journal *Educational Psychologist* devoted a 2007 volume to motivational interventions, including an article on preventing student disengagement. See contents at http://www.leaonline.com/toc/ep/42/4

CONCLUDING COMMENTS

Many students say that . . . they feel their classes are irrelevant and boring, that they are just passing time . . . (and) are not able to connect what they are being taught with what they feel they need for success in their later life. This disengagement from the learning process is manifested in many ways, one of which is the lack of student responsibility for learning. In many ways, the traditional educational structure, one in which teachers "pour knowledge into the vessel" (the student), has placed all responsibility for learning on the teacher; none on the student. Schools present lessons neatly packaged, without acknowledging or accepting the messiness of learning by doing and through experience and activity. Schools often do not provide students a chance to accept responsibility for learning, as that might actually empower students. Students in many schools have become accustomed to being spoon-fed the material to master tests, and they have lost their enthusiasm for exploration, dialogue, and reflection—all critical steps in the learning process.

—American Youth Policy Forum (2000)

Student disengagement, acting out behavior, bullying, truancy, dropouts and/or pushouts—no one doubts that motivation plays a key role in all this. In many cases, motivation is a causal factor; in all cases, it is a key facet of strategies to prevent and correct problems.

Motivational considerations are always taught in personnel preparation programs. However, what is taught often is narrowly focused on extrinsic motivators. Generations of school and mental health personnel have been taught about reinforcement theory with its emphasis on extrinsic controlling strategies. As a result, the major focus in schools is on strategies to *manage* behavior.

Just emerging is growing advocacy for professional preparation and development programs to incorporate a focus on what has been learned over many decades of research on intrinsic motivation and psychological reactance. In particular, the need is to move away from coercive intervention approaches and toward autonomy-supportive intervention approaches. As a 2006 research review by Vansteenkiste, Lens, and Deci notes, externally controlling contexts overrely on "overtly coercive strategies, such as salient reward contingencies, deadlines, and overtly controlling language" (p. 22). By way of contrast, personnel in autonomy-supportive school environments "empathize with the learner's perspective, allow opportunities for self-initiation and choice, provide a meaningful rationale if choice is constrained, refrain from the use of pressures and contingencies to motivate, and provide timely positive feedback" (p. 22). Personnel preparation of all who work in schools needs to address these matters.

In Part III, we offer concepts and practices for schools to help counter an over-reliance on social control interventions.

PART III

Moving Forward

School-Based Strategies for Addressing Behavior, Learning, and Emotional Problems

> *I find the great thing in this world is not so much where we stand, as in which direction we are moving.*
>
> —Oliver W. Holmes

The world around us is changing at an exponential rate and so must the way schools approach behavior, learning, and emotional problems. Now is the time to move forward in ensuring that all youngsters have an equal opportunity to succeed at school and to achieve productive and healthy lives. To these ends, this section highlights a comprehensive framework in which to embed mental health in schools.

As schools develop improvement plans, the roles and functions of all who provide student and learning supports require rethinking. In many schools, the need to address barriers to learning and teaching is critical but is not reflected in the plans that emerge. This disconnect helps explain the plateau effect related to achievement test scores and the continuing achievement gap.

In Part III, we highlight a broadened perspective of mental health in schools and various opportunities for being proactive in school improvement planning at this time of transformation in the education and mental health fields. The broadened view emphasizes that the work involves much more than providing mental health *services*. We caution that maintaining a narrow *service* orientation contributes to the marginalization of efforts to develop a comprehensive approach. We outline a comprehensive approach and emphasize the need to develop systematic and institutionalized interventions that can do the following:

1. Enhance the role schools play in promoting healthy social and emotional development

2. Help schools minimize the ways they contribute to mental health and psychosocial problems

3. Provide an integrated school-community system to promote mental health, prevent mental health and psychosocial problems, and provide special assistance for severe and pervasive mental health problems

6

A Period of Transition and Possible Transformation

Never doubt that a small group of thoughtful, committed citizens can change the world. Indeed, it is the only thing that ever has.

—Margaret Mead

Predicting specific types of change is a risky business. It is evident that the mental health and education fields are in flux (Adelman & Taylor, 2006c; Center for Mental Health in Schools, 2007a; Doll & Cummings, 2008; Taylor & Adelman, 2004). However, no one perspective or agenda dominates policy, practice, research, or training; and future directions are unspecified.

Based on what we see around the country, we venture the following prediction. Mental health in schools will move away from an orientation that mainly plans and implements services for a relatively few students. What will emerge is a broad approach that encompasses health promotion, problem prevention, and early-after-onset interventions, as well as special assistance for those with chronic and severe problems.

In this chapter, we outline such a broad approach. In doing so, we lay it out along an interconnected continuum of interventions. The continuum provides one basic dimension for guiding efforts to move the field forward in transforming ways.

SCHOOLS AND THE TRANSFORMATION
OF THE MENTAL HEALTH SYSTEM

Two parables help clarify the need for a broad perspective in working to transform how mental health is perceived in schools. The prevailing narrow perspective is illustrated by the *starfish* metaphor.

The day after a great storm had washed all sorts of sea life far up onto the beach, a youngster, set out to throw back as many of the still-living starfish as he could. After watching him toss one after the other into the ocean, an old man approached him and said, "It's no use your doing that, there are too many. You're not going to make any difference."

The boy looked at him in surprise, then bent over, picked up another starfish, threw it in, and replied, "It made a difference to that one!"

This parable, of course, reflects all the important clinical efforts undertaken by staff alone and when they meet together to work on specific cases. It is one way to think about providing student support.

What we refer to as the *bridge* parable underscores the need to put such clinical efforts into broader perspective.

In a small town, one weekend a group of school staff went fishing together down at the river. Not long after they got there, a child came floating down the rapids calling for help. One of the group on the shore quickly dived in and pulled the child out. Minutes later another, then another, and then many more children were coming down the river. Soon everyone was diving in and dragging children to the shore and then jumping back in to save as many as they could. In the midst of all this frenzy, one of the group was seen walking away. Her colleagues were irate. How could she leave when there were so many children to save? After long hours, to everyone's relief, the flow of children stopped, and the group could finally catch their breath. At that moment, their colleague came back. They turned on her and angrily shouted, "How could you walk off when we needed everyone here to save the children?"

She replied, "It occurred to me that someone ought to go upstream and find out why so many kids were falling into the river. What I found is that the old wooden bridge had several planks missing, and when some children tried to jump over the gap, they couldn't make it and fell through into the river. So I got someone to fix the bridge."

Fixing and building better bridges is a good way to think about the value of preventing problems. Devoting time to improve and enhance resources, programs, and systems is especially critical for schools since their mission encompasses *all* not just some students and calls for preventing problems and promoting development.

We take as a given that schools and communities are expected to meet the needs of all youngsters, not just those experiencing behavior, learning, and emotional problems. This provides both an opportunity and challenge to rethink interventions for mental health, compensatory and special education, and much more.

One perspective on the future comes from the work of the President's New Freedom Commission on Mental Health (2003) and the follow-up efforts of the New Freedom Initiative. The Commission's recommendations are designed to transform the mental health system. As the Commission's report notes, this is an era of sparse resources for public enterprises. The report recommends "policy and program changes that make the most of existing resources by increasing cost effectiveness and reducing unnecessary and burdensome regulatory barriers, coupled with a strong measure of accountability."

As the Commission's work underscores, the key aim of system transformation is to improve results; a companion aim is to invest resources wisely. With sparse resources, the emphasis is on redeploying what is already committed. The problem is how to redeploy resources in ways that evolve the system. With respect to mental health in schools, a broad perspective should be adopted to guide transformation.

A BROADENED PERSPECTIVE

Ending the marginalization of mental health in schools requires connecting in substantive ways with the mission of schools. It also requires embedding mental health concerns into the full range of student and learning supports designed to address behavior, learning, and emotional problems and promote personal and social growth. Special attention must be given to using natural opportunities that arise each day, over the school year, during every transition, and as soon as a student is identified as having a problem. Practices that don't connect well with the mission of schools must be secondary and tertiary items on the agenda. These include such controversial matters as screening and diagnoses of mental health problems, mainly providing clinical and other specialized services, and connecting community providers to schools to expand and integrate school-linked services.

More specifically, broadening the perspective of mental health in schools involves the following:

- *Defining mental health broadly*—that is, encompassing the agenda for mental health *in schools* within the broad context of the psychosocial and mental health concerns encountered each day at schools—including an emphasis on strengths as well as deficits and on the mental health of students' families and school staff

- *Enhancing collaboration among schools, communities, and the home*—for example, coalescing and enhancing the roles of schools, communities, and homes in addressing emotional, behavioral, and learning problems
- *Confronting equity considerations*—for example, stressing the role mental health in schools can play in ensuring all students have an equal opportunity to succeed at school; ensuring equity of access and availability
- *Addressing the related problems of marginalization, fragmentation, and counterproductive competition for sparse resources*—that is, coalescing policy, agencies, organizations, and daily practice
- *Designing and implementing appropriate interventions*—for example, accommodating diversity, using science-based theory and evidence to enhance results, applying high standards to improve quality and guide evaluation and accountability

With respect to embedding mental health into school improvement planning, the field must clarify how schools should do the following:

- Promote social-emotional development, prevent mental health and psychosocial problems, and enhance resiliency and protective buffers
- Intervene as early after the onset of emotional, behavior, and learning problems as is feasible and also assist with students who manifest severe and chronic problems
- Address systemic matters at schools that affect student and staff well-being, such as practices that engender bullying, alienation, and student disengagement from classroom learning
- Establish guidelines, standards, and accountability for mental health in schools in ways that confront equity considerations
- Build the infrastructure for and the capacity of all school staff to address emotional, behavioral, and learning problems and promote healthy social-emotional development
- Draw on all empirical evidence as an aid in developing a comprehensive, multifaceted, and cohesive continuum of school-community interventions to address emotional, behavioral, and learning problems
- Implement and validate prototypes of systems for addressing barriers to learning and teaching

AN INTERCONNECTED CONTINUUM
OF SYSTEMS AND PROGRAMS

Our position is that school improvement planning must encompass a comprehensive, multifaceted, and cohesive system of interventions that includes a focus on mental health and psychosocial concerns (Adelman & Taylor, 2000a, 2000b, 2000c, 2002; Center for Mental Health in Schools, 2005b, 2005d). In that context, mental health in schools can be conceived both as (1) *part of* essential learning supports systems that enable students to learn so that schools can achieve their mission and (2) a fundamental facet of the initiative to transform special education and the mental health system. Moreover, existing resources can be deployed and redeployed in ways that enhance equity with respect to availability, access, and effectiveness.

As illustrated in Exhibit 14, a broadened perspective embeds mental health into a continuum of systemically interconnected school and community interventions that encompass

- *a system for promotion* of healthy development *and prevention* of problems;
- *a system for intervening early* to address problems as soon after onset as is feasible;
- *a system for* assisting those with *chronic and severe problems.*

The goal is to develop the full continuum over time.

In most discussions, the continuum is conceived as encompassing a holistic and developmental emphasis. The focus is on individuals, families, and the contexts in which they live, learn, work, and play. A basic assumption in applying interventions is that the least restrictive and nonintrusive forms required are used initially to address problems and accommodate diversity. Another assumption is that problems are not discrete, and therefore, interventions should address root causes whenever feasible.

Note that this *systems-oriented* approach provides a marked contrast with the pyramid-like triangle graphic that is often used to represent levels of interventions. We have more to say about this in Chapter 7.

To further illustrate the nature of the continuum, we have transcribed the interconnected systems in Exhibit 14 into an array of programmatic examples (see Exhibit 15). Moving through the continuum as outlined in Exhibit 15, programs focus on (1) public health protection, promotion, and maintenance that foster positive development and wellness, (2) preschool-age support and assistance to enhance health and psychosocial development, (3) early schooling interventions, (4) improvement and augmentation of ongoing regular support, (5) other interventions prior to referral for intensive and ongoing targeted treatments, and (6) intensive treatments.

The continuum highlights the necessity of revisiting policy to foster comprehensiveness and cohesion. Before this can happen, a public health and public education commitment to fully develop such a continuum is required.

As noted, work is underway to establish the type of policy and practice shift that can institutionalize such a comprehensive approach.

Supportive Evidence

Research on comprehensive approaches is still in its infancy. For obvious reasons, no study has ever looked at the impact of implementing a comprehensive system in any geographic catchment area. Thus, research support for a comprehensive approach must be gleaned from a variety of sources, including project evaluations and dissertations.

Exhibit 14   Interconnected Systems for Meeting the Needs of All Children

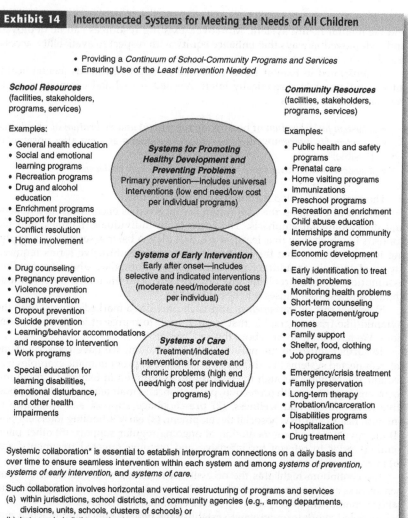

- Providing a *Continuum of School-Community Programs and Services*
- Ensuring Use of the *Least Intervention Needed*

School Resources
(facilities, stakeholders, programs, services)

Examples:

- General health education
- Social and emotional learning programs
- Recreation programs
- Drug and alcohol education
- Enrichment programs
- Support for transitions
- Conflict resolution
- Home involvement

- Drug counseling
- Pregnancy prevention
- Violence prevention
- Gang intervention
- Dropout prevention
- Suicide prevention
- Learning/behavior accommodations and response to intervention
- Work programs

- Special education for learning disabilities, emotional disturbance, and other health impairments

Community Resources
(facilities, stakeholders, programs, services)

Examples:

- Public health and safety programs
- Prenatal care
- Home visiting programs
- Immunizations
- Preschool programs
- Recreation and enrichment
- Child abuse education
- Internships and community service programs
- Economic development

- Early identification to treat health problems
- Monitoring health problems
- Short-term counseling
- Foster placement/group homes
- Family support
- Shelter, food, clothing
- Job programs

- Emergency/crisis treatment
- Family preservation
- Long-term therapy
- Probation/incarceration
- Disabilities programs
- Hospitalization
- Drug treatment

Systems for Promoting Healthy Development and Preventing Problems
Primary prevention—includes universal interventions (low end need/low cost per individual programs)

Systems of Early Intervention
Early after onset—includes selective and indicated interventions (moderate need/moderate cost per individual)

Systems of Care
Treatment/indicated interventions for severe and chronic problems (high end need/high cost per individual programs)

Systemic collaboration* is essential to establish interprogram connections on a daily basis and over time to ensure seamless intervention within each system and among *systems of prevention, systems of early intervention,* and *systems of care.*

Such collaboration involves horizontal and vertical restructuring of programs and services
(a) within jurisdictions, school districts, and community agencies (e.g., among departments, divisions, units, schools, clusters of schools) or
(b) between jurisdictions, school and community agencies, public and private sectors; among schools; among community agencies.

*Various venues, concepts, and initiatives permeate this continuum of intervention systems. For example, venues such as day care and preschools, concepts such as social and emotional learning and development, and initiatives such as positive behavior support, response to intervention, and coordinated school health. Also, a considerable variety of staff are involved.

Exhibit 15	From Primary Prevention to Treatment of Serious Problems: A Continuum of Community-School Programs to Address Barriers to Learning and Enhance Healthy Development

Intervention Continuum

Examples of Focus and Types of Intervention

(Programs and services aimed at system changes and individual needs)

Systems for health promotion and primary prevention

1. *Public health protection, promotion, and maintenance to foster opportunities, positive development, and wellness*
   - Economic enhancement of those living in poverty (e.g., work/welfare programs)
   - Safety (e.g., instruction, regulations, lead abatement programs)
   - Physical and mental health (including healthy start initiatives, immunizations, dental care, substance abuse prevention, violence prevention, health/mental health education, sex education and family planning, recreation, social services to access basic living resources, and so forth)

2. *Preschool-age support and assistance to enhance health and psychosocial development*
   - Systems enhancement through multidisciplinary teamwork, consultation, and staff development
   - Education and social support for parents of preschoolers
   - Quality day care
   - Quality early education
   - Appropriate screening and amelioration of physical and mental health and psychosocial problems

Systems for early-after-problem-onset intervention

3. *Interventions for early schooling*
   - Orientations, welcoming and transition support into school and community life for students and their families (especially immigrants)
   - Support and guidance to ameliorate school adjustment problems
   - Personalized instruction in the primary grades
   - Additional support to address specific learning and behavior problems
   - Parent involvement in problem solving
   - Comprehensive and accessible psychosocial and physical and mental health programs (including a focus on community and home violence and other problems identified through community needs assessment)

(Continued)

(Continued)

4. *Improvement and augmentation of ongoing regular support*
   - Systems enhancement through multidisciplinary teamwork, consultation, and staff development
   - Preparation and support for school and life transitions
   - Teaching "basics"of support and remediation to regular teachers (including use of available resource personnel, peer and volunteer support)
   - Parent involvement in problem solving
   - Resource support for parents-in-need (including assistance in finding work, legal aid, ELL and citizenship classes, and so forth)
   - Comprehensive and accessible psychosocial and physical and mental health interventions (including health and physical education, recreation, violence reduction programs, medical help, and so forth)
   - Academic guidance and assistance
   - Emergency and crisis prevention and response mechanisms

5. *Other interventions prior to referral for intensive, ongoing targeted treatments*
   - Systems enhancement through multidisciplinary teamwork, consultation, and staff development
   - Short-term specialized interventions (including resource teacher instruction and family mobilization; programs for suicide prevention, pregnant minors, substance abusers, gang members, and other potential dropouts)

6. *Intensive treatments*
   - Referral, triage, placement guidance and assistance, case management, and resource coordination
   - Family preservation programs and services
   - Special education and rehabilitation
   - Dropout recovery and follow-up support
   - Services for severe, chronic psychosocial/mental/physical health problems

Systems for treatment for severe/ chronic problems

Because of the fragmented nature of available research, findings are best appreciated in terms of the whole being greater than the sum of the parts, and implications are best derived from a broad conceptual framework. When a broad perspective is adopted, schools have a large research base to draw upon in addressing barriers to learning and enhancing healthy development. Examples of how to organize and use this research-base have been developed by our Center (Adelman & Taylor, 2006d; Center for Mental Health in Schools, 2004b). Additional data will be forthcoming from pioneering efforts to implement and validate the effectiveness of prototypes (Adelman & Taylor, 2003c; Elias, Zins, Graczyk, & Weissberg, 2003). Findings suggest positive outcomes (for school and society) associated with a wide range of practices.

Inferences also can be made from the daily evidence of what takes place in every wealthy and most upper-middle income communities. These natural *experiments* clearly show that families with financial resources, or who can avail themselves of such resources when necessary, purchase any of the interventions listed in Exhibits 14 and 15 to ensure their children's well-being. In a real sense, this represents empirical support for the value of such interventions that cannot be ignored.

> Jokingly, a colleague has suggested, "There is a new form of validation for some practices—it's called market validity!"

Mapping and Analysis of Resources

The continuum outlined in Exhibit 14 provides a reasonable basis for beginning to map and conduct analyses of existing resources. Such analyses help clarify how well the current state of the art approximates the ideal of having a comprehensive, multifaceted, and cohesive approach (Adelman & Taylor, 2006b).

Another guide for mapping and analysis is the set of guidelines for student support developed to outline the broadened perspective. The guidelines are included as a resource at the end of this chapter.

Mapping of needs and resources, gap analyses, and setting priorities are basic processes in transforming systems. Chapter 7 provides a more extensive framework for such work.

CONCLUDING COMMENTS

Any effort to enhance interventions for children's mental health must involve schools. Schools already provide a wide range of programs and services relevant to mental health and psychosocial concerns. Schools can and need to do much more. For this to happen, mental health in schools must be embedded into the basic mission of schools. To this end, all of us will need to help develop well-integrated, comprehensive, multifaceted support systems that enable students to learn in ways that ensure schools achieve their mandates. By doing so, we will ensure that mental health in schools is understood as fundamental to achieving their mission.

Before concluding, we want to emphasize that efforts to enhance mental health in schools should encompass a focus on promoting the well-being of teachers and other school staff so that they can do more to promote the well-being of students. Teachers, principals, student support personnel, office staff, and bus drivers all impact learning outcomes at a school. How staff work together and support each other makes a crucial difference. As is the case for students, the adults working at a school need supports that enhance protective buffers, reduce risks, and promote well-being.

Every school can foster staff and student resilience and create a school climate that encourages mutual support, caring, and sense of community. In a real sense, efforts to enhance school climate focus us not just on mental health in schools but also on the mental health *of* schools.

RESOURCE

Guidelines for an Enabling or Learning Supports Component*

1. Major Areas of Concern Related to Barriers to Student Learning

1.1 Addressing common educational and psychosocial problems (e.g., learning problems; language difficulties; attention problems; school adjustment and other life transition problems; attendance problems and dropouts; social, interpersonal, and familial problems; conduct and behavior problems; delinquency and gang-related problems; anxiety problems; affect and mood problems; sexual and/or physical abuse; neglect; substance abuse; psychological reactions to physical status and sexual activity; physical health problems)

1.2 Countering external stressors (e.g., reactions to objective or perceived stress, demands, crises, and deficits at home, school, and in the neighborhood;

inadequate basic resources such as food, clothing, and a sense of security; inadequate support systems; hostile and violent conditions)

1.3 Teaching, serving, and accommodating disorders and disabilities (e.g., learning disabilities; attention deficit hyperactivity disorder; school phobia; conduct disorder; depression; suicidal or homicidal ideation and behavior; post traumatic stress disorder; anorexia and bulimia; special education designated disorders such as emotional disturbance and developmental disabilities)

2. Timing and Nature of Problem–Oriented Interventions

2.1 Primary prevention

2.2 Intervening early after the onset of problems

2.3 Interventions for severe, pervasive, and/or chronic problems

3. General Domains for Intervention in Addressing Students' Needs and Problems

3.1 Ensuring academic success and also promoting healthy cognitive, social, emotional, and physical development and resilience (including promoting opportunities to enhance school performance and protective factors; fostering development of assets and general wellness; enhancing responsibility and integrity, self-efficacy, social and working relationships, self-evaluation and self-direction, personal safety, and safe behavior; health maintenance, effective physical functioning, careers and life roles; creativity)

3.2 Addressing external and internal barriers to student learning and performance

3.3 Providing social and emotional support for students, families, and staff

4. Specialized Student and Family Assistance (Individual and Group)

4.1 Assessment for initial (first level) screening of problems, as well as for diagnosis and intervention planning (including a focus on needs and assets)

4.2 Referral, triage, and monitoring and management of care

4.3 Direct services and instruction (e.g., primary prevention programs, including enhancement of wellness through instruction, skills development, guidance counseling, advocacy, schoolwide programs to foster safe and caring climates, and liaison connections between school and home; crisis intervention and assistance, including psychological and physical first aid; prereferral interventions; accommodations to allow for differences and disabilities; transition and follow-up programs; short- and long-term treatment, remediation, and rehabilitation)

4.4 Coordination, development, and leadership related to school-owned programs, services, resources, and systems—toward evolving a comprehensive, multifaceted, and integrated continuum of programs and services

4.5 Consultation, supervision, and inservice instruction with a transdisciplinary focus

4.6 Enhancing connections with and involvement of home and community resources (including but not limited to community agencies)

5. Ensuring Quality of Intervention

5.1 Systems and interventions are monitored and improved as necessary

5.2 Programs and services constitute a comprehensive, multifaceted continuum

5.3 Interveners have appropriate knowledge and skills for their roles and functions and provide guidance for continuing professional development

5.4 School-owned programs and services are coordinated and integrated

5.5 School-owned programs and services are connected to home and community resources

5.6 Programs and services are integrated with instructional and governance and management components at schools

5.7 Programs and services are available, accessible, and attractive

5.8 Empirically supported interventions are used when applicable

5.9 Differences among students and families are appropriately accounted for (e.g., diversity, disability, developmental levels, motivational levels, strengths, weaknesses)

5.10 Legal considerations are appropriately accounted for (e.g., mandated services, mandated reporting and its consequences)

5.11 Ethical issues are appropriately accounted for (e.g., privacy and confidentiality, coercion)

5.12 Contexts for intervention are appropriate (e.g., office, clinic, classroom, home)

6. Outcome Evaluation and Accountability

6.1 Short-term outcome data

6.2 Long-term outcome data

6.3 Reporting to key stakeholders and using outcome data to enhance intervention quality

---

* Adapted from: *Mental Health in Schools: Guidelines, Models, Resources, and Policy Considerations*, a document developed by the Policy Leadership Cadre for Mental in Schools. This document is available from the Center for Mental Health in Schools at UCLA, downloadable from the Center's Web site at http://smhp.psych.ucla.edu/pdfdocs/policymakers/guidelinesexecsumm.pdf. A separate document providing the rationale and science base for the version of the guidelines adapted for learning supports is available at http://smhp.psych.ucla.edu/summit2002/guidelinessupportdoc.pdf.

7

Strategies for Embedding Mental Health in School Improvement

It is not enough to say that all children can learn or that no child will be left behind; the work involves . . . achieving the vision of an American education system that enables all children to succeed in school, work, and life.

—Council for Chief State School Officers' mission statement

Moving forward requires ending the marginalization in school improvement policy and practice of mental health and other student support concerns. At best, school improvement plans maintain traditional approaches to student support. This perpetuates what critics call a *waiting for failure* approach and the overemphasis on services that cannot meet the needs of schools that have large numbers of students who are not doing well.

Recent policy and program analyses indicate that few student support staff are full participants at school and district tables where major school improvement decisions are made. It is no surprise, then, that school improvement planning does not appropriately account for mental health and other student support concerns. This state of affairs fundamentally undermines efforts to enable all students to have an equal opportunity to succeed at school.

Planning new directions for student support requires rethinking the multiple roles of all staff to enhance how necessary student supports are provided.

Moreover, leadership must be developed for designing and developing a comprehensive student and learning support system for all students. And such leadership must be at school improvement planning tables.

To further frame new directions, this chapter builds on the broadened perspective and the *systemic, integrated continuum* of interventions introduced in Chapter 6. We begin by introducing a unifying concept that captures the broadened perspective and embeds mental health concerns. Then, we meld the continuum with a multifaceted and cohesive set of *intervention content arenas* to create a comprehensive prototype framework for an Enabling or Learning Supports Component. We also briefly highlight implications for rethinking operational infrastructure at a school so that necessary mechanisms are in place to develop a comprehensive system for addressing barriers to learning and teaching.

UNIFYING CONCEPT

For marginalization and fragmentation of student support to end, all involved personnel must find better ways to work together. This means more than enhancing communication, cooperation, and coordination. The aim is to end *silo* activity and counterproductive competition among personnel who represent different programs and professional affiliations.

Part of the current problem is the term *student support*. It doesn't convey to policy makers an essential enterprise. The problem is compounded because the term often is interpreted as denoting the work of *specialists* who mainly provide *services* to a few of the many students who are not doing well at school.

We suggest that major inroads can result from adoption of a unifying umbrella concept that better conveys the role student and learning supports can play as a *fundamental* component in school improvement. Such a concept can convey a broad, *big-picture* understanding of the supports and why they are necessary. It can provide an unambiguous answer to the question, What is the overall direct and immediate function of student supports?

> A unifying umbrella concept embeds mental health and conveys the fundamental role of student and learning supports in school improvement so that all students have an equal opportunity to succeed at school.

Our work suggests the value of all of the following:

- Coalescing all student and learning supports under a rubric such as *addressing barriers to student learning*
- Configuring the activity into a *primary and essential component* of school improvement
- Defining the component as a comprehensive system for enabling learning by addressing barriers

Moreover, the component is framed as fully integrated with the instructional and management components at a school and districtwide (see Exhibit 16). The intent of all this is to move school improvement policy from its overemphasis on two components to adoption of a three-component model. (For more on this, see http://smhp.psych.ucla.edu/summit2002/assuringno child.pdf.)

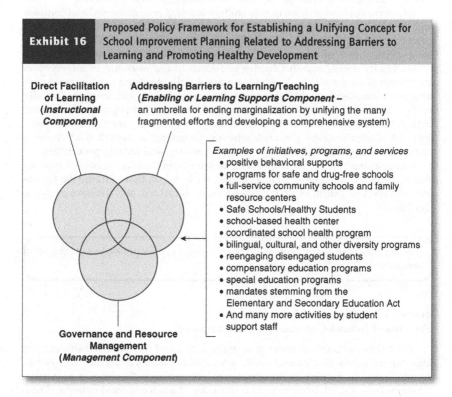

| Exhibit 16 | Proposed Policy Framework for Establishing a Unifying Concept for School Improvement Planning Related to Addressing Barriers to Learning and Promoting Healthy Development |

Direct Facilitation of Learning (*Instructional Component*)

Addressing Barriers to Learning/Teaching (*Enabling or Learning Supports Component* – an umbrella for ending marginalization by unifying the many fragmented efforts and developing a comprehensive system)

Examples of initiatives, programs, and services
- positive behavioral supports
- programs for safe and drug-free schools
- full-service community schools and family resource centers
- Safe Schools/Healthy Students
- school-based health center
- coordinated school health program
- bilingual, cultural, and other diversity programs
- reengaging disengaged students
- compensatory education programs
- special education programs
- mandates stemming from the Elementary and Secondary Education Act
- And many more activities by student support staff

Governance and Resource Management (*Management Component*)

A COMPREHENSIVE SYSTEMIC INTERVENTION FRAMEWORK

We call the component to address barriers to learning an *Enabling Component* (i.e., a component to enable learning by addressing the barriers). Various states and localities are moving to pursue school improvement in terms of the three primary and essential components graphically illustrated in Exhibit 16. In doing so, other designations often are used for the enabling component. For example, the state education agencies in California and Iowa and various districts across the country have adopted the term *Learning Supports*. The Hawaii Department of Education uses the term *Comprehensive Student Support System* (CSSS). Building on this, proposed legislation in California referred to a *Comprehensive Pupil Learning Supports System*. Whatever the component is called, the key policy and practice considerations are to define and elevate it as a primary and necessary component that complements and overlaps the instructional and management components.

Given that the range of barriers to student learning is multifaceted and complex and the number of students affected is quite large, the challenge is how to frame a comprehensive enabling component. The goal is to move away from simply itemizing specific interventions and listing various disciplines providing support.

As briefly mentioned in Chapter 6, a focus in the response to intervention movement is on three *tiers*. The tiers are graphically depicted as a pyramid continuum of interventions that at the base stresses universal interventions (for all); in the middle emphasizes targeted interventions (for selected groups designated with *at risk behavior*); and at the peak calls for individually indicated, intensive, specialized interventions (for a few who are designated as at high risk). Another categorization organizes around primary, secondary, and tertiary prevention.

Going a step further, we introduced an interconnected continuum of systems and programs in Chapter 6. In this chapter, we build on that to frame the fundamental *scope* and *content* of a comprehensive, multifaceted, and cohesive enabling component.

> The field must move from a "laundry list" of interventions to a comprehensive and cohesive framework.

Scope: A Continuum of Integrated Systems of School-Community Interventions

Over time, schools can move from fragmented and marginalized student and learning support activities into a fully *integrated continuum of intervention systems*. As illustrated in Exhibit 14 (in Chapter 6), we conceive the *scope* of activity as encompassing a school-community continuum of interconnected systems. These are framed as systems for

- *promoting* healthy development *and preventing* problems,
- *intervening early* to address problems as soon after onset as is feasible,
- *assisting* with *chronic and severe problems*.

Most schools have some programs and services that fit along the entire continuum. However, the interventions are not coalesced into integrated systems. Moreover, the tendency to focus on the most severe problems skews the process so that too little is done to prevent and intervene early after the onset of a problem.

In keeping with public education and public health perspectives, the continuum outlined in Exhibit 14 systematically spans the full spectrum of prevention efforts and incorporates a holistic and developmental emphasis that envelops individuals, families, and community contexts. It encompasses efforts to enable academic, social, emotional, and physical development and address behavior, learning, and emotional problems at every school. Properly implemented, it adheres to the principle of using the least restrictive and nonintrusive forms of intervention required to appropriately respond to problems and accommodate diversity.

Moreover, given that many problems overlap, the continuum can be designed to address root causes, thereby minimizing tendencies to develop separate programs for each observed problem. In turn, this enables improved coordination and integration of resources that can increase impact and cost effectiveness.

As graphically illustrated by the tapering of the three levels of intervention in Exhibit 14, development of a fully integrated set of *systems* is meant to reduce the number of individuals requiring specialized supports. That is, the aim in developing such a comprehensive approach is to prevent the majority of problems, deal with another significant segment as soon after problem onset as is feasible, and end up with relatively few needing specialized assistance and other intensive and costly interventions. For individual youngsters, this means preventing and minimizing as many problems as feasible and doing so in ways that maximize engagement in productive learning. For the school and community as a whole, the intent is to produce a safe, healthy, nurturing environment characterized by respect for differences, trust, caring, support, and high expectations.

Content: A Multifaceted and Cohesive Set of Content-Intervention Arenas

For any school and community, the above continuum encompasses many programs and services. In operationalizing the continuum, the focus turns to coalescing and categorizing the lengthy list of specific activities.

Pioneering efforts have grouped the many interventions at each level into intervention arenas that serve as a defined *content* or curriculum blueprint. In doing so, these trailblazers move from a laundry list to a defined and delimited set of general categories. The categories are formulated to capture the core content of what schools must do to enable *all* students to learn and *all* teachers to teach effectively.

Research has established that six arenas capture the essence of the multifaceted ways schools strive to comprehensively address barriers to learning and teaching. As illustrated in Exhibit 17 and highlighted in Exhibit 18, the categories include the following:

- *Classroom-focused enabling*—enhancing regular classroom strategies to enable learning (e.g., improving instruction for students with mild to moderate learning and behavior problems and reengaging those who have become disengaged from learning at school)

- *Support for transitions* (e.g., assisting students and families as they negotiate school and grade changes, daily transitions)
- *Home involvement with school*—strengthening families and home and school connections
- *Crisis response and prevention*—responding to, and where feasible, preventing school and personal crises
- *Community involvement and support* (e.g., outreach to develop greater community involvement and support, including enhanced use of volunteers)
- *Student and family assistance*—facilitating student and family access to effective services and special assistance as needed

Exhibit 17   Categories of Basic Content Arenas for Learning Supports Intervention

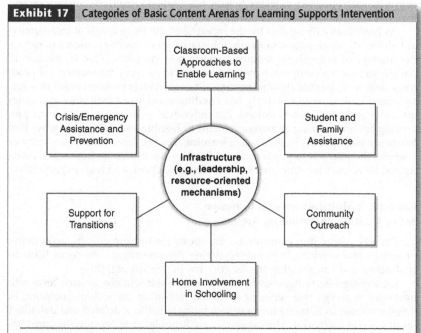

SOURCE: Adapted from Adelman and Taylor, 1994.

NOTE: *All categorical programs can be integrated into these six content arenas.* Examples of initiatives, programs, and services that can be unified into a system of learning supports include positive behavioral supports; programs for safe and drug-free schools; programs for social and emotional development and learning; full-service community schools and family resource and school-based health centers; Safe Schools/Healthy Students projects; CDC's Coordinated School Health Program; bilingual, cultural, and other diversity programs; compensatory education programs; special education programs; mandates stemming from the Elementary and Secondary Education Act; and many more. Schoolwide approaches are especially critical where large numbers of students are affected and at any school that is not yet paying adequate attention to equity and diversity concerns.

Exhibit 18	Major Examples of Activity in Each Content Arena

1. Classroom-Based Approaches encompass the following:

   • Opening the classroom door to bring available supports in (e.g., peer tutors, volunteers, aides trained to work with students in need; resource teachers and student support staff work in the classroom as part of the teaching team)

   • Redesigning classroom approaches to enhance teacher capability to prevent and handle problems and reduce need for out-of-class referrals (e.g., personalized instruction; special assistance as necessary; developing small group and independent learning options; reducing negative interactions and overreliance on social control; expanding the range of curricular and instructional options and choices; systematic use of prereferral interventions)

   • Enhancing and personalizing professional development (e.g., creating a learning community for teachers; ensuring opportunities to learn through coteaching, team teaching, and mentoring; teaching intrinsic motivation concepts and their application to schooling)

   • Curricular enrichment and adjunct programs (e.g., varied enrichment activities that are not tied to reinforcement schedules; visiting scholars from the community)

   • Classroom and schoolwide approaches used to create and maintain a caring and supportive climate

   Emphasis at all times is on enhancing feelings of competence, self-determination, and relatedness to others at school and reducing threats to such feelings.

2. Crisis Assistance and Prevention encompasses the following:

   • Ensuring immediate assistance in emergencies so students can resume learning

   • Providing follow-up care as necessary (e.g., brief and longer-term monitoring)

   • Forming a school-focused crisis team to formulate a response plan and take leadership for developing prevention programs

   • Mobilizing staff, students, and families to anticipate response plans and recovery efforts

   • Creating a caring and safe learning environment (e.g., developing systems to promote healthy development and prevent problems, bullying and harassment abatement programs)

   • Working with neighborhood schools and community to integrate planning for response and prevention

   • Capacity building to enhance crisis response and prevention (e.g., staff and stakeholder development, enhancing a caring and safe learning environment)

3. Support for Transitions encompasses the following:

   • Welcoming and social support programs for newcomers (e.g., welcoming signs, materials, and initial receptions; peer-buddy programs for students, families, staff, volunteers)

   • Daily transition programs (e.g., before school, breaks, lunch, afterschool)

   • Articulation programs (e.g., grade to grade—new classrooms, new teachers; elementary to middle school; middle to high school; in and out of special education programs)

   • Summer or intersession programs (e.g., catch-up, recreation, and enrichment programs)

(Continued)

(Continued)

- School-to-career and higher education (e.g., counseling, pathway, and mentor programs)
- Broad involvement of stakeholders in planning for transitions (e.g., students, staff, home, police, faith groups, recreation, business, higher education)
- Capacity building to enhance transition programs and activities

4. Home Involvement in Schooling encompasses the following:

- Addressing specific support and learning needs of family (e.g., support services for those in the home to assist in addressing basic survival needs and obligations to the children; adult education classes to enhance literacy, job skills, English as a second language, citizenship preparation)
- Improving mechanisms for communication and connecting school and home (e.g., opportunities at school for family networking and mutual support, learning, recreation, enrichment, and for family members to receive special assistance and to volunteer to help; phone calls and/or e-mail from teacher and other staff with good news; frequent and balanced conferences—student led when feasible; outreach to attract hard-to-reach families—including student dropouts)
- Involving homes in student decision making (e.g., families prepared for involvement in program planning and problem solving)
- Enhancing home support for learning and development (e.g., family literacy; family homework projects; family field trips)
- Recruiting families to strengthen school and community (e.g., volunteers to welcome and support new families and help in various capacities; families prepared for involvement in school governance)
- Capacity building to enhance home involvement

5. Community Outreach for Involvement and Support encompasses the following:

- Planning and implementing outreach to recruit a wide range of community resources (e.g., public and private agencies; colleges and universities; local residents; artists and cultural institutions, businesses, and professional organizations; service, volunteer, and faith-based organizations; community policy and decision makers)
- Systems to recruit, screen, prepare, and maintain community resource involvement (e.g., mechanisms to orient and welcome, enhance the volunteer pool, maintain current involvements, enhance a sense of community)
- Reaching out to students and families who don't come to school regularly, including truants and dropouts
- Connecting school and community efforts to promote child and youth development and a sense of community
- Capacity building to enhance community involvement and support (e.g., policies and mechanisms to enhance and sustain school-community involvement, staff and stakeholder development on the value of community involvement, *social marketing*)

6. Student and Family Assistance encompasses the following:

- Providing extra support as soon as a need is recognized and doing so in the least disruptive ways (e.g., prereferral interventions in classrooms; problem-solving conferences with parents; open access to school, district, and community support programs)
- Timely referral interventions for students and families with problems based on response to extra support (e.g., identification and screening processes, assessment, referrals, and follow-up—school based, school linked)
- Enhancing access to direct interventions for physical health, mental health, and economic assistance (e.g., school-based, school-linked, and community-based programs and services)
- Care monitoring, management, information sharing, and follow-up assessment to coordinate individual interventions and check whether referrals and services are adequate and effective
- Mechanisms for *resource* coordination and integration to avoid duplication, fill gaps, garner economies of scale, and enhance effectiveness (e.g., braiding resources from school-based and linked interveners, feeder pattern and family of schools, community-based programs; linking with community providers to fill gaps)
- Enhancing stakeholder awareness of programs and services
- Capacity building to enhance student- and family-assistance systems, programs, and services

FRAMEWORK FOR A COMPREHENSIVE ENABLING OR LEARNING SUPPORTS COMPONENT

Combining the six content arenas with the continuum of interventions provides a cohesive intervention framework for a comprehensive component to enable learning by addressing barriers and reengaging students in classroom instruction (i.e., an Enabling or a Learning Supports Component). The resultant matrix is illustrated in Exhibit 19.

The matrix framework helps convey a broad picture of a comprehensive, systemic approach. It provides a unifying intervention framework and an analytic tool for mapping, doing gap analyses, and setting priorities for moving forward.

In applying the framework, planners need to focus on classroom-based and schoolwide approaches. This requires

- addressing barriers and reengagement through a broader view of *basics* and through effective accommodation of individual differences and disabilities;
- enhancing the focus on motivational considerations with a special emphasis on intrinsic motivation as it relates to individual readiness and ongoing involvement with the intent of fostering intrinsic motivation as a basic outcome;
- adding remediation, treatment, and rehabilitation as necessary, but only as necessary.

Exhibit 19	Combined Continuum and Content Arenas Provide the Framework for a Comprehensive System of Learning Supports (an Enabling Component)*

Levels of Intervention

	Systems for Promoting Healthy Development and Preventing Problems	Systems for Early Intervention (Early After Problem Onset)	Systems of Care
Intervention Content Arenas			
Classroom-Focused Enabling			
Crisis/ Emergency Assistance and Prevention			
Support for Transitions			
Home Involvement in Schooling			
Community Outreach/ Volunteers			
Student and Family Assistance			

Accommodations for Differences and Disabilities

Specialized Assistance and Other Intensified Interventions (e.g., Special Education and School-Based Behavioral Health)

*The matrix creates a unifying guide for rethinking and restructuring the daily work of all staff at a school who focus on providing student and learning supports. It is used to map the current scope and content of how a school, a family of schools, and a school district address behavior, learning, and emotional problems. This information then is used to generate a gap analysis as a basis for school improvement planning and evaluation. (Related tools for moving forward are available online in a *Rebuilding Kit*–http://smhp .psych.ucla.edu/summit2002/resourceaids.htm)

Note also that various venues, concepts, and initiatives will fit into several cells of the matrix. Examples include venues such as day care centers, preschools, family centers, and school-based health centers; concepts such as social and emotional learning and development; and initiatives such as positive behavior support, response to intervention, and the coordinated school health program. The work of personnel who provide student supports also fits into one or more cells.

Finally, note in Exhibit 20 that addressing barriers to learning and teaching involves two major processes: (1) helping students around barriers *and* (2) engaging and reengaging them in classroom instruction. Interventions that do not accomplish the second consideration generally are insufficient in sustaining, over time, student involvement, good behavior, and effective learning at school.

> The intent is to prevent and minimize as many problems as feasible and to do so in ways that maximize engagement in productive learning.

In accomplishing all this, the focus is on reframing support programs and melding school, community, and home resources. Given sparse resources, this involves redeploying available resources. Toward these ends, the framework also facilitates mapping and analyzing the current scope and content for a family of schools (e.g., a feeder pattern of schools), a district, and the community.

Exhibit 20	**An Enabling Component to Address Barriers and Reengage Students in Classroom Instruction**

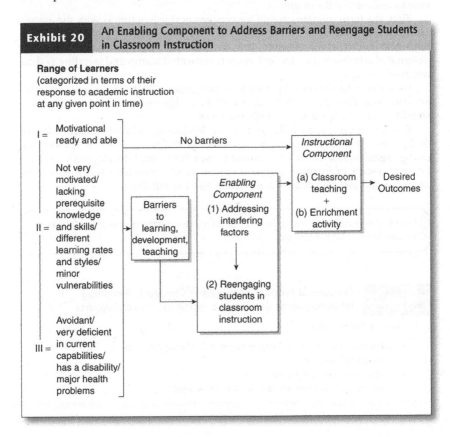

AN INTEGRATED INFRASTRUCTURE

Support personnel understand that addressing barriers to learning and teaching is axiomatic to school improvement. But many don't see why they should be concerned about school infrastructure, never mind infrastructure for connecting school and community. ("What's infrastructure got to do with helping kids?" they ask.)

A fundamental error is for school-improvement planning to ignore infrastructure changes to better account for student and learning supports. Another error is to focus only on ensuring development of case-oriented multidisciplinary teams and crisis response teams.

Prevailing organizational and operational infrastructure mechanisms marginalize the influence of those most directly concerned about addressing behavior, learning, and emotional problems. As a result, resource allocation and program planning is skewed.

Moving forward in addressing psychosocial and mental health concerns depends on rethinking school and district infrastructure. We offer a few points here to underscore the matter.

First, the term infrastructure: Our concern at this juncture is with the *organizational and operational mechanisms* that allow a system to accomplish critical functions and do so in an effective and efficient way. Of particular concern are designated administrative leaders, resource-oriented teams, and standing and ad hoc work groups.

Note that a fundamental principle in designing infrastructure is *structure follows function*. This means that infrastructure design begins with a clear understanding of roles, functions, and related tasks.

Roles, for example, include governance, leadership, administration, program design and development, capacity building, evaluation and accountability, change agent, and so forth. In pursuing these roles toward developing a comprehensive system of learning supports, a variety of immediate and longer-term functions and tasks must be accomplished (see Exhibit 21).

> Prevailing organizational and operational infrastructure mechanisms marginalize efforts to advance mental health in schools.

Exhibit 21	Examples of Functions and Tasks to Consider in Rethinking Infrastructure for Developing a System of Learning Supports

Functions—a few examples

- delineating and operationalizing the vision and defining standards
- reworking infrastructure
- conducting needs assessments
- mapping, analyzing strengths and weaknesses and gaps

- establishing priorities and making decisions about allocating resources for learning supports activity
- carrying out integrated planning, implementation, maintenance, and evaluation
- outreaching to create formal working relationships with community resources to bring some to a school and establish special linkages with others
- managing, redeploying, and braiding available resources
- gathering and analyzing process and outcome data

Tasks—a few examples

- ensuring coordination and integration for cohesively sharing facilities, equipment, and other resources
- enhancing information management, analysis, and communication
- developing strategies for enhancing resources and building capacity
- planning and implementing social marketing
- developing pools of nonprofessional volunteers and professional pro bono assistance

Dedicated and integrated infrastructure mechanisms are established with functions in mind. When the intent is to develop a comprehensive enabling component, such mechanisms not only must be integrated with each other, they must be fully enmeshed with those designed to enhance instruction and strengthen management and governance. This requires major changes in the organizational and operational infrastructure at a school and ultimately at district, regional, and state levels. It also means new roles and functions for administrators and staff.

Exhibit 22 illustrates how the infrastructure at a school might be reworked. Compare this example with what exists in most schools and districts.

A few points will help clarify the prototype infrastructure framework in Exhibit 22:

- *Leadership.* Learning Supports or Enabling Component Leadership consists of an administrator and other advocates and champions with responsibility and accountability for ensuring the vision for the component is not lost. The administrator meets with and provides regular input to the Learning Supports Resource Team.

- *Learning Supports Resource Team.* Every school that wants to improve its systems for providing student and learning supports needs a mechanism that focuses specifically on improving resource use and enhancement. A learning support resource team is a vital form of such a resource-oriented mechanism.

Most schools have case-oriented teams that focus on individual student and family problems (e.g., a student support team, an Individualized Education Plan [IEP] team). These teams focus on such functions as referral, triage, and care monitoring or management. In contrast to this case-by-case focus, a school's learning support resource team can take responsibility for enhancing use of all resources available to the school for addressing barriers to student learning and promoting healthy development. The team ensures component cohesion, integrated implementation, and ongoing development. This includes analyzing and redeploying existing resources and involving the community with a view to integrating human and financial resources from public and private sectors. The team meets weekly to guide and monitor daily implementation and development of a school's programs, services, initiatives, and systems providing learning supports and specialized assistance.

The number of team members varies with school size. Besides the administrator for the component, anyone concerned with developing a system of supports is welcome. Possible members are the student support staff at the school, a special education teacher, representatives of community agencies involved regularly with the school, and a student when appropriate and feasible.

• *Ad Hoc and Standing Work Groups.* Initially, these are *teams* that already exist related to initiatives and programs (e.g., a crisis team) and those that process *cases* (e.g., a student assistance team, an IEP team). Where redundancy exists, work groups are combined. The learning supports resource team forms others as needed to deal with specific concerns. Without these groups, many tasks cannot be accomplished.

Exhibit 22   Example of an Integrated Infrastructure at the School Level

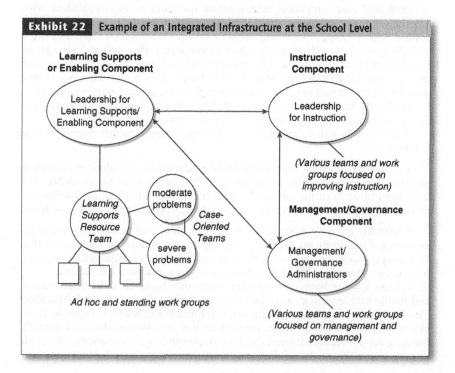

In sum, a well-designed and supported set of infrastructure mechanisms are required to establish, maintain, and evolve the type of a comprehensive approach outlined above. This includes mechanisms for administrative and staff leadership and for pursuing ongoing and ad hoc work. Such mechanisms are necessary for steering, coordinating among subsystems and specific interventions, enhancing resources by developing direct linkages between school and community programs, moving toward increased integration of school and community resources (see Chapter 13), and integrating the instructional, enabling, and management components.

WHAT MIGHT A FULLY FUNCTIONING ENABLING OR LEARNING SUPPORTS COMPONENT LOOK LIKE AT A SCHOOL?

Hawaii legislated what it calls a *Comprehensive Student Support System* (CSSS). The law was enacted to ensure that every school develops a comprehensive, multifaceted, and integrated component to address barriers to learning and promote healthy development as integral facets of school improvement (Center for Mental Health in Schools, 2007b). Adapted from a description developed for use by CSSS, the following outlines what a fully functioning enabling or learning supports component might look like at a school.

First, the school integrates the component as a primary facet of school improvement. The aim is to ensure the school develops a comprehensive, multifaceted, and cohesive approach to address barriers to learning and promote healthy development. Given limited resources, such a component is established by deploying, redeploying, and weaving all existing learning support resources together.

The school redesigns its infrastructure to establish an administrative leader who guides the component's development and is accountable for daily implementation, monitoring, and problem solving. A team (e.g., a Learning Supports Resource Team) exists that focuses on ensuring all relevant resources are woven together to install a comprehensive, multifaceted, and integrated continuum of interventions over a period of years. The team maps and analyzes available resources, sets priorities, and organizes work groups to plan program development. The goal is to establish a systemic, integrated *continuum of interventions* and a multifaceted and cohesive set of *intervention content arenas*.

While the focus of the team is on resource use and program development, it also ensures mechanisms are functioning effectively for responding rapidly when specific students are identified as having mild to moderate problems.

For most students, problems are resolved through relatively straightforward situational and program changes and problem-solving strategies. Based on analyses of their response to such interventions, additional assistance *in the classroom* is provided if needed. Those whose problems persist are referred for additional and sometimes specialized assistance. Before such interventions are set in motion, in-depth analyses are made of the reasons for their problems in order to ensure appropriate assistance is planned.

All special interventions are carefully monitored and coordinated. Through a sequential strategy that begins with the least intervention needed and that gauges students' responses to intervention at every stage, the number requiring intensive help and referral for specialized assistance is significantly reduced.

Because of the emphasis on programs and activities that create a schoolwide culture of caring and nurturing, students, families, staff, and the community feel the school is a welcoming and supportive place, accommodating of diversity, and committed to promoting equal opportunities for all students to succeed at school. When problems arise, they are responded to positively, quickly, and effectively. Morale is high. See Exhibit 23 for some more specifics.

Let the main objective . . . be as follows: To seek and to find a method of instruction, by which teachers may teach less, but learners learn more; by which schools may be the scene of less noise, aversion, and useless labor, but of more leisure, enjoyment, and solid progress.

—Comenius (1632)

Exhibit 23   Some Examples of a School's Use of a Learning Supports Component

The following should be understood as examples of the types of interventions that might be used with any student who experiences barriers to learning. Remember the point is to ensure a full continuum is available at schools. The emphasis is on ensuring a school can provide the most appropriate and least disruptive and restrictive strategies and use a student's response to intervention to gauge whether more intensive help and referrals for specialized assistance are required. When such a sequential approach is followed, schools can expect a significant reduction in the flow of referrals for specialized assistance

**Focusing on Helping the Teacher With Student Reengagement
Rather Than Overemphasizing Discipline and Referral for Services**

A third-grade teacher has several students who have not been doing well at school. They often are in trouble on the school playground before school and during lunch. Prior to establishment of a learning supports component, the teacher constantly had to discipline and send them to the principal's office. Referrals made to the Student Success Team just put the students on a long waiting list. With the learning supports component in place, the first emphasis is on how to enhance what goes on in the classroom and on schoolwide changes that minimize negative encounters; this minimizes the need for classroom management, discipline, and referral out for expensive special services.

In particular, the focus on enhancing teacher capacity to reengage students in daily learning activities helps the teacher learn more about matching individual interests and skills and how to design the instructional day to provide additional supports using peers and community volunteers. Rather than seeing the solution in terms of discipline, she learns how to understand what is motivating problems and is able to provide a more personalized approach to instruction and extra in-classroom support to reengage the students in learning. Over time, all student support staff not already involved in classroom instruction will be taught how to work in the classroom to help the teacher learn and implement new approaches for all students who are not well engaged in classroom learning.

At the same time, strategies to enhance support for transition times (such as before school and lunch) will increase recreational and enrichment opportunities for all students to have positive options for interaction. Personnel providing playground supervision are asked to play a greater role in helping engage the students in an activity that interests them (e.g., a sport's tournament, an extramural club activity). They monitor involvement to ensure the students are truly engaged and use these natural opportunities to help these and other students enhance interpersonal skills.

Newcomers: One Example of Support for Transitions and Home Involvement

To increase family involvement in schooling, special attention is placed on enhancing welcoming and social support strategies for new students and families. Student support personnel work with office staff to develop welcoming programs and establish social support networks (e.g., peer-buddy systems for students; parent-parent connections). As a result, newcomers (and all others) are greeted promptly and with an inviting attitude. Those without correct enrollment records are helped to access what they need. Parents are connected with another parent who helps them learn about school and neighborhood resources. Upon entering the new classroom, teachers connect the newcomer with a trained peer-buddy who sticks with the newcomer for a few weeks while they learn the ropes.

Support staff work with each teacher to identify any student who hasn't made a good transition. Together, they determine why and work with the family to turn things around.

Crisis Prevention

To reduce the number of crises, student support personnel analyze what is preventable (usually related to human relations problems) and then design a range of schoolwide prevention approaches. Among these are strategies to involve all school staff (credentialed and classified) in activities that promote positive interactions and natural opportunities for learning prosocial behavior and mutual respect.

Fewer Referrals, Better Response

As in-classroom and schoolwide approaches emerge, the need for out-of-classroom referrals declines. This allows for rapid and early response when a student has problems, and it enables more effective linking of students to community services when necessary.

CONCLUDING COMMENTS

Given the tremendous pressure on schools to improve academics, instructional improvements appropriately are the central concern. For too many students, however, teachers find the educational mission thwarted because of multifaceted factors interfering with youngsters' learning and performance. Addition of a comprehensive classroom and schoolwide system for addressing such factors enables teachers and students to succeed and contributes to well-being. Everyone seems to understand the matter. But too little thought and less action is directed at reframing how schools can address behavior, learning, and emotional problems in more effective ways and for all students.

In this chapter, we stressed that the immediate opportunity for moving forward is to fill a major void related to school improvement. As guides for enhancing school improvement planning, we outlined the following:

- A unifying concept that makes all learning supports fit together
- An overall comprehensive framework to guide intervention planning and development
- Infrastructure changes that facilitate development of a comprehensive system of learning supports and ensure full integration into school improvement decision making and planning

These provide a general foundation for moving forward. Chapters 8 through 11 offer a range of specific practices.

A self-study survey is included as an addendum to this chapter to provide an overview related to developing an enabling or learning supports component at a school.

For more on infrastructure concerns at school, feeder pattern, and district levels, see *Notes on Infrastructure for Learning Supports at District, Regional, and State Offices* available at http://smhp.psych.ucla.edu/pdfdocs/studentsupport/toolkit/aidk.pdf

---

Some Additional Center Resources on These Matters

Addressing What's Missing in School Improvement Planning: Expanding Standards and Accountability to Encompass an Enabling or Learning Supports Component

- http://smhp.psych.ucla.edu/pdfdocs/enabling/standards.pdf

Designing Schoolwide Programs in Title I Schools: Using the Nonregulatory Guidance in Ways That Address Barriers to Learning and Teaching

- http://smhp.psych.ucla.edu/pdfdocs/briefs/DOEguidance.pdf

Another Initiative? Where Does It Fit? A Unifying Framework and an Integrated Infrastructure for Schools to Address Barriers to Learning and Promote Healthy Development

- http://smhp.psych.ucla.edu/pdfdocs/infrastructure/anotherinitiative-exec.pdf

The School Leader's Guide to Student Learning Supports: New Directions for Addressing Barriers to Learning

- http://www.corwinpress.com/book.aspx?pid'11343

The Implementation Guide to Student Learning Supports: New Directions for Addressing Barriers to Learning

- http://www.corwinpress.com/book.aspx?pid'11371

RESOURCE

Survey of Learning Supports System Status

As a school sets out to enhance the usefulness of learning supports designed to address barriers to learning, it helps to clarify what you have in place as a basis for determining what needs to be done. You will want to pay special attention to the following:

- Clarifying what resources already are available
- How the resources are organized to work in a coordinated way
- What procedures are in place for enhancing resource usefulness?

This survey provides a starting point.

The first form provides a template that you can fill in to clarify the people and their positions at your school who provide services and programs related to addressing barriers to learning. This also is a logical group of people to bring together in establishing a resource-oriented team for learning supports at the school.

Following this is a survey designed to help you review how well systems for learning supports have been developed and are functioning.

The other self-study surveys are available at http://smhp.psych.ucla.edu/pdfdocs/Surveys/Set1.pdf

LEARNING SUPPORTS STAFF AT THE SCHOOL

In a sense, each staff member is a special resource for each other. A few individuals are highlighted here to underscore some special functions.

Administrative Leader for Learning Supports _____	*Title I and Bilingual Coordinators* _____
School Psychologist _____ times at the school _____ • Provides assessment and testing of students for special services. Counseling for students and parents. Support services for teachers. Prevention, crisis, conflict resolution, program modification for special learning and/or behavioral needs.	times at the school _____ • Coordinates categorical programs, provides services to identified Title I students, implements Bilingual Master Plan (supervising the curriculum, testing, and so forth).
School Nurse _____ times at the school _____ • Provides immunizations, follow-up, communicable disease control, vision and hearing screening and follow-up, health assessments and referrals, health counseling and information for students and families.	*Resource and Special Education Teachers* _____ _____ _____ times at the school _____ • Provides information on program modifications for students in regular classrooms as well as providing services for special education.

Pupil Services and Attendance Counselor	School-Based Crisis Team (list by name and title)
times at the school _____	_____ _____
• Provides a liaison between school and home to maximize school attendance, transition counseling for returnees, enhancing attendance improvement activities.	_____ _____ _____ _____ _____ _____ _____ _____ _____ _____
Social Worker _____	School Improvement Program Planners
times at the school _____	_____ _____
• Assists in identifying students at risk and provides follow-up counseling for students and parents. Refers families for additional services if needed.	_____ _____ _____ _____ Community Resources • Providing school-linked or school-based interventions and resources

Counselors	times at the school	Who	What they do	When
_____	_____	_____	_____	_____
_____	_____	_____	_____	_____
• General and special counseling/ guidance services. Consultation with parents and school staff.		_____	_____	_____
Dropout Prevention Program Coordinator		_____	_____	_____
_____		_____	_____	_____
times at the school _____	Other important resources:			
• Coordinates activity designed to promote dropout prevention.				

SURVEY OF LEARNING SUPPORTS SYSTEM STATUS

Items 1–9 ask about what processes are in place.

Use the following ratings in responding to these items.

DK = don't know

1 = not yet

2 = planned

3 = just recently initiated

4 = has been functional for a while

5 = well institutionalized (well established with a commitment to maintenance)

1. Is someone at the school designated as the administrative leader for activity designed to address barriers to learning (e.g., learning supports, health and social services—the Enabling Component)?   DK 1 2 3 4 5

2. Is there a time and place when personnel involved in activity designed to address barriers to learning meet together?   DK 1 2 3 4 5

3. Is there a resource-oriented team (e.g., a Learning Supports Resource Team) as contrasted to a case-oriented team?   DK 1 2 3 4 5

   a. Does the team analyze data trends at the school with respect to the following?
   - Attendance   DK 1 2 3 4 5
   - Dropouts   DK 1 2 3 4 5
   - Achievement   DK 1 2 3 4 5

   b. Does the team map learning supports programs to determine whether the following exists?
   - Identified priorities are being addressed adequately   DK 1 2 3 4 5
   - Program quality is up to standards   DK 1 2 3 4 5
   - Gaps have been identified and priorities for the future are set   DK 1 2 3 4 5

c. Which of the following areas of learning
support are reviewed regularly?
  - Classroom-based approaches to enable and   DK 1   2   3   4   5
    reengage students in classroom learning
  - Crisis assistance and prevention   DK 1   2   3   4   5
  - Support for transitions   DK 1   2   3   4   5
  - Home involvement in schooling   DK 1   2   3   4   5
  - Community outreach for involvement and   DK 1   2   3   4   5
    support
  - Student and family assistance   DK 1   2   3   4   5

4. Are there *written descriptions* of learning supports
   programs available to give to the following people?
   a. Staff   DK 1   2   3   4   5
   b. Families   DK 1   2   3   4   5
   c. Students   DK 1   2   3   4   5
   d. Community stakeholders   DK 1   2   3   4   5

5. Are there case-oriented systems in place for the
   following?
   a. Concerned parties to use in making referrals   DK 1   2   3   4   5
   b. Triage (to decide how to respond when a   DK 1   2   3   4   5
      referral is made)   DK 1   2   3   4   5
   c. Case monitoring and management   DK 1   2   3   4   5
   d. A student review team   DK 1   2   3   4   5
   e. A crisis team   DK 1   2   3   4   5

6. Are there *written descriptions* available to give to
   staff and others about the following?
   a. How to make referrals   DK 1   2   3   4   5
   b. The triage process   DK 1   2   3   4   5
   c. The process for case monitoring and management DK 1   2   3   4   5
   d. The process for student review   DK 1   2   3   4   5

7. Are there systems in place to support staff wellness? DK 1   2   3   4   5

8. Are there processes by which staff and families
   learn the following?
   a. What is available in the way of   DK 1   2   3   4   5
      programs/services at school?
   b. What is available in the way of   DK 1   2   3   4   5
      programs/services in the community?
   c. How to access programs/services they need?   DK 1   2   3   4   5

9. Has someone at the school been designated as a   DK 1   2   3   4   5
   representative to meet with the other schools in
   the feeder pattern to enhance coordination and
   integration of learning supports among the
   schools and with community resources?

The following items ask about effectiveness of existing processes.

Use the following ratings in responding to these items.

DK = don't know

1 = hardly ever effective

2 = effective about 25% of the time

3 = effective about half the time

4 = effective about 75% of the time

5 = almost always effective

10. How effective are the processes for the following?

a. Planning, implementing, and evaluating learning supports system improvements   DK   1   2   3   4   5

b. Enhancing learning supports resources (e.g., through budget decisions, staff development; developing or bringing new programs/services to the site; making formal linkages with programs/services in the community)   DK   1   2   3   4   5

11. How effective are the processes for ensuring the following?

a. Resources are properly allocated and coordinated   DK   1   2   3   4   5

b. Community resources linked with the school are effectively coordinated and integrated with related school activities   DK   1   2   3   4   5

12. How effective are the processes for ensuring that resources available to the whole feeder pattern of schools are properly allocated, shared, and coordinated?   DK   1   2   3   4   5

13. How effective is each of the following?

a. Referral system   DK   1   2   3   4   5
b. Triage system   DK   1   2   3   4   5
c. Case monitoring and management system   DK   1   2   3   4   5
d. Student review team   DK   1   2   3   4   5
e. Crisis team   DK   1   2   3   4   5

14. List community resources with which you have formal relationships.

a. Those that bring program(s) to the school site

b. Those not at the school site but which have made a special commitment to respond to the school's referrals and needs

8

Social and Emotional Learning and Promotion of Mental Health

Implications for Addressing Behavior Problems

Kids need us most when they are at their worst.

The goals of school encompass teaching academics and turning out productive and healthy citizens. With respect to the latter, the underlying concern includes promoting mental health with an emphasis on facilitating positive social and emotional development and learning.

Behavior problems clearly get in the way of schools achieving their goals. As noted in Chapter 5, misbehavior disrupts. Observing misbehavior can disinhibit others. Thus, discipline and classroom management are daily topics at every school. Unfortunately, strategies usually are reactive rather than preventive.

Concerns about promoting mental health and responding to behavior problems are highly related. Such concerns are embedded in the six content arenas discussed in Chapter 7. How these concerns are addressed is critical to the type of school and classroom climate that emerges and to student engagement and reengagement in classroom learning.

In this chapter, we approach these matters first from the perspective of promoting mental health and preventing problems. Then, we consider enhanced ways to think about and deal with behavior problems.

PROMOTION OF MENTAL HEALTH AND PREVENTION OF PROBLEMS

While screening and diagnosing problems and providing clinical services are fundamental to any mental health system, a public health approach and the broad definitions discussed in Chapter 2 require more. The comprehensive approach presented in this book calls for interventions that promote mental health, as well as preventing problems and dealing with those that can't be avoided. To these ends, mental health in schools must address risk factors, protective buffers, and promotion of full development.

Promotion of mental health encompasses enhancing knowledge, skills, and attitudes in order to foster social and emotional development, a healthy lifestyle, and personal well-being. The scope of work overlaps primary, secondary, and tertiary interventions for preventing mental health and psychosocial problems. The desired outcomes encompass those designated as 21st-century skills in the framework for 21st-century learning.

Interventions to promote mental health encompass not only strengthening individuals but also enhancing nurturing and supportive conditions at school, at home, and in the neighborhood. All this includes a particular emphasis on increasing opportunities for personal development and empowerment by promoting conditions that foster and strengthen positive attitudes and behaviors (e.g., enhancing motivation and capability to pursue positive goals, resist negative influences, and overcome barriers). It also includes efforts to maintain and enhance physical health and safety and *inoculate* against problems (e.g., providing positive and negative information, skill instruction, and fostering attitudes that build resistance and resilience).

Promoting healthy development, well-being, and a value-based life are important ends unto themselves. Exhibit 24 outlines a synthesis of major areas of focus for mental health promotion.

While schools alone are not responsible for all that is outlined in Exhibit 24, they do play a significant role, albeit sometimes not a positive one, in social and emotional development. School improvement plans need to specify ways schools (1) *directly facilitate* social and emotional (as well as physical) development and (2) *minimize threats* to positive development (Collaboration for Academic, Social, and Emotional Learning, 2003; Graczyk, Domitrovich, & Zins, 2003; Gray, Young, & Barnekow, 2006; Jané-Llopis & Barry, 2005; Power, DuPaul, Shapiro, & Kazak, 2003; Stewart-Brown, 2006; Weare, 2000; World Health Organization, 2004). In doing such planning, appreciation of differences in levels of development and developmental demands at different ages is fundamental, as is personalized implementation to account for individual differences.

Exhibit 24	Areas of Focus in Enhancing Healthy Psychosocial Development

- *Responsibility and integrity* (e.g., understanding and valuing of societal expectations and moral courses of action)
- *Self-esteem* (e.g., feelings of competence, self-determination, and being connected to others)
- *Social and working relationships* (e.g., social awareness, empathy, respect, communication, interpersonal cooperation and problem solving, critical thinking, judgment, and decision making)
- *Self-evaluation, self-direction, and self-regulation* (e.g., understanding of self and impact on others, development of personal goals, initiative, and functional autonomy)
- *Temperament* (e.g., emotional stability and responsiveness)
- *Personal safety and safe behavior* (e.g., understanding and valuing of ways to maintain safety, avoid violence, resist drug abuse, and prevent sexual abuse)
- *Health maintenance* (e.g., understanding and valuing of ways to maintain physical and mental health)
- *Effective physical functioning* (e.g., understanding and valuing of how to develop and maintain physical fitness)
- *Careers and life roles* (e.g., awareness of vocational options, changing nature of sex roles, stress management)
- *Creativity* (e.g., breaking set, thinking outside the box)

From a mental health perspective, helpful guidelines are found in research clarifying normal trends for school-age youngsters' efforts to feel *competent, self-determining,* and *connected with significant others* (Deci & Ryan, 2002). Measurement of such feelings can provide indicators of the impact of a school on mental health. Positive findings are expected to correlate with school engagement and academic progress. Negative findings are expected to correlate with student anxiety, fear, anger, alienation, a sense of losing control, and feelings of hopelessness and powerlessness. In turn, these negative thoughts, feelings, and attitudes can lead to externalizing (aggressive, *acting out*) or internalizing (withdrawal, self-punishing, delusional) behaviors.

Promoting mental health has definite payoffs both for academic performance and reducing problems at schools. As noted, promoting healthy development, well-being, and a value-based life are important ends unto themselves. Therefore, an enhanced commitment to mental health promotion should be a key facet of the renewed emphasis on the whole child by education leaders (Association for Supervision and Curriculum Development, 2007).

Protective Buffers and Promoting Full Development

A comprehensive approach strengthens individuals and enhances conditions at school, at home, and in the neighborhood (Catalano, Berglund, Ryan, Lonczak, & Hawkins, 2004). There is a particular emphasis on increasing opportunities for personal development and empowerment by promoting conditions that foster and enhance positive attitudes and behaviors (e.g., enhancing motivation and capability to pursue positive goals, resist negative influences, and overcome barriers).

While *prevention* promotes well-being, the primary concern is to reduce risks and enhance buffers through programs designed for the general population—often referred to as universal interventions—or for selected groups designated as at risk. The focus on contextual conditions recognizes that the primary causes for most youngsters' emotional, behavior, and learning problems are external factors (e.g., such as extreme economic deprivation, community disorganization, high levels of mobility, violence, drugs, poor quality or abusive caretaking, poor quality schools, negative encounters with peers, inappropriate peer models, immigrant status).

At the same time, continuing concern is given to problems stemming from individual disorders and differences (e.g., medical problems, low birth weight and neurodevelopmental delay, psychophysiological problems, difficult temperament and adjustment problems). For more on this, see *A Good Beginning: Sending America's Children to School With the Social and Emotional Competence They Need to Succeed* (Peth-Pierce, 2000) and *Preventing Mental, Emotional, and Behavioral Disorders Among Young People: Progress and Possibilities* (O'Connell et al., 2009).

Protective factors *buffer* against risks. The term *resilience* usually refers to an individual's ability to cope in ways that buffer against the impact of risks. Protective buffers prevent or counter risk-producing conditions by fostering individual, neighborhood, family, school, and/or peer strengths, assets, and coping mechanisms. Intervention strategies are designed to develop special relationships and provide special assistance and accommodations.

Examples of Protective Buffers

Conditions that prevent or counter risk-producing conditions—strengths, assets, corrective interventions, coping mechanisms, special assistance, and accommodations

Environmental Conditions*			Person Factors*
Neighborhood	Family	School and Peers	Individual
• Strong economic conditions/ emerging economic opportunities • Safe and stable communities	• Adequate financial resources • Nurturing supportive family members who are positive models	• Success at school • Safe, caring, supportive, and healthy school environment	• Higher cognitive functioning • Psychophysiological health • Easy temperament, outgoing personality, and positive behavior

Environmental Conditions*			Person Factors*
Neighborhood	Family	School and Peers	Individual
• Available and accessible services • Strong bond with positive other(s) • Appropriate expectations and standards • Opportunities to successfully participate, contribute, and be recognized	• Safe and stable (organized and predictable) home environment • Family literacy • Provision of high-quality child care • Secure attachments—early and ongoing	• Positive relationships with one or more teachers • Positive relationships with peers and appropriate peer models • Strong bond with positive other(s)	• Strong abilities for involvement and problem solving • Sense of purpose and future • Gender (girls less apt to develop certain problems)

*A reciprocal determinist view of behavior recognizes the interplay of environment and person variables.

Focusing just on enhancing assets is insufficient. As Scales and Leffert (1999) indicate in their work on developmental assets:

> Young people also need adequate food, shelter, clothing, caregivers who at the minimum are not abusive or neglectful, families with adequate incomes, schools where both children and teachers feel safe, and economically and culturally vibrant neighborhoods—not ones beset with drugs, violent crime, and infrastructural decay. For example, young people who are disadvantaged by living in poor neighborhoods are consistently more likely to engage in risky behavior at higher rates than their affluent peers, and they show consistently lower rates of positive outcomes (Brooks-Gunn & Duncan, 1997). Moreover, young people who live in abusive homes or in neighborhoods with high levels of violence are more likely to become both victims and perpetrators of violence (Garbarino, 1995).

Note that reducing risks and enhancing protection can minimize problems but are insufficient for fostering full development, well-being, and a value-based life. Those concerned with establishing systems for promoting healthy development stress that being problem free is not the same as promoting positive development. They advocate for strategies that directly facilitate development and empowerment, including the mobilization of individuals for problem solving and self-direction.

In many cases, interventions to create buffers and foster full development are identical, and the pay-off is the cultivation of developmental strengths and assets. However, promoting healthy development is not limited to countering risks and engendering protective factors. Promotion of full development is intended to produce ends valued in and of themselves and to which most of us aspire.

Examples of Conditions for Promoting Full Development

Conditions over and beyond those that create protective buffers that enhance healthy development, well-being, and a value-based life

Environmental Conditions*			Person Factors*
Neighborhood	Family	School and Peers	Individual
• Nurturing and supportive conditions • Policy and practice promotes healthy development and sense of community	• Conditions that foster positive physical and mental health among all family members	• Nurturing and supportive climate schoolwide and in classrooms • Conditions that foster feelings of competence, self-determination, and connectedness	• Pursues opportunities for personal development and empowerment • Intrinsically motivated to pursue full development, well-being, and a value-based life

*A reciprocal determinist view of behavior recognizes the interplay of environment and person variables.

Personnel working in schools can encourage youngsters and their families to take advantage of opportunities at school and in the community to prevent problems, enhance protective buffers, and promote mental health. Examples include enrollment in the following:

- Direct instruction designed to enhance specific areas of knowledge, skills, and attitudes
- Enrichment programs and service learning opportunities at school and/or in the community
- Afterschool youth-development programs

In addition, personnel working in schools have a role to play in special mental health initiatives. For example, the National Strategy for Suicide Prevention has as its first goal promoting awareness that suicide is a preventable public health problem. Strategies include developing public education campaigns, sponsoring national conferences on suicide prevention, organizing special-issue forums, and disseminating information (Mazza & Reynolds, 2008; also available at http://mentalhealth.samhsa.gov/suicideprevention/).

With respect to school environment, the aim should be to ensure it is inviting and accommodating. This requires restructuring that promotes a sense of community. Examples include establishing welcoming programs for new students and families and strategies to support other transitions, developing *families* of students and teachers to create schools within schools, and teaching peers and volunteer adults to provide support and mentoring. Strategies at this environmental level also encompass working with community agencies and businesses to enhance the range of opportunities students have with respect to recreation, work, and community service.

About Mental Health Education as a Contributor to Prevention

Mental health education helps protect, promote, and maintain the well-being of students. Mental health education ranges from disseminating mental health information to actual course instruction related to positive social and emotional development and wellness. It also encompasses many open-enrollment programs.

Every school can and should contribute to educational activity that helps protect, promote, and maintain the physical and mental well-being of students. School personnel already play a major role in disseminating health information. This includes information about the following:

- Positive opportunities for recreation and enrichment
- Opportunities to earn money
- How to stay healthy—physically and mentally (This encompasses instruction using curricula on special topics such as social skills and interpersonal relationships, substance abuse, violence prevention, physical and sexual abuse prevention, sex education, and so forth.)
- Early identification of problems
- What students and parents should do when problems arise
- Warm lines and hotlines
- Services on and off campus.

In general, schools can capitalize on the strengths of staff by facilitating a greater range of mental health roles for them to play. For instance, during the instructional day, curricula in many classes touch upon matters related to positive social and emotional development and wellness. Incorporating mental health as a major facet of health education is a natural venue. Schools can also offer a range of open-enrollment programs designed to foster positive mental health and socio-emotional functioning. In addition, school personnel can learn to respond more effectively each day as mental health and psychosocial concerns inevitably arise.

A comprehensive framework addresses risk factors, protective buffers, and promotion of full development. By preventing mild to moderate problems from developing into severe ones, schools reduce the number of students who need specialized interventions and help reserve such assistance for those who require it.

FACILITATING SOCIAL AND EMOTIONAL DEVELOPMENT AND LEARNING

One facet of proactively promoting mental health is promoting healthy social and emotional development. This meshes well with a school's goals for enhancing students' personal and social well-being. It also supports efforts to transform classroom and school climate by creating an atmosphere of *caring, cooperative learning,* and a *sense of community.*

Agenda for promoting social and emotional learning encourage a holistic and family-centered orientation and practices that increase positive engagement in learning at school. Encompassed are strategies to enhance personal responsibility (social and moral), integrity, self-regulation (self-discipline), a work ethic, diverse talents, and positive feelings about self and others.

The commitment to fostering students' personal and social functioning is supported by an understanding that social and emotional growth

- enhance the daily smooth functioning of schools and the emergence of a safe, caring, and supportive school climate;
- facilitate students' holistic development;
- enable student motivation and capability for academic learning;
- optimize life beyond schooling.

What Is Social and Emotional Learning?

For most individuals, learning social skills and emotional regulation are part of normal development and socialization. Thus, social and emotional learning is not primarily a formal training process. This can be true even for individuals who have behavior and emotional problems. (While poor social skills are identified as a symptom and contributing factor in a wide range of educational, psychosocial, and mental health problems, remember that symptoms are only correlates not validated indicators of cause.)

As formulated by the Collaborative for Academic, Social, and Emotional Learning (CASEL), social and emotional learning (SEL)

is a process for helping children and even adults develop the fundamental skills for life effectiveness. SEL teaches the skills we all need to handle ourselves, our relationships, and our work, effectively and ethically. These skills include recognizing and managing our emotions, developing caring and concern for others, establishing positive relationships, making responsible decisions, and handling challenging situations constructively and ethically. They are the skills that allow children to calm themselves when angry, make friends, resolve conflicts respectfully, and make ethical and safe choices. (Collaboration for Academic, Social, and Emotional Learning, 2003)

CASEL also views SEL as

. . . providing a framework for school improvement. Teaching SEL skills helps create and maintain safe, caring learning environments. The most beneficial programs provide sequential and developmentally appropriate instruction in SEL skills. They are implemented in a coordinated manner, schoolwide, from preschool through high school. Lessons are reinforced in the classroom, during out-of-school activities, and at home. Educators receive ongoing professional development in SEL. And families and schools work together to promote children's social, emotional, and academic success. (Collaboration for Academic, Social, and Emotional Learning, 2003)

Because of the scope of SEL programming, the work is conceived as multi-year. The process stresses adult modeling and coaching and student practice to solidify learning social and emotional awareness of self and others, self-management, responsible decision making, and relationship skills (Collaboration for Academic, Social, and Emotional Learning, 2003; Elias & Barbarasch, 2009; Greenberg, Weissberg, et al., 2003; Merrill, Gueldner, & Tran, 2008).

Natural Opportunities to Promote Social and Emotional Learning

Sometimes promoting social and emotional learning takes the form of a special curriculum (e.g., social skills training, character education, assets development) or is incorporated into the regular curricula. Even if this is not the case, classroom and schoolwide practices can and should do much more to (1) capitalize on *natural* opportunities at schools to promote social and emotional development and (2) minimize transactions that interfere with positive growth in these areas. Natural opportunities are authentic examples of *teachable moments.*

Observations during a school day and over the school year provide ample sightings of natural opportunities. For example, watch for whether instruction is carried out in ways that strengthen or hinder development of interpersonal skills and connections. Is cooperative learning and sharing promoted? Is student understanding of self and others facilitated? Is counterproductive competition minimized? Are interpersonal conflicts mainly suppressed, or are they used as learning opportunities? Are roles provided for all students to become positive helpers throughout the school and community?

More generally, pay attention to the following:

• *Daily opportunities.* Schools are social milieus. Each day in the classroom and around the school, students interact with their peers and various adults in formal and informal ways. Every encounter—positive and negative—represents a potential learning experience. All school staff, and especially teachers, can be taught ways to capitalize on such encounters to enhance social-emotional learning and minimize transactions that work against positive growth.

• *Yearly patterns.* The culture of most schools yields fairly predictable patterns over the course of the year. The beginning of the school year, for example, typically is a period of hope. As the year progresses, a variety of stressors are encountered. Examples include homework assignments that are experienced as increasingly difficult, interpersonal conflicts, and testing and grading pressures. Special circumstances also are associated with holidays, social events, sports, grade promotions, and graduation.

Each month strategies can be implemented that encourage school staff to enhance coping and minimize stressors through social-emotional learning and shared problem solving. The point is to establish a focus each month and build the capacity of school staff to evolve the school culture in ways that reduce unnecessary stressors and naturally promote social and emotional development. Monthly themes are readily generated; a few examples are listed in Section II of Exhibit 25.

• *Transitions.* Students are regularly confronted with a variety of transitions—changing schools, changing grades, and encountering a range of other minor and major transitory demands. Every transition can exacerbate problems or be used to promote positive learning and attitudes and reduce alienation. However, institutionalized efforts to support students through such transitions often are neglected. Examples of schoolwide and classroom-specific opportunities to address transitions proactively include a focus on welcoming new arrivals (students, their families, staff); providing ongoing social supports as students adjust to new grades, schools, programs; and using before and afterschool and intersession activities as times for ensuring generalization and enrichment of such learning.

• *Early after a problem arises.* Stated simply, every student problem represents a need and an opportunity for learning. A theme throughout this volume is that, whatever the first response, the second response to such problems should include a focus on promoting personal and social growth.

Exhibit 25 summarizes examples of natural opportunities for promoting personal and social growth related to each of the above groupings. The exhibit can be shared at schools as a stimulus to encourage greater attention to social and emotional development.

Exhibit 25	Examples of *Natural* Opportunities at School to *Promote* Social-Emotional Learning

I. *Using Natural Daily Opportunities*

    A. In the classroom (e.g., when students interact with each other and to staff during class and group instruction; when cooperative learning, peer sharing, and tutoring are used; as one facet of addressing interpersonal and learning problems)

    B. Schoolwide (e.g., providing roles for all students to be positive helpers and leaders throughout the school and community; engaging students in strategies to enhance a caring, supportive, and safe school climate; as aspects of conflict resolution and crisis prevention)

II. *In Response to Yearly Patterns*—Schools have a yearly rhythm, changing with the cycle and demands of the school calendar. The following are examples of monthly themes developed for schools to draw upon and go beyond. The idea is to establish focal points for minimizing potential problems and pursuing natural opportunities to promote social-emotional learning.

September—Getting Off to a Good Start

October—Enabling School Adjustment

November—Responding to Referrals in Ways That Can *Stem the Tide*

December—Reengaging Students: Using a Student's Time Off in Ways That Pay Off!

January—New Year's Resolutions—A Time for Renewal; A New Start for Everyone

February—The Midpoint of a Schoolyear—Report Cards and Conferences: Another Barrier or a Challenging Opportunity

March—Reducing Stress; Preventing Burnout

April—Spring Can Be a High Risk Time for Students

May—Time to Help Students and Families Plan Successful Transitions to a New Grade or School

June—Summer and the *Living Ain't Easy*

July—Using *Downtime* to Plan Better Ways to Work Together in Providing Learning Supports

August—Now Is the Time to Develop Ways to Avoid Burnout

(For resources to pursue these monthly themes, go to the Center for Mental Health in Schools at UCLA—http://smhp.psych.ucla.edu)

III. *During Transitions*

    A. Daily (e.g., capturing opportunities before school, during breaks, lunch, afterschool)

    B. Newcomers (e.g., as part of welcoming and social support processes; in addressing school adjustment difficulties)

    C. Grade to Grade (e.g., preparing students for the next year; addressing adjustment difficulties as the year begins)

(Continued)

(Continued)

IV. *At the First Indication That a Student Is Experiencing Problems*—Enhancing social and emotional functioning is a natural focus of early-after-onset interventions for behavior, learning, and emotional problems.

The Promise of Promoting Social and Emotional Learning

Programs to improve social skills and interpersonal problem solving are described as having promise both for prevention and correction. Early research was conducted mainly with students manifesting emotional and behavior disorders. The majority of this research found limited skills were acquired, and outcome maintenance and generalizability was poor. This was the case for training of specific skills (e.g., what to say and do in a specific situation), general strategies (e.g., how to generate a wider range of interpersonal problem-solving options), as well as efforts to develop cognitive-affective orientations (e.g., empathy training).

Recent analyses by researchers involved with the CASEL suggest

> . . . students who receive SEL programming academically outperform their peers, compared to those who do not receive SEL. Those students also get better grades and graduate at higher rates. Effective SEL programming drives academic learning, and it also drives social outcomes such as positive peer relationships, caring and empathy, and social engagement. Social and emotional instruction also leads to reductions in problem behavior such as drug use, violence, and delinquency (Collaboration for Academic, Social, and Emotional Learning, 2003; also see Payton et al., 2008). However, note that such findings have been critiqued not only on empirical grounds but also with respect to the political, cultural, and educational assumptions upon which contemporary practices are based. (Hoffman, 2009)

RESPONDING TO BEHAVIOR PROBLEMS

What are ways to respond to behavior problems that are consistent with promoting mental health?

After making broad programmatic changes to the degree feasible, intervention with a misbehaving student involves steps directed at underlying factors. For instance, with intrinsic motivation in mind, the following assessment questions arise:

- Is the misbehavior unintentional or intentional?
- If intentional, is it reactive or proactive?
- If the misbehavior is reactive, is it a reaction to threats to self-determination, competence, or relatedness?

- If proactive, are there other interests that might successfully compete with satisfaction derived from deviant behavior?

In general, intrinsic motivation theory suggests that corrective interventions for those misbehaving reactively must reduce reactance and enhance positive motivation for participation. For youngsters highly motivated to pursue deviance (e.g., those who proactively engage in criminal acts), even more is needed. Intervention might focus on helping these youngsters identify and follow through on a range of valued, socially appropriate alternatives to deviant activity. Such alternatives must be capable of producing greater feelings of self-determination, competence, and relatedness than usually result from the youngster's deviant actions. To these ends, motivational analyses of the problem can point to specific strategies for implementation by teachers, clinicians, parents, or students themselves.

Disengaged Students, Misbehavior, and Social Control

Disengagement is associated with behavior and learning problems and eventual dropout. As noted in Chapter 5, engagement is associated with supportive teachers, peers, and classrooms with challenging and authentic tasks, opportunities for choice, and sufficient structure (Fredericks et al., 2004).

Among the various supports are strategies that reengage students who have become disengaged and perhaps resistant to broad-band (nonpersonalized) teaching approaches. To the dismay of most teachers, however, strategies for reengaging students in *learning* rarely are a prominent part of preservice or inservice preparation and seldom are the focus of interventions pursued by professionals whose role is to support teachers and students (National Research Council and the Institute of Medicine, 2004).

For years, schools have been criticized for overemphasizing punishment. To move schools beyond overreliance on punishment, ongoing advocacy stresses initiating social skills training, asset development, character education, and positive behavior interventions and supports (Bear, 2008). The move from punishment to positive approaches is a welcome one. However, most of the new initiatives pay too little attention to helping teachers deal with student engagement problems and other related motivational concerns (Wentzel & Wigfield, 2007).

From a motivational perspective, addressing behavior problems does not end with implementing social control techniques and eliminating situational triggers. Strategies also must enhance teachers' understanding of how to reengage a student in classroom learning. Such strategies also may enable a teacher to prevent many behavior problems.

Reacting to Misbehavior

Unfortunately, too many people see punishment as the only recourse in dealing with misbehavior. They use the most potent negative consequences available to them in a desperate effort to control an individual and make it clear to others that acting in such a fashion is not tolerated.

Because of the frequency of student misbehavior, teachers often feel they must deal with the behavior problem before they can work on the matters of engagement and accommodation. This is especially the case when deviant and devious behavior creates an unsafe environment.

As a result, teachers and other school staff increasingly have adopted social control strategies. These include some *discipline* and *classroom management* practices that model behavior that fosters (rather than counters) development of negative values. Exhibit 26 presents an overview of prevailing discipline practices.

Exhibit 26   Defining and Categorizing Discipline Practices

Historically, the two mandates that have shaped much of current practice include the following:

1. Schools must teach self-discipline to students.
2. Teachers must learn to use disciplinary practices effectively to deal with misbehavior.

In 1987, Knoff offered three definitions of discipline as applied in schools:

> (a) ... punitive intervention; (b) ... a means of suppressing or eliminating inappropriate behavior, of teaching or reinforcing appropriate behavior, and of redirecting potentially inappropriate behavior toward acceptable ends; and (c) ... a process of self-control whereby the (potentially) misbehaving student applies techniques that interrupt inappropriate behavior, and that replace it with acceptable behavior. (p. 119)

In contrast to the first definition that specifies discipline as punishment, Knoff viewed the other two as nonpunitive or as he called them "positive, best-practices approaches" (p. 119).

In 1982, Hyman, Flanagan, and Smith categorized models shaping disciplinary practices into five groups: psychodynamic-interpersonal models, behavioral models, sociological models, eclectic-ecological models, and human-potential models

In 1986, Wolfgang and Glickman grouped disciplinary practices in terms of a process-oriented framework:

- Relationship-listening models
- Confronting-contracting models
- Rules and rewards-punishment

In 1995, Bear categorized three goals of the practice—with a secondary nod to processes, strategies, and techniques used to reach the goals:

- Preventive discipline models (e.g., models that stress classroom management, prosocial behavior, moral/character education, social problem solving, peer mediation, affective education and communication models)
- Corrective models (e.g., behavior management, Reality Therapy)
- Treatment models (e.g., social skills training, aggression replacement training, parent management training, family therapy, behavior therapy)

We find noteworthy that so much of the literature stresses the negative impact of harsh discipline. Findings from parenting studies point to increases in child aggression, formation of a maladaptive social information processing style, and internalization of negative values. Significant correlations also are reported between corporeal punishment of adolescents and depression, suicide, alcohol abuse, and domestic abuse.

In schools, short of suspending the individual, punishment takes the form of a decision to do something to students that they do not want done. In addition, a demand for future compliance usually is made, along with threats of harsher punishment if compliance is not forthcoming. The discipline may be administered in ways that suggest the student is seen as an undesirable person. As students get older, suspension increasingly comes into play. Indeed, suspension remains one of the most common disciplinary responses for the transgressions of secondary students.

As with many emergency procedures, the benefits of using punishment may be offset by many negative consequences. These include increased negative attitudes toward school and school personnel. These attitudes often lead to more behavior problems, antisocial acts, and various mental health problems. Disciplinary procedures also are associated with dropping out of school. Extreme disciplinary practices often constitute *pushout* strategies.

Most school guidelines for managing misbehavior stress that discipline should be reasonable, fair, and nondenigrating (e.g., should be experienced by recipients as legitimate reactions that neither denigrate one's sense of worth nor reduce one's sense of autonomy). With this in mind, classroom management practices usually emphasize establishing and administering *logical consequences*. Such an idea is generalized from situations where naturally occurring consequences are present, such as touching a hot stove causes a burn. (See Exhibit 27 for more on the topic of logical consequences.)

Exhibit 27   About Logical Consequences

In classrooms, little ambiguity may exist about the rules; unfortunately, the same often cannot be said about *logical* penalties. Even when the consequence for a particular rule infraction is specified ahead of time, the logic may be more in the mind of the teacher than in the eyes of the students. In the recipient's view, any act of discipline may be experienced as punitive—unreasonable, unfair, denigrating, disempowering.

Basically, consequences involve depriving students of things they want and/or making them experience something they don't want. Consequences take the form of (1) removal and/or deprivation (e.g., loss of privileges, removal from an activity), (2) reprimands (e.g., public censure), (3) reparations (e.g., to compensate for losses caused by misbehavior), and (4) recantations (e.g., apologies, plans for avoiding future problems). For instance, teachers commonly deal with acting out behavior by removing a student from an activity. To the teacher, this step (often described as *time-out*) may be a logical way to stop students from disrupting others by isolating them, or the logic may be that the students need a cooling off period. The reasoning is that (1) by misbehaving, students show they do not deserve the privilege of participating (assuming the students like the activity), and (2) the loss will lead to improved behavior in order to avoid future deprivation.

Most teachers have little difficulty explaining their reasons for using a consequence. However, if the intent really is for students to perceive consequences as logical and nondebilitating, logic calls for determining whether the recipient sees the discipline as a legitimate response to misbehavior. Moreover, difficulties arise about how to administer consequences in ways that minimize negative impact on a student's perceptions of self. Although the intent is to stress that the misbehavior and its impact are bad, students too easily can experience the process as characterizing them as bad people.

Organized sports such as youth basketball and soccer offer a prototype of an established and accepted set of consequences administered with a recipient's perceptions given major consideration. In these arenas, referees are able to use the rules and related criteria to identify inappropriate acts and apply penalties; moreover, they are expected to do so with positive concern for maintaining a youngster's dignity and engendering respect for all.

If discipline is to be perceived as a logical consequence, steps must be taken to convey that a response is not a personally motivated act of power (e.g., an authoritarian action) and indeed, is a rational and socially agreed upon reaction. Also, if the intent is long-term reduction in future misbehavior, time must be taken to help students learn right from wrong, to respect others rights, and to accept responsibility.

From a motivational perspective, logical consequences are based on understanding a student's perceptions and are used in ways that minimize negative repercussions. To these ends, motivation theory suggests (1) establishing publicly accepted consequences to increase the likelihood they are experienced as socially just (e.g., reasonable, firm but fair) and (2) administering such consequences in ways that allow students to maintain a sense of integrity, dignity, and autonomy. These ends are best achieved under conditions where students are *empowered* (e.g., are involved in deciding how to make improvements and avoid future misbehavior and have opportunities for positive involvement and reputation building at school).

Specific discipline practices ignore the broader picture that every classroom teacher must keep in mind. The immediate objective of stopping misbehavior must be accomplished in ways that maximize the likelihood that the teacher can engage and reengage the student in instruction and positive learning.

From a prevention viewpoint, few doubt that program improvements that engage and reengage students can reduce behavior (and learning) problems significantly. Application of consequences also is recognized as an insufficient step in preventing future misbehavior. Therefore, as outlined in Exhibit 28, strategies for dealing with misbehavior should encompass interventions for

- preventing and anticipating misbehavior,
- reacting during misbehavior,
- following up.

Exhibit 28   Intervention Focus in Dealing With Misbehavior

I. Preventing Misbehavior

  A. Expand Social Programs

    1. Increase economic opportunity for low-income groups.

    2. Augment health and safety prevention and maintenance (encompassing parent education and direct child services).

    3. Extend quality day care and early education.

  B. Improve Schooling

    1. Personalize classroom instruction (e.g., accommodating a wide range of motivational and developmental differences.

    2. Provide status opportunities for nonpopular students (e.g., special roles as assistants and tutors).

    3. Identify and remedy skill deficiencies early.

  C. Follow Up All Occurrences of Misbehavior to Remedy Causes

    1. Identify underlying motivation for misbehavior.

    2. For unintentional misbehavior, strengthen coping skills (e.g., social skills, problem-solving strategies).

    3. If misbehavior is intentional but reactive, work to eliminate conditions that produce reactions (e.g., conditions that make the student feel incompetent, controlled, or unrelated to significant others).

    4. For proactive misbehavior, offer appropriate and attractive alternative ways the student can pursue a sense of competence, control, and relatedness.

    5. Equip the individual with acceptable steps to take instead of misbehaving (e.g., options to withdraw from a situation or to try relaxation techniques).

    6. Enhance the individual's motivation and skills for overcoming behavior problems (including altering negative attitudes toward school).

(Continued)

(Continued)

II. Anticipating Misbehavior

  A. Personalize Classroom Structure for High-Risk Students

    1. Identify underlying motivation for misbehavior.
    2. Design curricula to consist primarily of activities that are a good match with the identified individual's intrinsic motivation and developmental capability.
    3. Provide extra support and direction so the identified individual can cope with difficult situations (including steps that can be taken instead of misbehaving).

  B. Develop Consequences for Misbehavior That Are Perceived by Students as Logical (i.e., that are perceived by the student as reasonably fair, and nondenigrating reactions that do not reduce one's sense of autonomy)

III. During Misbehavior

  A. Try to base response on understanding of underlying motivation (if uncertain, start with assumption the misbehavior is unintentional).

  B. Reestablish a calm and safe atmosphere

    1. Use understanding of student's underlying motivation for misbehaving to clarify what occurred (if feasible involve participants in discussion of events).
    2. Validate each participant's perspective and feelings.
    3. Indicate how the matter will be resolved emphasizing use of previously agreed upon logical consequences that have been personalized in keeping with understanding of underlying motivation.
    4. If the misbehavior continues, revert to a firm but nonauthoritarian statement.
    5. As a last resort use crises back-up resources.

      a. If appropriate, ask student's classroom friends to help.
      b. Call for help from identified back-up personnel.

    6. Throughout the process, keep others calm by dealing with the situation with a calm and protective demeanor.

IV. After Misbehavior

  A. Implement Discipline—Logical Consequences/Punishment

    1. Objectives in using consequences
      a. Deprive student of something she or he wants.
      b. Make student experience something she or he doesn't want.

    2. Forms of consequences
      a. Removal and/or deprivation (e.g., loss of privileges, removal from activity)
      b. Reprimands (e.g., public censure)
      c. Reparations (e.g., of damaged or stolen property)
      d. Recantations (e.g., apologies, plans for avoiding future problems)

  B. Discuss the Problem With Parents

    1. Explain how they can avoid exacerbating the problem.
    2. Mobilize them to work preventively with school.

  C. Work Toward Prevention of Further Occurrences (see I & II)

Positive Behavioral Interventions and Supports

One reaction to all the negative approaches to discipline has been the development of initiatives for using positive behavioral interventions and supports. For various reasons, the first such initiatives came from special education. As noted by the U.S. Department of Education (2005):

> Students who receive special education as a result of behavior problems must have individualized education programs that include behavior goals, objectives, and intervention plans. While current laws driving special education do not require specific procedures and plans for these students, it is recommended that their IEPs be based on functional behavioral assessments and include proactive positive behavioral interventions and supports—Positive Behavioral Support (PBS).

PBS encompasses a range of interventions that are implemented in a systematic manner based on a student's demonstrated level of need. It is supposed to address factors in the environment that are relevant to the causes and correction of behavior problems.

While the focus was first on special education, the initiative has expanded into schoolwide applications of behavioral techniques, with an emphasis on teaching specific social skills (Bear, 2008). Here is how the U.S. Department of Education (2005) emphasizes use of schoolwide PBS, including universal, group, and individual interventions.

> In the past, schoolwide discipline has focused mainly on reacting to specific student misbehavior by implementing punishment-based strategies, including reprimands, loss of privileges, office referrals, suspensions, and expulsions. Research has shown that the implementation of punishment, especially when it is used inconsistently and in the absence of other positive strategies, is ineffective. Introducing, modeling, and reinforcing positive social behavior is an important part of a student's educational experience. Teaching behavioral expectations and rewarding students for following them is a much more positive approach than waiting for misbehavior to occur before responding.
>
> The purpose of schoolwide PBS is to establish a climate in which appropriate behavior is the norm. A major advance in schoolwide discipline is the emphasis on schoolwide systems of support that include proactive strategies for defining, teaching, and supporting appropriate student behaviors to create positive school environments. Instead of using a patchwork of individual behavioral management plans, a continuum of positive behavior support for all students within a school is implemented in areas, including the classroom and nonclassroom settings (such as hallways, restrooms). Positive behavior support is an application of a behaviorally based systems approach to enhance the capacity of schools, families, and communities to design effective environments that improve the link between research-validated practices and the environments in

which teaching and learning occur. Attention is focused on creating and sustaining primary (schoolwide), secondary (classroom), and tertiary (individual) systems of support that improve lifestyle results (personal, health, social, family, work, recreation) for all children and youth by making problem behavior less effective, efficient, and relevant, and desired behavior more functional.

The schoolwide PBS process emphasizes the creation of systems that support the adoption and durable implementation of evidence-based practices and procedures, and fit within ongoing school reform efforts. An interactive approach that includes opportunities to correct and improve four key elements is used in schoolwide PBS focusing on the following:

- Outcomes: academic and behavior targets that are endorsed and emphasized by students, families, and educators.
- Practices: interventions and strategies that are evidence based.
- Data: information that is used to identify status, need for change, and effects of interventions.
- Systems: supports that are needed to enable the accurate and durable implementation of the practices of PBS.

All effective schoolwide systems have seven major components in common: (a) an agreed upon and common approach to discipline, (b) a positive statement of purpose, (c) a small number of positively stated expectations for all students and staff, (d) procedures for teaching these expectations to students, (e) a continuum of procedures for encouraging displays and maintenance of these expectations, (f) a continuum of procedures for discouraging displays of rule-violating behavior, and (g) procedures for monitoring and evaluating the effectiveness of the discipline system on a regular and frequent basis.

With the growing interest in response to intervention (RtI) initiatives, educators are tying PBS and RtI together in a shared problem-solving approach. The intent is to both correct and prevent problems. PBS also is discussed as a way to enhance school climate (Swearer, Espelage, Loe, & Kingsbury, 2008).

Focusing on Underlying Motivation to Address Concerns About Engagement

Moving beyond socialization, social control, and behavior modification and with an emphasis on engagement, strategies must address the roots of misbehavior, especially the underlying motivational bases for such behavior.

Consider students who spend most of the day trying to avoid all or part of the instructional program. An intrinsic motivational interpretation suggests that many of these youngsters do not perceive school as a place where they experience a sense of competence, autonomy, and or relatedness to others. Over time, these perceptions develop into strong motivational dispositions and related patterns of misbehavior.

Misbehavior can reflect proactive (approach) or reactive (avoidance) motivation. Uncooperative, disruptive, and aggressive behavior patterns that are *proactive* tend to be rewarding and satisfying to an individual because the behavior itself is exciting or because the behavior leads to desired outcomes (e.g., peer recognition, feelings of competence, or autonomy). Intentional negative behavior stemming from such approach motivation is viewed as pursuit of deviance.

Misbehavior in the classroom often also is *reactive*, stemming from avoidance motivation. This behavior is viewed as a protective reaction. Students with learning problems often are motivated to avoid and to protest against being forced into situations in which they cannot cope effectively. For such students, many teaching and therapy situations are perceived in this way. Under such circumstances, individuals can be expected to react by trying to protect themselves from the unpleasant thoughts and feelings that the situations stimulate (e.g., feelings of incompetence, loss of autonomy, negative relationships). In effect, the misbehavior reflects efforts to cope and defend against aversive experiences. The actions may be direct or indirect and include defiance, physical and psychological withdrawal, and diversionary tactics.

Interventions for reactive and proactive behavior problems begin with major program changes. From a motivational perspective, the aims are to (1) prevent and overcome negative attitudes toward school and learning; (2) enhance motivational readiness for learning and overcoming problems; (3) maintain intrinsic motivation throughout learning and problem solving; and (4) nurture the type of continuing motivation that results in students engaging in activities away from school that foster maintenance, generalization, and expansion of learning and problem solving. Failure to attend to motivational concerns in a comprehensive, normative way results in approaching passive and often hostile students with practices that instigate and exacerbate problems.

Social control techniques may be necessary initially, but they are insufficient for reengaging students in classroom learning. For this reason, the developmental trend in responding to misbehavior must be toward practices that embrace an expanded view of engagement and human motivation and a focus on social and emotional learning (see Exhibit 29).

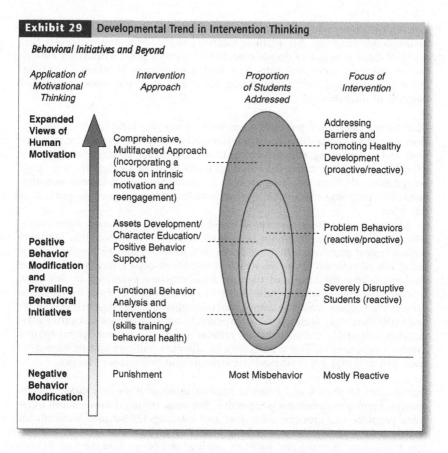

Exhibit 29 Developmental Trend in Intervention Thinking

Behavioral Initiatives and Beyond

Application of Motivational Thinking	Intervention Approach	Proportion of Students Addressed	Focus of Intervention
Expanded Views of Human Motivation	Comprehensive, Multifaceted Approach (incorporating a focus on intrinsic motivation and reengagement)		Addressing Barriers and Promoting Healthy Development (proactive/reactive)
Positive Behavior Modification and Prevailing Behavioral Initiatives	Assets Development/ Character Education/ Positive Behavior Support		Problem Behaviors (reactive/proactive)
	Functional Behavior Analysis and Interventions (skills training/ behavioral health)		Severely Disruptive Students (reactive)
Negative Behavior Modification	Punishment	Most Misbehavior	Mostly Reactive

CONCLUDING COMMENTS

As John Holt (1989) noted half seriously: *I suspect that many children would learn arithmetic, and learn it better, if it were illegal.*

Concern for social and emotional learning and for student misbehavior is leading to an increasing appreciation for the power of intrinsic motivation (Deci & Ryan, 2002). Motivation research and theory provide ample guidance for developing strategies to counter student disengagement and promote mental health (Adelman & Taylor, 2006a; Brophy, 2004; National Research Council and the Institute of Medicine, 2004; Vansteenkiste et al., 2006).

As we discuss in the next few chapters, enhancing intrinsic motivation is a core consideration in the overall redesign of classrooms and for all facets of mental health in schools.

9

Challenges and Opportunities for Promoting Mental Health in the Classroom

*. . . there's no bigger challenge than trying to insert kids in a one-size-fits-all
[classroom] and then having to deal with the spillover of emotional and behavioral reactions. If kids are not in a place where they can learn, they let us know
loud and clear.*

—Patricia Woodin-Weaver, cited in Willis and Mann (2000)

Effectively addressing students' behavior, learning, and emotional problems
requires transforming what transpires in classrooms. To this end, student-
support staff and others who can help must spend more time teaming with
teachers *in the classroom*.

One frequently mentioned challenge and opportunity for doing so stems
from the interest in response to intervention (RtI) initiatives. Wisely, such initiatives stress the unacceptability of waiting for students to fail. However, as with so
many ways of addressing students' behavior, learning, and emotional problems,
this budding movement often is pursued as just another piecemeal approach
(Samuels, 2008).

Fragmentary endeavors cannot address the complex realities confronting teachers and student support staff. A fact of life in too many classrooms is that a significant proportion of students lack enthusiasm for the day's lesson plans. Moreover, an alarming number are totally disengaged from classroom instruction and are disruptive and/or dropping out. To reverse all this requires interventions that enable such students to (1) get around interfering barriers and (2) reengage in classroom instruction. Properly designed, the RtI movement can help, but it represents only one strategy in the complex process of transforming struggling classrooms into effective learning environments.

Breakthroughs in reducing behavior, learning, and emotional problems are unlikely until school improvement planners face up to developing a comprehensive system of learning supports. One major facet of such a system is the redesign of regular classroom strategies to better enable learning. The redesign includes the following:

- Opening the classroom door (a) to bring in more help (e.g., volunteers trained to work with students in need; resource teachers and student support staff to team up with the teacher in the classroom) and (b) to facilitate personalized professional development
- Ensuring what goes on in the classroom (and schoolwide) establishes and maintains a stimulating, caring, and supportive climate
- Enhancing teacher capability to prevent and handle problems and reduce the need for out-of-class referrals (e.g., personalizing instruction; expanding the range of curricular and instructional options and choices; systematic use of prereferral interventions, response to intervention, and in-class special assistance; turning big classes into smaller units; reducing overreliance on social control)

OPENING THE CLASSROOM DOOR AND CREATING STIMULATING, CARING, AND SUPPORTIVE CLASSROOMS

Opening the classroom door allows for many forms of assistance, mentoring, partnership, and other collegial practices. Opening the classroom door means ensuring those who enter are welcomed and supported.

Teachers, especially new teachers, need more in-classroom support and personalized on-the-job education than they receive. All teachers want to learn more about how to enable learning among students, especially those with problems. All school personnel want support from each other in enhancing outcomes for such students. They also need to work closely with parents, volunteers, professionals in training, and so forth.

An open classroom door allows colleagues to do much more than *consult*. It encourages collaboration and teaming that are key facets of (1) addressing barriers to learning and teaching and (2) promoting engagement, learning, performance, and healthy development. However, before colleagues such as student support staff can effectively team with a teacher in a classroom, they must learn much more about classroom life and teaching. They must especially learn about what it takes to engage and reengage students in classroom instruction.

Opening the classroom door helps to create a stimulating, caring, and supportive context that promotes academic achievement and social and emotional learning.

How classrooms are arranged and how instruction is organized helps or hinders learning and teaching and affects behavior. The aim is to design the classroom to promote personalized and holistic learning and minimize behavior, learning, and emotional problems. Student engagement is especially critical in preventing problems. When a problem does arise, the goal is to address it immediately using RtI strategies (including *prereferral* interventions).

Minimally, classroom practices must enhance motivation to learn and facilitate active learning and do so in ways that promote a climate and culture of mutual caring and respect. The ideal is to create an environment where students and teachers feel positively stimulated, well supported, and engaged in pursuing the learning objectives of the day.

Stimulating, caring, and supportive classrooms do much more than motivate learning of subject matter and academic skills. They provide conditions for social and emotional learning. Students learn to cooperate, share responsibility, develop understanding and skills related to conflict resolution and mediation, and much more. For staff, such classrooms provide a context for collaborating with colleagues and with a variety of volunteers to ensure mutual support and counter staff burnout (see Exhibit 30).

Exhibit 30   About School and Classroom Climate
Climate is a key concept in planning to enhance the quality of school life, teaching, learning, and support. School and classroom climate sometimes are referred to as the learning environment, as well as by terms such as atmosphere, ambience, ecology, and milieu.   Classroom climate influences classroom behavior and learning. The impact on students and staff can be beneficial or another barrier to learning and teaching. Understanding the nature of classroom climate is a basic element in improving schools. Implied is the intent to establish and maintain a positive context that facilitates classroom learning. In practice, classroom climates range from hostile or toxic to welcoming and supportive and can fluctuate daily and over the schoolyear.

School and classroom climate are temporal, and somewhat fluid, perceived qualities of the immediate setting that emerge from the complex transaction of many factors. In turn, the climate reflects the influence of the underlying, institutionalized values and belief systems, norms, ideologies, rituals, and traditions that constitute the school *culture*. And of course, the climate and culture at a school are affected by the surrounding political, social, cultural, and economic contexts (e.g., home, neighborhood, city, state, country).

Related concepts for understanding school and classroom climate are social system organization; social attitudes; staff and student morale; power, control, guidance, support, and evaluation structures; curricular and instructional practices; communicated expectations; efficacy; accountability demands; cohesion; competition; *fit* between learner and classroom; system maintenance, growth, and change; orderliness; and safety. Moos (1979) groups such concepts into three dimensions: (1) Relationship (i.e., the nature and intensity of personal relationships within the environment—the extent to which people are involved in the environment and support and help each other); (2) Personal development (i.e., basic directions along which personal growth and self-enhancement tend to occur); and (3) System maintenance and change (i.e., the extent to which the environment is orderly, clear in expectations, maintains control, and is responsive to change).

Prevailing approaches to measuring classroom climate use (1) teacher and student perceptions, (2) external observer's ratings and systematic coding, and/or (3) naturalistic inquiry, ethnography, case study, and interpretative assessment techniques (Fraser, 1998; Freiberg, 1999). Because the concept is a psychological construct, climate in a given classroom can be perceived differently by observers. With this in mind, Moos (1979) measured classroom environment in terms of the shared perceptions of those in the classroom.

Analyses of research suggest significant relationships between classroom climate and matters such as student engagement, behavior, self-efficacy, achievement, and social and emotional development; principal leadership style; stages of educational reform; teacher burnout; and overall quality of school life. For example, studies report strong associations between achievement levels and classrooms that are perceived as having greater cohesion and goal direction and less disorganization and conflict. Research also suggests that the impact of classroom climate may be greater on students from low-income homes and groups that often are discriminated against.

Given the correlational nature of classroom climate research, cause-and-effect interpretations remain speculative. The broader body of organizational research does indicate the profound role accountability pressures play in shaping organizational climate (Mahony & Hextall, 2000). Thus, it is likely that the increasing demands for higher achievement test scores and control of student behavior contribute to a classroom climate that is reactive, overcontrolling, and overreliant on external reinforcement to motivate positive functioning.

Opening the classroom door expands and facilitates active learning.

Simply stated, active learning is *learning by doing, listening, looking,* and *asking;* but just being active is not what counts. The objective is mobilization of the student to seek out and learn. Specific activities are designed to capitalize on student interests and curiosity, involve them in problem solving and guided inquiry, and elicit their thinking through reflective discussions and appropriate products. Moreover, the activities are designed to do all this in ways that minimize threats to and enhance feelings of competence, self-determination, and relatedness to others.

Examples abound of ways to facilitate active learning at all grade levels. It can take the form of class discussions, problem-based and discovery learning, a project approach, involvement in learning centers at school, experiences outside the classroom, and independent learning in or out of school. Obviously, computers and the worldwide Internet are valuable tools in all this. Opening classroom doors allows the world to come in and students to go out in ways that enhance motivation and learning.

The many mental health implications of opening the classroom door and creating a positive climate in the classroom and throughout the school are clear. In addition, research has indicated a range of strategies for enhancing a positive climate.

Opening the classroom door enables all school personnel to play a role in establishing a proactive approach for developing a positive climate in the class and throughout the school. Analyses suggest that a proactive approach requires careful attention to (1) enhancing the quality of life at school and especially in the classroom for students and staff, (2) pursuing a curriculum that promotes not only academic but also social and emotional learning, (3) enabling teachers and other staff to be effective with a wide range of students, and (4) fostering intrinsic motivation for learning and teaching. With respect to all this, the literature advocates

- a welcoming, caring, and hopeful atmosphere;
- social support mechanisms for students and staff;
- an array of options for pursuing goals;
- meaningful participation by students and staff in decision making;
- transforming the classroom infrastructure from a big classroom into a set of smaller units organized to maximize intrinsic motivation for learning and not based on ability or problem-oriented grouping;
- providing instruction and responding to problems in a personalized way;
- use of a variety of strategies for preventing and addressing problems as soon as they arise;
- a healthy and attractive physical environment that is conducive to learning and teaching.

For any school, a welcoming induction and ongoing support are critical elements both in creating a positive sense of community and in facilitating staff and student school adjustment and performance. Schoolwide strategies for welcoming and supporting staff, students, and families at school *every day* are part of creating a mentally healthy school—one where staff, students, and families interact positively with each other and identify with the school and its goals.

Using Aides and Volunteers in Targeted Ways

Every teacher has had the experience of planning a wonderful lesson and having the class disrupted by one or two unengaged students (who often are more interested in interacting with a classmate than pursuing the lesson). The first tendency usually is to use some simple form of social control to stop the disruptive behavior (e.g., using proximity and/or a mild verbal intervention). Because so many students today are not easily intimidated, teachers often find such strategies don't work. So, the control efforts are escalated. The teacher reprimands, warns, and finally sends the student to *time-out* or to the front office for discipline. In the process, the other students start to titter about what is happening and learning is disrupted.

In contrast to this scenario, teachers can train qualified volunteers to work in ways that help all concerned by minimizing disruptions and reengaging an errant student. The objective is to train volunteers to watch for and move quickly at the first indication that a student needs special guidance and support. For instance, a volunteer is taught to go and sit next to the student and quietly try to reengage the youngster in the lesson. If this proves undoable, the volunteer takes the student to a quiet area in the classroom and initiates another type of activity. If necessary and feasible, the volunteer and student may go out for a brief walk. While this means the student won't get the benefit of instruction during that period, that wouldn't have happened anyway.

None of this is a matter of rewarding student bad behavior. Rather, the strategy avoids the tragedy of disrupting the whole class while the teacher reprimands the culprit and in the process increases that student's negative attitudes toward teaching and school. This use of a volunteer allows teaching to continue, and as soon as time permits, it makes it possible for staff to explore with the student ways to make the classroom a mutually satisfying place to be. Moreover, by handling the matter in this way, the teacher is likely to find the student more receptive to discussing things than if the usual *logical consequences* have been administered (e.g., loss of privileges, sending the student to time-out or to the assistant principal).

Using this approach and not having to shift into a discipline mode has multiple benefits. For one, the teacher is able to carry out the day's lesson plan. For another, the other students do not have the experience of seeing the teacher having a control contest with a student. (Even if the teacher wins such contests, it may have a negative effect on how students perceive him or her; and if the teacher somehow "loses it," that definitely conveys a wrong message. Either outcome can be counterproductive with respect to a caring climate and a sense of community.) Finally, the teacher has not had a negative encounter with the targeted student. Such encounters build up negative attitudes on both sides that can be counterproductive with respect to future teaching, learning, and behavior. Because no negative encounter has taken place, the teacher can reach out to the student after the lesson is over and start to think about how to use an aide or volunteers to work with the student to prevent future problems.

For more on volunteers as an invaluable resource, see Resource B at the end of this chapter.

REDESIGNING CLASSROOM STRATEGIES

The old adage: "Meet learners where they are" captures the commonsense view of good classroom practices. Unfortunately, this adage often is interpreted only as a call for *matching* a student's current *capabilities* (e.g., knowledge and skills). The irony, of course, is that most school personnel know that motivational factors (e.g., attitudes) play a key role in poor instructional outcomes. One of the most frequent laments about students is, "They could do it if only they *wanted* to!"

We all also know that good abilities are more likely to emerge when students are motivated not only to pursue assignments but also are interested in using what they learn. The point is that good classroom practices involve matching *motivation* (especially *intrinsic* motivation), and this often involves overcoming *avoidance* motivation (Adelman & Taylor, 2006d; Deci & Ryan, 1985, 2002).

With respect to facilitating learning, the desire to meet learners where they are is based on the concept of the *match* or the problem of *fit*. Schools strive to design instruction that is an optimal match, but the reality is they often must settle for a reasonably good fit. The best approximation probably emerges from *personalizing instruction*.

Personalization

The concepts of individualized or personalized instruction overlap in emphasizing developmental differences. That is, most *individualized* approaches stress individual differences in developmental capability. *Personalization*, however, is defined as the process of accounting for individual differences in *both capability* and *motivation* (Adelman & Taylor, 2006a; Taylor & Adelman, 1999).

We approach personalization as a psychological construct. Psychologically, a *learner's perception* is a critical factor in defining whether the environment is a good fit. Given this, effective practice involves ensuring learning opportunities are *perceived by learners* as good ways to reach their goals. From this perspective, a basic assessment concern is that of eliciting learners' perceptions of how well what is offered matches both their interests and abilities.

Outlined in Exhibit 31 are underlying assumptions and major elements of personalized classrooms. Properly designed and carried out, personalizing instruction is sufficient in facilitating classroom learning for most students, and this reduces the need for specialized assistance.

Exhibit 31	Underlying Assumptions and Major Program Elements of a Personalized Program

I. Underlying Assumptions

The following are basic assumptions underlying personalized programs as we conceive them:

- Learning is a function of the ongoing transactions between the learner and the learning environment.

- Optimal learning is a function of an optimal match between the learner's accumulated capacities and attitudes and current state of being and the program's processes and context.
- Matching both learner motivation and capacities must be primary procedural objectives.
- The learner's perception is the critical criterion for evaluating whether a good match or fit exists between the learner and the learning environment.
- The wider the range of options that can be offered and the more the learner is made aware of the options and has a choice about which to pursue, the greater the likelihood that he or she will perceive the match as a good one.
- Besides improved learning, personalized programs enhance intrinsic valuing of learning and a sense of personal responsibility for learning. Furthermore, such programs increase acceptance and even appreciation of individual differences, as well as independent and cooperative functioning and problem solving.

II. Program Elements

Major elements of personalized programs as we have identified them are as follows:

- Turning large classes into small units (many small group and individual learning opportunities— see Resource A at the end of this chapter)
- Regular use of informal and formal conferences for discussing options, making decisions, exploring learners' perceptions, and mutually evaluating progress
- A broad range of options from which learners can make choices with regard to types of learning content, processes, needed support and guidance, and desired outcomes
- Active decision making by learners in making choices (with appropriate guidance and support) and in evaluating how well the chosen options match their motivation and capability
- Establishment of program plans and mutual agreements about the ongoing relationships between the learners and the program personnel
- Regular reevaluations of decisions, reformulation of plans, and renegotiation of agreements based on mutual evaluations of progress, problems, and learners' perceptions of the match

Personalizing regular classroom programs also can improve the effectiveness of prevention, inclusion, RtI, and prereferral interventions. In such classrooms, personalization represents a regular classroom application of the principle of using the least intervention required to meet a need (which encompasses the concept of least restrictive environment).

Enhancing Motivation Is a Core Concern

The emphasis on motivation has fundamental intervention implications (Vansteenkiste et al., 2006). In particular, classroom redesign should ensure instructional strategies encompass a broad range of content, outcome, and procedural *options*, including a personalized structure to facilitate learning. Real options generate substantive opportunities for *involving learners in decision making*. A motivational focus also stresses development of nonthreatening ways to provide information about learning and performance.

Student support personnel can contribute greatly by helping ensure that classrooms address motivation as a primary consideration. For example, teachers often require assistance in the classroom when determining what is likely to affect a student's positive and negative motivation to learn.

Many instructional approaches are effective when a student is motivated to learn what is taught. For students with behavior, learning, and emotional problems, however, enhancing motivation for classroom learning often is the primary concern. The seeds of significant problems are planted when instruction is not a good fit. For example, learning problems generate an emotional overlay and usually behavior problems. Thus, while motivation is a basic concern for all students, strategies to enhance motivation are essential for those with problems.

In transforming classrooms, the following points about motivation warrant particular attention:

1. *Optimal performance and learning require motivational readiness.* Motivation is a key antecedent condition in any learning situation. *Readiness* is understood in terms of offering stimulating and supportive environments where learning can be perceived as vivid, valued, and attainable. Readiness is a prerequisite to student attention, involvement, and performance. Poor motivational readiness may cause poor learning and a factor maintaining behavior, learning, and emotional problems. Thus, the need for strategies that produce a high level of motivational readiness (and reduce avoidance motivation and reactance) so students are mobilized to participate.

2. *Motivation represents both a process and an outcome concern.* Individuals can value learning something but may not be motivated to pursue the processes used. Many students are motivated to learn when they first encounter a topic but do not maintain that motivation. Processes must elicit, enhance, and maintain motivation so that students stay mobilized. Programs must be designed to maintain, enhance, and expand intrinsic motivation so that what is learned is not limited to immediate lessons and is applied in the world beyond the schoolhouse door.

Negative motivation and avoidance reactions and any conditions likely to generate them must be circumvented or at least minimized. Of particular concern are activities students perceive as unchallenging, uninteresting, overdemanding, or overwhelming. Most people react against structures that seriously limit their range of options or that are overcontrolling and coercive. Examples of conditions that can have a negative impact on a person's motivation are sparse resources, excessive rules, and a restrictive day-in, day-out emphasis on drill and remediation.

Students experiencing problems at school usually have extremely negative perceptions of and avoidance tendencies toward teachers and activities that look like *the same old thing.* Major changes in approach must be made if such students are to change these perceptions. Ultimately, success may depend on the degree to which the students view the adults at school and in the classroom as supportive rather than indifferent or controlling and intended outcomes as personally valuable and obtainable.

3.   *School staff not only need to increase motivation—especially intrinsic motivation—but also must avoid practices that decrease it.* Students may learn a specific lesson at school (e.g., some basic skills). However, they may have little or no interest in using the new knowledge and skills outside the classroom. Increasing the desire to do so requires procedures that can reduce negative and increase positive feelings, thoughts, and coping strategies.

Identifying and minimizing experiences that maintain or increase avoidance motivation is of special concern with respect to students manifesting behavior, learning, and emotional problems. Care must be taken to avoid over-reliance on extrinsics to entice and reward since such strategies can decrease intrinsic motivation.

The point is to enhance stable, positive, intrinsic attitudes that mobilize ongoing pursuit of desired ends, throughout the school, and away from school. Developing intrinsic attitudes is basic to increasing the type of motivated practice (e.g., reading for pleasure) that is necessary for mastering and assimilating new learning.

GOSH, MRS. THOMPSON, I WAS READY TO LEARN MATH YESTERDAY. TODAY I'M READY TO LEARN TO READ.

Personalize First; Add Special Assistance If Necessary

Small, personalized learning communities foster productive learning both by removing developmentally hazardous conditions that may be present in the school context and by providing opportunities to learn, opportunities to teach, and learning supports that enable a school to become a positive, developmentally enhancing context.

—Felner, Seitsinger, Brand, Burns, and Bolton (2008)

A sequential and hierarchical framework can guide efforts to provide a good match and determine the most appropriate and least disruptive intervention needed for individuals with learning and behavior problems (see Exhibit 32). The first step personalizes instruction in regular classrooms. The intent is to ensure the program is highly responsive to learner differences in both motivation and development and, in the process, enhance a caring context for learning.

With personalized instruction in place, the next step provides special assistance as necessary. Note that this second step is introduced only if learners continue to have problems. As outlined in Exhibit 32, Step 2 involves three levels of focus.

To be a bit more specific:

Step 1 involves *personalizing instruction*. The intent is to ensure a student *perceives* instructional processes, content, and outcomes as a good match with his or her interests and capabilities. The first emphasis is on *motivation*. Thus, Step 1a stresses use of motivation-oriented strategies to (re)engage the student in classroom instruction. This step draws on the broad science base related to human motivation with special attention paid to research on intrinsic motivation and psychological reactance. The aim is to enhance student perceptions of significant options and involvement in decision making.

The next concern is *developmental capabilities*. Thus, Step 1b stresses use of teaching strategies that account for current knowledge and skills. In this respect, the emphasis on tutoring (designated as "Supplemental Services" in Title I) can be useful if the student perceives the tutoring as a good fit for learning. Then, if necessary, intervention expands to encompass *special assistance*. Step 2 stresses use of special assistance strategies to address any major barriers to learning and teaching. In this respect, the range of strategies referred to as "Prereferral Interventions" (see Exhibit 33) and the programs and services that constitute learning supports are of considerable importance. (Again, the impact depends on students' perceptions of how well interventions fit their needs.)

With a sequential approach, students who do not respond sufficiently to regular classroom interventions next receive supportive assistance designed to help them remain in the regular program. Only after all this is found insufficient is a referral made for special education assessment. (If the problem proves to be severe and disruptive, an alternative setting may be necessary on a temporary basis to provide more intensive and specialized assessments and assistance.)

Exhibit 32   Learning Sequence and Levels

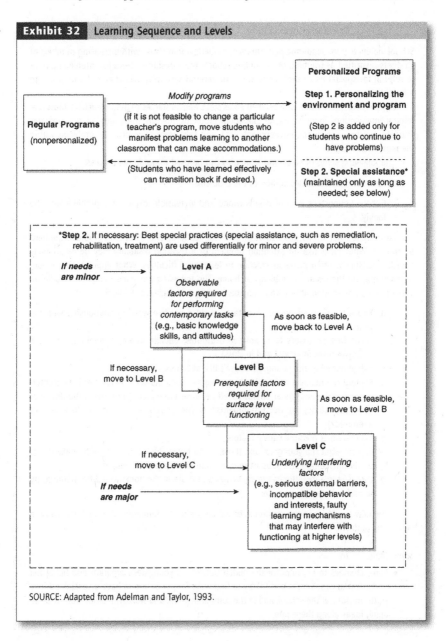

SOURCE: Adapted from Adelman and Taylor, 1993.

Exhibit 33   Prereferral Intervening

School violence, poor academic performance, misbehavior in class—with increasing numbers of students identified as troubled or in trouble, schools must design systems for intervening prior to referral for special assistance. Otherwise, the referral system is overwhelmed and grinds to a halt.

A *prereferral intervention* process delineates steps and strategies to guide teachers. Most prereferral interventions identify regular classroom problems, identify the source of the problems (student, teacher, curriculum, environment, etc.), and take steps to resolve the problems within the regular classroom.

The following series of steps and strategies can be used to guide the process:

1. Formulate an initial description of the problem.

2. Get the youngster's view of what's wrong and as feasible, explore the problem with the family.

As every teacher knows, the causes of behavior, learning, and emotional problems are hard to analyze. What looks like an attention problem or a learning disability may be emotionally based. Misbehavior often arises in reaction to learning difficulties. What appears as a school problem may be the result of problems at home. The following are some things to consider in seeking more information about what may be causing a youngster's problem.

   a. Through enhanced personal contacts, build a positive working relationship with the youngster and family.
   b. Focus first on assets (e.g., positive attributes, outside interests, hobbies, what the youngster likes at school and in class).
   c. Ask about what the youngster doesn't like at school.
   d. Explore the reasons for dislikes (e.g., Are assignments seen as too hard, as uninteresting? Is the youngster embarrassed because others will think she or he does not have the ability to do assignments? Is the youngster picked on, rejected, or alienated?)
   e. Explore other possible causal factors.
   f. Explore what the youngster and those in the home think can be done to make things better (including extra support from a volunteer, a peer, a friend, etc.).
   g. Discuss some new things the youngster and those in the home would be *willing* to try to make the situation better.

3. Try new strategies in the classroom based on the best information about what is causing the problem.

Some Things to Try

- Make changes to (1) improve the match between a youngster's program and his or her interests and capabilities and (2) try to find ways for her or him to have a special, positive status in class, at the school, and in the community. Talk and work with other staff in developing ideas along these lines.

- Add resources for extra support (aide, volunteers, peer tutors) to help the youngster's efforts to learn and perform. Create time to interact and relate with the youngster as an individual.
- Discuss with the youngster (and those in the home) why the problems are occurring.
- Specifically focus on exploring matters with the youngster that will suggest ways to enhance positive motivation.
- Change aspects of the program (e.g., materials, environment) to provide a better match with his or her interests and skills.
- Provide enrichment options (in and out of class).
- Use resources such as volunteers, aides, and peers to enhance the youngster's social support network.
- Specifically focus on exploring ways those in the home can enhance their problem-solving efforts.
- If necessary include other staff (e.g., counselor, principal) in a special discussion with the youngster exploring reasons for the problem and ways to enhance positive involvement at school and in class.

4. If the new strategies don't work, *talk to others* at school to learn about what they find helpful (e.g., reach out for support, mentoring, coaching; participate with others in clusters and teams; observe how others teach in ways that effectively address differences in motivation and capability; request additional staff development on working with such youngsters).

5. If necessary, use the *school's referral processes* to ask for additional specialized assistance.

6. Work with referral resources to *coordinate your efforts* with theirs for classroom success.

Responding as Early After Problem Onset as Feasible and Applying Response to Intervention

For many years, the impetus for identifying problems was to make referrals for special assistance. This produced increasing numbers of referrals, many of which led to assessment for special education. As it became evident that too many students were inappropriately diagnosed, *prereferral intervening* was proposed (again see Exhibit 33).

Given the value of responding early after the onset of problems, the last reauthorization of the federal Individuals with Disabilities Education Act (IDEA) (2005) called for (1) early intervening and (2) response to intervention. For all practical purposes, prereferral strategies are embedded in these efforts.

1. *Early Intervening Services.* IDEA regulations (2005) call for a district to use up to 15% of the amount it receives each year under Part B of IDEA to develop and implement coordinated, early intervening services. These may include interagency financing structures for students in kindergarten through Grade 12 (with

a particular emphasis on students in kindergarten through Grade 3) who are not currently identified as needing special education or related services but who need additional academic and behavioral support to succeed in a general education environment.

   2. *Response to Intervention.* As Sprague (2006) notes, "Response to intervention (RtI) has become a major stimulus for discussion and action. . . . Schools are increasingly adopting an RtI logic to organize and deliver both academic and behavioral support for *all* students." The concept is supported by the federal government in its effort to reduce inappropriate diagnoses for special education. Federal support has led to creation of the National Center on Response to Intervention (for more information, see http://www.rti4success.org/).

   Properly conceived and implemented, the strategy is expected to improve the learning opportunities for many students and reduce the number *inappropriately* diagnosed with learning disabilities and behavioral disorders. The intent is to minimize identification of students who don't need expensive special education.

   As noted, the approach overlaps ideas about prereferral interventions. However, the intent is to increase systematic implementation with special attention to enhancing teacher capability to carry out "well-designed and well-implemented early intervention" in the regular classroom. While variability in practice is inevitable, the tendency is to over-rely on direct instructional strategies. However, when direct instruction does not solve the problem, additional interventions are indicated (Martinez & Nellis, 2008).

   Therefore, as a screening process, RtI helps determine if more intensive or specialized assistance is required and whether a referral for formal diagnosis may be indicated. A core difficulty in this respect is that of mobilizing unmotivated students (and particularly those who have become actively disengaged from classroom instruction). If motivational considerations are not effectively addressed, valid assessments cannot be made.

   Essentially, the process reflects the sequential and hierarchical approach illustrated in Exhibit 32. It calls for making changes in the classroom designed to improve the student's learning and behavior as soon as problems are noted and using the information gleaned from the student's responses to make further modifications if needed. This work continues until problems cannot be resolved through regular classroom interventions.

   RtI has the potential to build teacher capacity so that similar problems are prevented in the future. Implied in all this is that someone is working to ensure (1) classroom teachers have or are learning how to implement *well-designed early intervention* in the classroom, and (2) support staff are learning how to play a role, sometimes directly in the classroom, to expand intervention strategies as needed. The strategy is meant to provide specific and well-monitored plans for *identified* students and is not intended to delay providing students with necessary assistance.

Building Capacity for Early Intervening and RtI

Professional development must ensure teachers know how to implement well-designed early interventions in the classroom. And support staff must learn how to play a role directly in the classroom to expand the nature and scope of interventions.

Two capacity-building concerns are particularly necessary. One is professional development on how to implement the Step 1 and 2 interventions described above and illustrated in Exhibit 32; the other involves ensuring classrooms and student support programs are designed in ways that allow enough time for implementation.

Central to all this is learning how to create a positive classroom climate—one that uses practices that enhance motivation to learn and perform, while avoiding practices that decrease motivation and/or produce avoidance motivation and that focuses on mobilizing unmotivated students (and particularly those who have become actively disengaged from classroom instruction). Such practices include the following:

- Regular use of informal and formal conferences with students to discuss options, make decisions, explore learners' perceptions, and mutually evaluate progress
- A broad range of options from which learners can make *choices* about types of learning content, activities, and desired outcomes
- A broad range of options from which learners can make choices about their need for *support* and *guidance* during decision making and learning processes
- Active decision making by learners in making choices and in evaluating how well the chosen options match their motivation and capability
- Establishment of program plans and mutual agreements about the ongoing relationships between the learners and program personnel
- Regular reevaluations and reformulation of plans and renegotiation of agreements based on mutual evaluations of progress, problems, and learners' perceptions of how well instruction matches his or her interests and capabilities

Teachers and support staff also must learn how to approach *special assistance* in a sequential and hierarchical manner. This requires the ability to (1) use reteaching strategies in ways that accommodate individual needs and differences; (2) teach prerequisite knowledge, skills, and attitudes the student may not have learned yet; and (3) play a role in addressing major barriers interfering with student learning and performance. To ensure strategies are implemented in a personalized way, schools must promote the type of collaborative classrooms and grouping strategies that have the effect of turning big classes into smaller units (see Resources A and B at the end of this chapter).

By themselves, early intervening and RtI strategies, especially if narrowly conceived, do not address major barriers to student learning. Instruction must be supported by interventions focusing on matters such as enhancing supports for transitions and crisis events and home and community involvement and other forms of supportive assistance.

The need, then, is for a broad-based system to reduce behavior, learning, and emotional problems, promote social and emotional development, and effectively reengage students in classroom learning. A comprehensive system not only will reduce the number of students inappropriately referred for special education or specialized services but also can address problems effectively early after onset and prevent many from occurring.

CONCLUDING COMMENTS

Working in classrooms is a highly demanding job. It is particularly difficult in school settings where a large proportion of the student population is not performing well.

The problem of improving classrooms is exacerbated by the growing teacher shortage. More and more schools must employ novices, including individuals with little or no preservice teacher preparation. And many of these newcomers are placed in schools where many students come to class each day not particularly enthusiastic about what they are expected to do and often without the background of knowledge and skills to connect with the day's lesson plans.

Given this state of affairs, schools must become settings where many stakeholders enter the classroom to work with the teacher to help students around barriers and enhance their perception that classroom instruction is worth pursuing.

From a psychological perspective, learning and teaching are experienced most positively when the learner cares about learning and the teacher cares about teaching. *Moreover, the whole process benefits greatly when all the participants care about each other.* Thus, good schools and good teachers work diligently to create an atmosphere that encourages mutual support, caring, and a sense of community and social justice. Such an atmosphere can play a key role in preventing behavior, learning, emotional, and health problems and promoting social and emotional learning and well-being.

Classroom and school climate have moral, social, and personal facets. When all facets are present and balanced, they can nurture individuals and facilitate the process of learning.

On an ongoing basis, a positive classroom climate is best maintained through use of personalized instruction, regular student conferences, activity fostering social and emotional development, and opportunities for students to attain positive status. Efforts to establish and maintain a caring classroom climate benefit from strategies that promote welcoming and social support, cooperative learning, peer tutoring, mentoring, advocacy, peer counseling and mediation, human relations, and conflict resolution. Clearly, myriad strategies contribute to students feeling positively connected to the classroom and school.

Given the importance of home involvement in schooling, attention also must be paid to creating a caring atmosphere for family members. Increased home involvement is more likely if families feel welcome and have access to social support at school. Thus, teachers and other school staff need to establish interventions that effectively welcome and connect families with school staff and other families to generate ongoing social support and greater participation.

Also, just as with students and their families, school staff need to feel truly welcome and socially supported. Rather than leaving this to chance, a caring school develops and institutionalizes ways to welcome and connect new staff with those with whom they will be working. And it does so in ways that effectively inducts newcomers into the organization. We discuss this further in Chapter 11.

RESOURCE A

Turning Big Classes Into Smaller Units

Just as schools with large enrollments need to be turned into sets of small schools, so must classrooms be arranged into small units every day. As a report in 2000 from the American Youth Policy Forum states:

> The structure and organization of a High School of the Millennium is very different than that of the conventional high school. First and foremost, [the school] is designed to provide small, personalized, and caring learning communities for students. . . . The smaller groups allow a number of adults . . . to work together with the students . . . as a way to develop more meaningful relationships and as a way for the teachers to better understand the learning needs of each student.

The Key Is Grouping

Aside from times when a learning objective is best accomplished with the whole class, creating small classes out of the whole is desirable. This involves grouping students in various ways, as well as providing opportunities for individual activity. At a fundamental level, grouping is a strategy in turning classrooms with large enrollments into a set of simultaneously operating small classes.

Clearly, students should never be grouped in ways that harm them (e.g., putting them in low-ability tracks, segregating those with problems). But grouping is a necessity for effective teaching. *Appropriate grouping* facilitates student engagement, learning, and performance. Besides enhancing academic learning, it can increase intrinsic motivation by promoting feelings of personal and interpersonal competence, self-determination, and positive connection with others. Moreover, it can foster autonomous learning skills, personal responsibility for learning, and healthy social-emotional attitudes and skills.

A well-designed classroom enables teachers to spend most of their time rotating among small self-monitored groups (e.g., two to six members) and individual learners. With team teaching and staff collaboration, such grouping can be done across classrooms.

Effective grouping is facilitated by ensuring teachers have adequate resources, including space, materials, and help. The key to effective grouping, however, is to take the time needed for youngsters to learn to work well with each other, with other resource personnel, and at times independently. Students are grouped and regrouped flexibly and regularly based on individual interests, needs, and for the benefits to be derived from diversity. Small learning groups are established for cooperative inquiry and learning, concept and skill development, problem solving, motivated practice, peer- and cross-age tutoring, and other forms of activity that can be facilitated by peers, aides, and/or volunteers. In a small group, students have more opportunities to participate. In heterogeneous, cooperative learning groups, each student has an interdependent role in pursuing a common learning goal and can contribute on a par with their capabilities.

Three types of groupings that are common include the following:

- *Needs-Based Grouping:* Short-term groupings are established for students with similar learning needs (e.g., to teach or reteach them particular skills and to do so in keeping with their current interests and capabilities).
- *Interest-Based Grouping:* Students who already are motivated to pursue an activity usually can be taught to work together well on active learning tasks.
- *Designed-Diversity Grouping:* For some objectives, combining sets of students from different backgrounds and who have different abilities and interests is desirable (e.g., to discuss certain topics, foster certain social capabilities, engender mutual support for learning).

All three types provide opportunities to enhance interpersonal functioning and an understanding of working relationships and of factors affecting group functioning. In all forms of grouping, approaches such as cooperative learning and computer-assisted instruction are relevant.

Recognize and Accommodate Diversity

Every classroom is diverse to some degree. Diversity arises from many factors: gender, ethnicity, race, socioeconomic status, religion, capability, disability, interests, and so forth. In grouping students, drawing on the strengths of diversity can be productive. For example, a multiethnic classroom enables teachers to group students across ethnic lines bring different perspectives to the learning activity. Students not only learn about other perspectives, the situation helps enhance critical thinking and other higher order conceptual abilities. It also can foster the type of intergroup understanding and relationships that contributes to a school climate of caring and mutual respect. Of course, the entire curriculum and all instructional activities must incorporate an appreciation of diversity, and teachers must plan ways to appropriately accommodate individual and group differences.

Collaborative or Team Teaching

As Hargreaves (1994) notes,

The way to relieve the uncertainty and open-endedness that characterizes classroom teaching is to create communities of colleagues who work collaboratively [in cultures of shared learning and positive risk-taking] to set their own professional limits and standards, while still remaining committed to continuous improvement. Such communities can also bring together the professional and personal lives of teachers in a way that supports growth and allows problems to be discussed without fear of disapproval or punishment. (p. 156)

Obviously, it helps to have multiple collaborators in the classroom. An aide and/or volunteers, for example, can assist with establishing and maintaining well-functioning groups, as well as providing special support and guidance for designated individuals. As teachers increasingly open their doors to others, assistance can be solicited from paid tutors, resource and special education teachers, pupil services personnel, and an ever widening range of volunteers (e.g., tutors, peer buddies, parents, mentors, and any others who can bring special abilities into the classroom and offer additional options for learning). Of course, team teaching offers a potent way to expand the range of options for personalizing instruction. Not only can teaming benefit students, it can be a great boon to teachers. A good collaboration is one where colleagues mesh professionally and personally. It doesn't mean that agreement exists about everything, but agreement about what constitutes good classroom practices is fundamental.

Collaborations can take various forms. For example, teaming may take the form of any of the following:

- *Parallel Work*—team members combine their classes or other work and teach to their strengths. This may involve specific facets of the curriculum (e.g., one person covers math, another reading; they both cover different aspects of science) or different students (e.g., for specific activities, they divide the students and work with those to whom each relates to best or can support in the best way).
- *Complementary Work*—one team member takes the lead and another facilitates follow-up activity.
- *Special Assistance*—while one team member provides basic instruction, another focuses on those students who need special assistance.

Usually, the tendency is to think in terms of two or more teachers teaming to share the instructional load. We stress, however, the value of expanding the team to include support staff, aides, volunteers, and designated students to help in creating small groupings. Teachers and support staff can work together to recruit and train others to join in the collaborative effort. And with access to the Internet and distance learning, the nature and scope of collaboration has the potential to expand in dramatic fashion.

A Note About Students as Collaborative Helpers

Besides the mutual benefits students get from cooperative learning groups and other informal ways they help each other, formal peer programs can be invaluable assets. Students can be taught to be peer tutors, group discussion leaders, role models, and mentors. Other useful roles include peer buddies (to welcome, orient, and provide social support as a new student transitions into the class and school), peer-conflict mediators, and much more. Student helpers benefit their peers, themselves, and the school staff, and enhance the school's efforts to create a caring climate and a sense of community.

RESOURCE B

Volunteers as an Invaluable Resource

Volunteers can be a multifaceted resource in a classroom and throughout a school. For this to be the case, however, the school staff must value volunteers and learn how to recruit, train, nurture, and use them effectively. When implemented properly, school volunteer programs can enable teachers to personalize instruction, free teachers and other school personnel to meet students' needs more effectively, broaden students' experiences, strengthen school-community understanding and relations, enhance home involvement, and enrich the lives of volunteers. In the classroom, volunteers can provide just the type of extra support needed to enable staff to conference and work with students who require special assistance.

Volunteers may help students on a one-to-one basis or in small groups. Group interactions are especially important in enhancing a student's cooperative interactions with peers. One-to-one work is often needed to develop a positive relationship with a particularly aggressive or withdrawn student, in reengaging a student who has disengaged from classroom learning, and in fostering successful task completion with a student easily distracted by peers. Volunteers can help enhance a student's motivation and skills and at the very least, can help counter negative effects that arise when a student has difficulty adjusting to school. Working under the direction of the teacher and student support staff, they can be especially helpful in establishing a supportive relationship with students who are having trouble adjusting to school.

The Many Roles for Volunteers in the Classroom and Throughout the School

I. Welcoming and Social Support

   A. In the Front Office

      1. Greeting and welcoming

      2. Providing information to those who come to the front desk

      3. Escorting guests, new students, and families to destinations on the campus

      4. Orienting newcomers

    B. Staffing a Welcoming Club
       1. Connecting newly arrived parents with peer buddies
       2. Helping develop orientation and other information resources for newcomers
       3. Helping establish newcomer support groups

II. Working With Designated Students in the Classroom
    A. Helping to orient new students
    B. Engaging disinterested, distracted, and distracting students
    C. Providing personal guidance and support for specific students in class to help them stay focused and engaged

III. Providing Additional Opportunities and Support in Class and on the Campus
    A. Recreation
    B. Enrichment
    C. Tutoring
    D. Mentoring

IV. Helping Enhance Positive Climate Throughout the School (including assisting with chores)
    A. Assisting with supervision in class and throughout the campus
    B. Contributing to campus beautification
    C. Helping to get materials ready

Volunteers can be recruited from a variety of sources: parents and other family members, others in the community such as senior citizens and workers in local businesses, college students, and peers and older students at the school. Other organized programs also can provide volunteers such as local service clubs. Increasingly, institutions of higher education are requiring students to participate in learning through service. Schools committed to enhancing home and community involvement in schooling can pursue volunteer programs as a productive element in their efforts to do so.

Few teachers have the time to recruit and train a cadre of volunteers. Teachers can work with student support staff and the school administration to set up a volunteer program for the school. Initially, a small group of volunteers can be recruited and taught how to implement and maintain the volunteer program (e.g., how to recruit a large pool of volunteers, help train them, nurture them, work with them to recruit replacements).

The cost of volunteer programs is relatively small compared to the impact they can have on school climate and the quality of life for students and school staff.

For more on this topic, see the technical aid packet titled *Volunteers to Help Teachers and Schools Address Barriers to Learning* from the Center for Mental Health in Schools. Online at http://smhp.psych.ucla.edu/pdfdocs/volunteer/volunt.pdf.

10

Mental Health Assistance for Students at School

"To take care of them" can and should be read with two meanings: to give children help and to exclude them from the community.

—Nicholas Hobbs (1975)

As stressed throughout this book, focusing *only* on the problems of specific students and pursuing clinical interventions limits thinking about cause and correction. That is, such an orientation biases perceptions and attributions.

Adopting a broad, transactional perspective underscores that the first question in addressing behavior, learning, and emotional problems is *not* necessarily, "What's wrong with the students?" An equally justifiable first question is, "Are external factors causing the problem?"

For a significant number of problems, changing environments and improving programs are necessary and sometimes sufficient steps in preventing and correcting a problem at school. Of course, whether or not the problem resides with the environment, students may require some special assistance. Such practices and processes are covered in this chapter.

MENTAL HEALTH ASSISTANCE
FOR STUDENTS AT SCHOOL

Concepts, Practices, and Resources

Before highlighting specific interventions and strategies, we want to emphasize the value of adopting a consumer orientation to mental health in schools.

In the helping professions, processes that inappropriately distance, depersonalize, and desensitize practitioners from those they serve are long-standing concerns. Also of concern are power imbalances. Special attention is required to avoid disempowering individuals and groups and increasing their dependency on professionals.

The complexity of these matters increases for those working with minors and in schools. Questions arise daily about *What is in a youngster's best interest?* and *Who should decide?*

In school settings, adults make many decisions for students, often without involving the youngster or their caregivers. As professionals know all too well, decisions made about referral and *case* management often have profound, life-shaping effects. Even the best interventions have potential negative consequences (often minimized by referring to them as *side effects*).

In the United States, federal guidelines stress the obligation of schools to identify certain problems, inform parents of their rights related to special programs, and ensure that proper assistance is provided. For the most part, schools proceed in ways that are not consumer-oriented. For example, referrals tend to be made in a rather directive manner without much information and discussion.

From another perspective, research indicates that decisions made about—rather than with—individuals often are not effective. Good intervention usually depends less on the intervener's perspective and preferences than on the match between the intervention and the practical and psychological requirements of the client (financial costs, geographical location, intervener and intervention characteristics).

Because of all this, a basic principle underlying the following discussion is that *students must be involved in major decisions designed to provide them with special assistance.* Except in rare instances, this principle also applies to parents or guardians. For us, this readily blends over into a consumer orientation. We suggest that the more a profession is consumer-oriented, the greater the likelihood of good practice with the benefits for most young people and for society far outweighing the costs involved.

The goals of consumer-oriented practices are to

- clarify the range of relevant intervention options;
- provide good information about each (cost, location, intervention rationale and features, evidence about positive, and negative effects, and, where feasible, previous consumer evaluations);
- use consultation processes that effectively involve clients in decisions.

The best consumer protection, of course, is a good professional (see Exhibit 34).

Exhibit 34 The Best Consumer Protection Is a *Good* Professional

All professionals, of course, mean to do good. But what constitutes a *good* professional? For consumer advocates, a consumer orientation is at the heart of the matter. Indeed, such an orientation is found in a set of professional guidelines formulated by the American Psychological Association. These guidelines state that members of a good profession do the following:

1. Guide their practices and policies by a sense of social responsibility

2. Devote more of their energies to serving the public interest than to *guild* functions and to building in-group strength

3. Represent accurately to the public their demonstrable competence

4. Develop and enforce a code of ethics primarily to protect the client and only secondarily to protect themselves

5. Identify their unique pattern of competencies and focus their efforts to carrying out those functions for which they are best equipped

6. Engage in cooperative relations with other professions having related or overlapping competencies and common purposes

7. Seek an adaptive balance among efforts devoted to research, teaching, and application

8. Maintain open channels of communication among *discoverers,* teachers, and appliers of knowledge

9. Avoid nonfunctional entrance requirements into the profession, such as those based on race, nationality, creed, or arbitrary personality considerations

10. Ensure that their training is meaningfully related to the subsequent functions of the members of the profession

11. Guard against premature espousal of any technique or theory as a final solution to substantive problems

12. Strive to make their services accessible to all persons seeking such services regardless of social and financial considerations

---

TYPES OF MENTAL HEALTH ASSISTANCE AT SCHOOLS

Schools provide a particularly good place for students to seek help. A challenge for school staff is how to create an environment that encourages students (and families)

to do so. In creating such an environment, schools must ensure students receive and understand information about available programs and services and how to access them. School personnel also must build student and family confidence in those providing services and ensure privacy and confidentiality.

A 2008 report done for the Centers for Disease Control and Prevention reviews school laws and policies concerning child and adolescent health (Centers for Law and the Public's Health, 2008). It provides the following information about mental health *services* in schools:

All states allow for the provision of counseling, psychological, and social services in school settings, but the scope and content of these services vary across states, school districts, and individual schools. State laws do not typically require that all students have access to specific services at school or outline how services should be provided. Nevertheless, access to and eligibility for mental health services in schools are widespread. A recent report by Substance Abuse and Mental Health Services Administration (SAMHSA; 2008) concluded that all students were eligible to receive mental health services in 87% of schools surveyed. . . . These services include individual and group assessments, interventions, and referrals. . . .

Students may need treatment for mental health conditions ranging from depression and suicidality to attention deficit hyperactivity disorder (ADHD) and stress. Schools may also provide a number of other counseling and social services, such as counseling and treatment for eating disorders, substance abuse, tobacco use, and physical, sexual, or emotional abuse. . . .

Schools may facilitate counseling, psychological, and social services through multiple mechanisms, including onsite services by a variety of professionals employed by the school (e.g., school counselors, psychologists, nurses, and social workers), delivery of services by School-Based Health Centers (SBHCs) and referrals to offsite health providers (with appropriate prior written consent if personal information is disclosed). . . .

Treatment services or referrals are widely available in schools. Some states have initiated proactive measures to expand access to school mental health services. . . . Others mandate that schools implement programs to detect and treat substance abuse. . . .

Recommending the use of psychotropic drugs has been a contentious issue at the state level. Several states, including Connecticut, Illinois, Texas, and Virginia, prohibit school officials from recommending that students use psychotropic drugs.

In our work, we broaden the discussion from *services* to types of special *assistance* needed and provided. By way of overview, Exhibit 35 outlines a flow chart of special assistance interventions at schools.

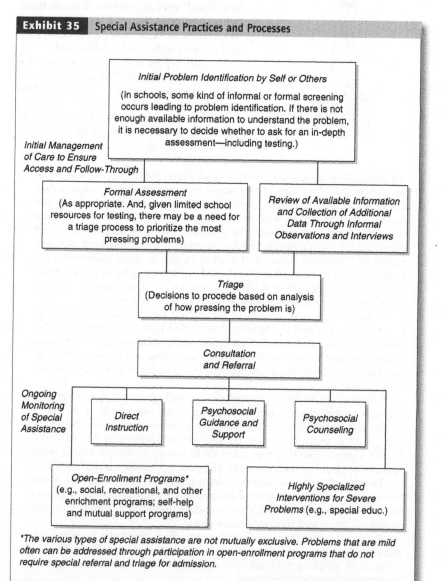

Exhibit 35   Special Assistance Practices and Processes

Initial Problem Identification by Self or Others

(In schools, some kind of informal or formal screening occurs leading to problem identification. If there is not enough available information to understand the problem, it is necessary to decide whether to ask for an in-depth assessment—including testing.)

Initial Management of Care to Ensure Access and Follow-Through

Formal Assessment
(As appropriate. And, given limited school resources for testing, there may be a need for a triage process to prioritize the most pressing problems)

Review of Available Information and Collection of Additional Data Through Informal Observations and Interviews

Triage
(Decisions to procede based on analysis of how pressing the problem is)

Consultation and Referral

Ongoing Monitoring of Special Assistance

Direct Instruction

Psychosocial Guidance and Support

Psychosocial Counseling

Open-Enrollment Programs*
(e.g., social, recreational, and other enrichment programs; self-help and mutual support programs)

Highly Specialized Interventions for Severe Problems (e.g., special educ.)

*The various types of special assistance are not mutually exclusive. Problems that are mild often can be addressed through participation in open-enrollment programs that do not require special referral and triage for admission.

Our discussion of special assistance begins with the forms of corrective intervention outlined toward the bottom of Exhibit 35. Following this, we explore what is involved in connecting students with such help. After that, we highlight psychological first aid as a response to crises.

Five forms of corrective intervention are represented in Exhibit 35 and highlighted as follows: (1) open-enrollment programs, (2) direct instruction, (3) psychosocial guidance and support, (4) psychosocial counseling, and (5) highly specialized interventions for severe problems.

1. *Open-Enrollment Programs*—Schools can offer a variety of open-enrollment programs designed to foster and enhance positive mental health and socio-emotional functioning. These encompass a host of recreation, community service, and work opportunities. Examples include afterschool clubs and intramural sports; service learning and job shadowing programs; and music, drama, art, and crafts classes. Students can take leadership roles in welcoming programs for new students and families and in peer tutoring, mediation, counseling, and mentoring programs. They can also help establish strategies to change the school environment in ways that make it safer, more inviting, and accommodating.

2. *Direct Instruction*—To enhance coping with mental health problems, this form of intervention uses didactic approaches to teach specific knowledge, skills, and attitudes and compensatory strategies. The work is done individually or in a small group and in or out of the classroom. Manuals are available detailing cognitive and metacognitive strategies.

3. *Psychosocial Guidance and Support*—Each day many students require a small dose of personalized guidance and support to enhance their motivation and capability for coping with stressors. Others involved in therapeutic treatment (e.g., personal counseling, psychotherapy, psychotropic medication) need someone who understands the treatment and can deal with related concerns that arise at school.

Personalized guidance and support is best provided on a regular basis in the classroom and at home. Student support staff can (a) help teachers function in ways where they directly provide such support or do so through use of various activities and peer support strategies and (b) mobilize and enhance support from those in the home.

Student support personnel also are logical staff for a student to contact if something is amiss between a student's therapeutic regimen and what else is happening at school. Such staff are also good resources for interfacing with a student's off-campus counselor or therapist. In general, they can assume the role of school-site care manager, providing coordination between the school's efforts to teach and any treatment the student is receiving.

Guidance and support involves a range of potential activity:

- Advising
- Advocacy and protection

- Providing support for transitions (e.g., orienting new students and connecting them with social support networks, facilitating students with special needs as they transition to and from programs and services)
- Mediation and conflict resolution
- Promoting and fostering opportunities for social and emotional development
- Being a liaison between school and home
- Being a liaison between school and other professionals serving a student

Note: Special considerations and concerns arise related to students taking psychotropic medications (see the end of the chapter for some resources on this topic).

4. *Psychosocial Counseling*—Good counseling builds on caring, which is a foundational aspect of helping relationships. Also encompassed are the fundamentals of any good *working* relationship. In general, counseling requires the ability to carry on a *productive dialogue,* that is, to talk with, not at, others. This begins with active listening and not prying and being judgmental. It also encompasses knowing when to share information and appropriately relate one's own experiences.

Counseling also requires the ability to create a working relationship that quickly conveys to the student

- *positive value and expectation* (that something of value can and will be gained from the experience);
- *personal credibility* (that the counselor is someone who can help and can be trusted to keep his or her word, be fair, and be consistent, yet flexible);
- *permission and protection to engage in exploration and change* (that the situation is one with clear guidelines making it okay and safe to say what's on one's mind).

All this enables the counselor to elicit a student's concerns. Then, the process requires the ability to respond with

- *empathy, warmth, and nurturance* (e.g., the ability to understand and appreciate what others are thinking and feeling, transmit a sense of liking, express appropriate reassurance and praise, minimize criticism and confrontation);
- *genuine regard and respect* (e.g., the ability to transmit real interest, acceptance, and validation of the other's feelings and to interact in a way that enables others to maintain a feeling of integrity and personal control).

Personal counseling for students aims at enabling them to increase their sense of competence, personal control, and self-direction—all with a view to enhancing ability to relate better to others and perform better at school.

When a counseling relationship is established, care must be taken not to undermine it by allowing the student to become dependent. Ways to minimize dependency include the following:

- Giving advice rarely, if at all
- Ensuring that a student takes personal responsibility for dealing with problems and assumes credit for progress
- Ensuring that the student doesn't misinterpret efforts to help or lose sight of the limits of the relationship
- Helping the student identify when to seek support and clarifying a wide range of ways to do so
- Planning a careful transition for termination

Most counseling at a school site is short-term. Some is informal—brief encounters with students who drop in or are encountered somewhere on campus. All encounters are potentially productive as long as one attends to student motivation as key antecedent and process conditions and as an important outcome concern.

Regardless of how long a student is seen for counseling, if a relationship has been established, it eventually must end. In effect, such *termination* is a transition. It involves discussing the fact that the counseling is coming to an end, exploring any anxiety the student has about this, and reassuring the student about how to deal with subsequent problems (e.g., by establishing a connection with staff, peers, family who agree to be a support network). If feasible, an invitation is extended to the student to share periodically how things are going. If the student is referred for more counseling, support is provided for a smooth transition, including clarifying what should be shared with the new counselor and by whom.

5. *Highly Specialized Interventions for Severe Problems*—Any and all of the above can apply to students who have severe mental health problems. In addition, such students require extensive accommodations and specialized, intensive help.

Legislation spells out the rights and entitlements of such students to access appropriate special assistance. For example, Section 504 of the 1973 Rehabilitation Act (anti-discrimination, civil rights legislation) provides a basis for a school to provide special accommodations for any student identified as having some physical or mental impairment that affects a major life activity, such as learning at school. Section 504 protects all school-age children who qualify as disabled: (1) has or (2) has had a physical or mental impairment that substantially limits a major life activity or (3) is regarded as disabled by others. The disabling condition need only limit one major life activity in order for the student to be eligible. Children receiving special education services under the Individuals with Disabilities Education Improvement Act are also protected by Section 504.

Accommodations should be considered when

- a student shows a pattern of not benefiting from instruction,
- retention is being considered,
- a student exhibits a chronic health or mental health condition,
- a student returns to school after being hospitalized,
- long-tem suspension or expulsion is being considered,
- a student is evaluated and found ineligible for special education services or is transitioning out of special education,
- substance abuse is an issue,
- a student is *at risk* for dropping out,
- a student is taking medication at school.

Accommodations to meet educational needs focus on the curriculum, classroom and homework assignments, testing, grading, and so forth. Such accommodations primarily are offered in regular classrooms (see Chapter 9).

A school's student review team provides a major mechanism for ensuring that appropriate accommodations are planned (see Exhibit 36). A 504 plan provides the following:

- An evaluation based on current levels of performance, teacher reports, and documentation of areas of concern
- Development and/or implementation of an accommodation plan that specifies *reasonable* modifications in order for students to benefit from their educational program
- Procedural safeguards for students and parents, including written notification of all district decisions concerning the student's evaluation or educational placement and due process
- Review and reevaluation of modifications and placement on a regular basis and prior to any change in placement

If special education services and/or placements are considered, a school's Individualized Education Plan (IEP) team comes into play.

When decisions are made to include psychotherapy or behavior change interventions, increasing attention is given to empirically supported treatments (see Chapters 4 and 14).

Exhibit 36	About Special Assistance Teams

As discussed in Chapter 7, schools need both case- and resource-oriented teams to address student behavior, learning, and emotional problems. Many schools already have two case-oriented teams—a student review team and an individual education planning team. In addition to these mechanisms, schools need a resource-oriented mechanism (e.g., a learning supports resource team). Such a team is designed to bring together representatives from all major school and community programs and services colocated at or closely linked to the school.

A student review team mostly focuses on students who teachers identify as having mild to moderate problems interfering with their classroom learning and/or performance. Different schools use different names for this team (e.g., student study or success team, student assistance team, teacher assistance team). Such a team is the gatekeeper for all but *open-enrollment* programs, and it often is step on the pathway to special education. However, an individual education planning team, usually referred to as an IEP team, is responsible for determining eligibility for special education services and for establishing the general plan for meeting the student's needs.

From the time a student is first identified as having a problem, someone should be assigned to monitor and manage what happens. Such a role can be played by members of case-oriented teams. The process encompasses constant evaluation of the appropriateness and effectiveness of what is done and taking appropriate steps if the intervention is not effective. Such *case management* can include coordination among all who are involved (e.g., other services and programs, including the efforts of the classroom teacher and those at home).

Many of the individuals on case-oriented teams also are on resource teams. Remember that the latter differs from a case-oriented team in that its focus is on managing and enhancing *systems* to coordinate, integrate, and strengthen interventions. Also, much is gained when complexes of schools work collaboratively with an orientation to maximize resource use. Schools in the same neighborhood (e.g., a high school and its feeder middle and elementary schools) often deal with the same families (e.g., families with children at each level of schooling) and link with the same community resources. A complex resource *council* brings together representatives from each school's resource team to facilitate coordination and equity among schools in using school and community resources.

Whenever special education placements are considered, attention must be given to inclusion and transitions. Appropriate inclusion for students with special needs begins with ensuring that only those who cannot be helped effectively in the mainstream are referred to special placements. When data indicate that a person is not making progress, whatever the cause, special services and placements are considered. Such a decision often includes the profound move of transferring an individual out of a mainstream setting into a special environment. The decision usually is based on whether the person's problem is viewed as mild to moderate or severe and pervasive and whether it affects learning, behavior, emotional, or physical functioning.

Most mild to moderate problems belong in mainstream settings. This is feasible through modifying the physical setting, instituting special accommodations, and/or adding extra (ancillary) services (see Chapter 9). Ancillary assistance includes (1) extra instruction such as tutoring; (2) enrichment opportunities such as pursuit of hobbies, arts and crafts, and recreation; (3) psychologically oriented treatments such as individual and family therapy; and (4) biologically oriented treatments such as medication.

Persons with severe and pervasive problems often are placed in specialized settings such as remedial classrooms, *alternative* schools, and institutions. Even when special placements are made, students must have the opportunity to spend part of the time in regular classrooms and other *mainstream* programs in which they can function with appropriate accommodations and assistance.

Placement decisions focus first on major intervention needs, then on which, if any, extra assistance seems indicated. In many instances, decisions about secondary ancillary interventions are best made after primary interventions are given an adequate trial and found insufficient. In all instances, *appropriate attention must be given to inclusion and transitions.*

And remember, as outlined in Chapter 9, *all* special assistance must attend to the following:

- *Motivation as a key antecedent condition*—a prerequisite. Poor motivational readiness often is (a) a cause of inadequate and problem functioning, (b) a factor maintaining such problems, or (c) both. Thus, strategies are required that reduce avoidance motivation and enhance motivational readiness so that the student is mobilized to participate.
- *Motivation as a key ongoing process concern*—Processes must elicit, enhance, and maintain motivation so that the student stays mobilized (e.g., strategies to counter boredom).
- *Enhancing intrinsic motivation as a basic outcome concern*—A student may be motivated to work on a problem during an intervention session but not elsewhere. Responding to this concern requires strategies to enhance stable, positive attitudes that mobilize the student to act outside the intervention context and after the intervention is terminated.

In general, conditions likely to lead to negative motivation and avoidance reactions must be avoided or at least minimized. Of particular concern are activities students perceive as unchallenging, uninteresting, overdemanding, or overwhelming and structure that seriously limits their range of options or that is overcontrolling and coercive. Examples of conditions that can have a negative impact on a student's motivation are excessive rules, criticism, and confrontation.

The less one understands the background and experiences that have shaped a student, the harder it may be to create a good fit. This problem is at the root of concerns about working with students who come from different cultures and about accounting for individual differences in general. (More on this later in this chapter.)

CONNECTING A STUDENT WITH THE RIGHT MENTAL HEALTH ASSISTANCE

School personnel identify many mental health problems each day, and requests for specialized assistance to address such problems are common. As we have stressed, many problems can be prevented and corrected through classroom redesign. For those students for whom special assistance is necessary, schools also must have well-designed processes to connect them with the right special assistance (review Exhibit 35).

By way of overview, Exhibit 37 highlights some specific practices for connecting a student with help and monitoring what happens. In what follows, we explore (1) identifying and clarifying need, (2) conducting triage, (3) providing client consultation and referral, and (4) monitoring and managing care. Several of the exhibits in this section are designed as resource tools, and a list of relevant resources is provided at the end of the chapter.

Exhibit 37	Some Specific Practices Involved in Connecting a Student With the Right Help and Monitoring the Processes

Problem Identification

    a. Problems may be identified by anyone (staff, parent, student).

    b. Provide an identification form that everyone can access and fill out.

    c. Ensure an easily accessible place for people to turn in forms.

    d. Inform all stakeholders regarding the availability of forms, where to turn them in, and what will happen after they do so.

Triage Processing

    a. Review submitted forms each day; sort, and direct them to appropriate resources. (Designate and train a triage processor; several individuals can share this task—for example, different persons can do it on a specific day or for specified weeks.)

    b. After the sorting is done, send a status information form to the person who identified the problem (assuming it was not a self-referral).

Clients Directed to Resources or for
Further Problem Analysis and Recommendations

    a. For basic necessities of daily living (e.g., food, clothing, etc.), the triage process includes providing information about resources either through the person who identified the problem or directly to the student and family in need.

    b. If the problem requires a few sessions of immediate counseling to help a student or family through a crisis, the triage process includes sending the form to the person making assignments to on-campus counselors.

    c. The forms for all others are directed to a small triage *team* (one to three trained professionals) for further analysis and recommendations. (Large caseloads may require putting several teams into operation.) Members of such a team may not have to meet on all cases; some could be reviewed independently with recommendations made and passed on to the next reviewer for validation. In complex situations, however, not only might a team meeting be indicated, it may be necessary to gather more information from concerned parties (e.g., teacher, parent, student).

(Continued)

(Continued)

**Interventions To Ensure Recommendations
and Referrals Are Pursued Appropriately**

a. In many instances, additional prereferral interventions should be recommended. Some of these will reflect analyses that suggest the student's problem is really a system problem (e.g., the problem is more a function of the teacher or other environmental factors). Other analyses will lead to specific strategies for the student's problem that don't require referral for outside the class assistance. Such analyses also lead to clarifying ways in which a site must be equipped to implement and monitor the impact of prereferral recommendations.

b. When students and families require referral for health and social services, procedures should be in place to enhance motivation and ability for follow-through. Care management should provide follow-through, coordination, impact, and additional referrals as necessary.

c. Referrals to assess the need for special or compensatory education often are delayed because of a waiting list. Backlogs should be monitored and arrangements made to catch up (e.g., by organizing enough release time to do the assessments and reviews).

Management of Care

a. Some situations require only a limited form of monitoring (e.g., to ensure follow-through). A system must be developed for assigning care monitors as needed. Aides and paraprofessionals might be trained for this function.

b. Other situations require intensive management by specially trained professionals to (1) ensure interventions are coordinated, integrated, and appropriate; (2) continue problem analysis and determine progress; (3) determine whether additional assistance is needed; and so forth. There are many models for intensive management of care. A common approach is to assign the responsibility to the professional who has the greatest involvement (or best relationship) with the student or family.

c. One key and often neglected function of the care manager is to provide appropriate status updates to all parties who should be kept informed.

Identifying and Clarifying Need

In many instances, the primary causes of a student's behavior, learning, and emotional problems cannot be determined. Is the problem due to a central nervous dysfunction or some other biological disorder (e.g., true ADHD, LD, clinical depression)? Is it the result of early deprivation (e.g., a lack of school readiness opportunities, living in an unhappy home environment, the product of negative peer influences)? Determining underlying cause is especially difficult after a student becomes unmotivated to perform.

Commonly, students are identified as candidates for special assistance through a formal or informal initial assessment—which, in essence, is a first-level screening process. Formally done, such screening provides an initial set of data about the nature, extent, and severity of a problem. It also can help clarify the student's motivation for addressing the problem. The involvement of significant others, such as family members, also can be explored. First-level screening provides a foundation for more in-depth assessment and if appropriate, a formal diagnosis.

At the same time, because of the deficiencies of first-level screening (see Chapter 3), a systematic process is required to ensure initial identification is done as validly as possible and with appropriate safeguards. To this end, those requesting special assistance for a student should provide a detailed description about the nature and scope of the identified problem. This includes any information on the contributing role of environmental factors. In addition, to create a balanced picture, information should be provided on a student's assets as well as weaknesses.

Once a request is made, several other sources of available information should be gathered. Useful sources are teachers, administrators, school support staff, recreation supervisors, parents, others who have made professional assessments, and of course, the student. Good practice calls for assessing the student's environment as a possible cause. The seeds of a problem may be stressors in the classroom, home, and/or neighborhood. A home visit is useful.

In gathering information from a student, a screening interview can be conducted. The nature of this interview varies depending on the age of the student and whether concerns raised are general ones about misbehavior and poor school performance or specific concerns about lack of attention; overactivity; major learning problems; suicidal ideation; or about physical, sexual, or substance abuse.

Some behavioral and emotional symptoms may stem from physical problems, and of course, a student may respond to stress with somatic symptoms. Some students are just a bit immature or exhibit behavior that is fairly common at a particular development stage. As the examples outlined below indicate, age, severity, pervasiveness, and chronicity are important considerations in analyzing mental health problems. Depending on such matters, some problems are common and transient; others are low-frequency and serious disorders.

Prematurely concluding a student has a pathological disorder is unwarranted.

Age	Common Transient Problem	Low-Frequency Serious Disorder
0–3	Concern about monsters under the bed	Sleep Behavior Disorder
3–5	Anxious about separating from parent	Separation Anxiety Disorder (crying & clinging)
5–8	Shy and anxious with peers (sometimes with somatic complaints)	Reactive Attachment Disorder
	Disobedient, temper outbursts	Conduct Disorder
	Very active and doesn't follow directions	Attention Deficit Hyperactivity Disorder
	Has trouble learning at school	Learning Disorder
8–12	Low self-esteem	Depression
12–15	Defiant and/or reactive	Oppositional Defiant Disorder
15–18	Experimental substance use	Substance abuse

If screening suggests the need for more in-depth assessment to prescribe specific forms of specialized assistance (either at the school or in the community), the next step is referral for such assessment. To be of value, such assessment must lead to help; in the process, a diagnosis and recommendation for special education services may be generated.

However, in analyzing assessment findings, remember that a student's behavior, learning, and emotional problems are *symptoms* (i.e., correlates). Unless valid *signs* are present clarifying what is causing problems, prematurely concluding the student has a pathological disorder is unwarranted.

A Note About Mental Health Screening

State laws set up a framework within which schools may conduct screening for mental health conditions among students. Screening may occur for a number of conditions, including depression, suicide, substance abuse, eating disorders, ADHD, and physical and emotional abuse. Research indicates that assessment of mental health problems or disorders (including behavioral observation, psychosocial assessment, and psychological testing) is offered in nearly 90% of schools. . . .

—Centers for Law and the Public's Health (2008)

In Chapter 3, we explored concerns that arise around formal mental health *screening*. Formal screening to identify students who have problems or who are at risk is accomplished through individual or group procedures. Most such procedures are *first-level* screens and are expected to overidentify problems. That is, they identify many students who do not really have significant problems (false positive errors). This certainly is the case for screens used with infants and primary grade children, but false positives are not uncommon when adolescents are screened. Errors are supposed to be detected by follow-up assessments. Because of the frequency of false positive errors, serious concerns arise when screening data are used to diagnose students and prescribe remediation and special treatment.

Minimal controversy exists about one form of first-level screening. Each year a great many parents and teachers identify significant numbers of children soon after the onset of a problem. This natural screening can be helpful in initiating supportive accommodations that can be incorporated into regular school and home practice. Then, by assessing the response of these children to such interventions (e.g., RtI), it can be determined whether more specialized intervention is needed to overcome a problem.

Whether formal or natural, first-level screening primarily is meant to sensitize responsible professionals. No one wants to ignore indicators of significant problems. At the same time, constant vigilance is necessary to guard against tendencies to see *normal variations* in students' development and behavior and other facets of human diversity as problems. First-level screens do not allow for definitive statements about a student's problems and need. At best, most such screening procedures provide a preliminary indication that something may be wrong. In considering formal diagnosis and prescriptions for how to correct the problem, one needs data from assessment procedures that have greater validity. Remember that many symptoms of problems also are common characteristics of young people, especially in adolescence.

Extreme caution clearly must be exercised to avoid misidentifying and inappropriately stigmatizing children and adolescents. Overestimating the significance of a few indicators is a common error. Moreover, many formal screening instruments add little predictive validity to natural screening.

At best, first-level screening procedures provide a preliminary indication that something may be wrong.

Triage

Given schools never have enough resources for all the students who need special assistance, processing such students inevitably involves a form of gatekeeping—referred to in clinical circles as triage. A paradox related to this is that the better a school develops processes for problem identification and student review, the greater the number of students sent for review. We call this the "field of dreams" effect. (*Build it and they will come.*)

Ideally, a school will stem the tide of students sent for review by enhancing its prevention practices (e.g., welcoming and providing social supports and ensuring that students make a good adjustment to a new school and/or a new classroom). And, as discussed in Chapter 9, increasing emphasis on well-designed prereferral interventions and response to intervention strategies will cut down on the need for special assistance outside the classroom.

When referrals are made to on-site resources, it falls to the school to decide which students need immediate attention and which can be put on a waiting list. Working alone or on a team, student support personnel usually play a key role in making this determination.

To further stem the tide of students sent for review, those who process the requests need to spend some time

- analyzing the general nature of the problems being sent with a view to identifying changes in the classroom and school that could minimize the need for similar requests in the future;
- helping develop and implement the changes.

This work is best accomplished by forming a resource-oriented team.

Consultation and Referral

Using all information gathered, the next step is to sit down with concerned parties (student, family, other school staff) to explore what's wrong and what to do about it. This intervention is a consultation and referral process. The objective is to assist family and school staff with problem solving and decision making in ways that lead to appropriate forms of help.

Referrals for special assistance are commonplace at school sites and relatively easy to make; the process of arriving at *appropriate* referrals is harder. And, *ensuring access and follow-through* is the most difficult process. To these ends, schools can

ᵗ provide ready reference to information about appropriate school- or community-based referrals;
• maximize follow-through by using a *consumer-oriented consultation process* that involves students and families in all decisions and helps them deal with potential barriers.

> Referrals are easy to make ... unfortunately, data suggest follow-through rates of less than 50% for referrals made by schools.

Ensuring the process is consumer oriented begins with full appreciation of the nature and scope of a student's problems *as perceived by the student, the family, and school staff.* Then, the consultation process is designed as a shared problem-solving approach with the final decisions controlled by the student and family. The steps in the problem-solving process are

• analyzing the problem (Are environmental factors a concern? Are there concerns about underlying disorders?);
• clarifying possible alternative ways to proceed given what's available;
• deciding on a course of action (evaluating costs vs. benefits of various alternatives for meeting needs);
• detailing the steps involved in connecting with potential resources and formulating a sound plan for access and follow-through on decisions;
• following up to be certain of access and follow-through.

In many instances, a referral is not necessary. What is called for is mobilizing the school staff to improve programs. Key is expanding students' opportunities in ways that increase expectations about a positive future as a way to counter prevailing student frustration, unhappiness, apathy, and hopelessness.

The following is a benchmark checklist for a consumer-oriented, problem-solving consultation process.

___ *Provides readily accessible basic information about relevant resources to students, families, and school personnel*

Entails widespread circulation of general information about on- and off-campus programs and services and ways to readily access such resources.

____ *Helps students, families, and school personnel appreciate whether a referral is necessary and, if so, clarifies the value of a potential resource*

Involves reviewing with the student, family, staff how referral options can assist. A resource file and handouts can be developed to aid in identifying and providing information about appropriate services and programs—on- and off-campus—for specific types of concerns (e.g., individual/ group/ family/ professional or peer counseling for psychological, drug, and alcohol problems, hospitalization for suicide prevention). Many students benefit from group counseling. And, if a student's problems are based mainly in the home, one or both parents may need counseling— with or without the student's involvement as appropriate. Of course, if the parents won't pursue counseling for themselves, the student may require other forms of special assistance to cope with and minimize the impact of the negative home situation.

____ *Analyzes options with student, family, and staff and helps with decision making as to which are the most appropriate resources*

Involves evaluating the pros and cons of potential options (including location, fees, least restrictive and intrusive intervention) and, if more than one option emerges as promising, rank ordering them. For example, because students often are reluctant to follow through with off-campus referrals, first consideration may be on-campus. Off-campus district programs and those offered by community agencies can follow as needed. Off-campus referrals are made with due recognition of school district policies.

____ *Identifies and explores with the student/family/staff all factors that might be potential barriers to pursuing the most appropriate option*

Is there a financial problem? A transportation problem? A problem about parental consent? Too much anxiety, fear, and/or apathy? Concerns about language and cultural sensitivity? At this point, be certain that the student (and where appropriate the family) truly feels an intervention is a good way to meet her or his needs.

____ *Works on strategies for dealing with barriers to follow-through*

Strategies must provide sufficient support and guidance to enable students and families to connect with resources This often overlooked step is basic to follow-through and entails taking time to clarify specific ways to handle barriers to following through.

(Continued)

(Continued)

_____ *Sends the student, family, and staff off with a written summary of what was decided, including follow-through strategies*

A referral decision form can summarize (a) specific directions about enrolling in the first-choice resource, (b) how to deal with problems that might interfere with successful enrollment, and (c) what to do if the first choice doesn't work out. A copy of a referral decision form can be given to the student and family as a reminder of decisions made; the original can be kept on file for purposes of case monitoring. Before students leave, evaluate the likelihood of follow-through. (Do they have a sound plan for how to get from here to there?) If the likelihood is low, the above tasks bear repeating.

_____ *Also sends them off with a follow-through status report form*

Such a form is intended to let the school know whether the referral worked out, and if not, whether additional help is called for in connecting the student and family to needed resources. Also, remember that teachers and other school staff who asked for a student review will want to know that something was done. Without violating any confidentiality considerations, a quick response can be sent reassuring them that the process is proceeding.

_____ *Follows through with student and family and other concerned parties to determine current status of needs and whether previous decisions were appropriate*

Requires establishing a reminder (tickler) system so that follow-up is made after an appropriate period of time.

Obviously, the above processes can take more than one session and may require repeating if follow-through is a problem. In many cases, one must take specific actions to help with follow-through, such as making direct connections (e.g., by phone) to the intake coordinator for a program. Extreme cases may require extreme measures such as arranging for transportation or for someone to actually go along to facilitate enrollment. Do an immediate check about follow-through (e.g., within 1–2 weeks) to see how well a student has connected with help. If the student hasn't, the contact can be used to find out what needs to be done next.

In using a consumer-oriented approach, the hope is that a positive side effect will be a higher degree of student, family, and teacher self-reliance in problem solving, decision making, and consumer awareness.

Exhibit 38 is a resource tool that summarizes steps in the assessment and consultation process.

Exhibit 38	Examples of Some Specific Steps in Assessment and Consultation Processes

1. Initial screening of student and family (initial contacts with the home may be via phone conversations)

2. Filling out of questionnaires by each concerned party (parents and student) regarding perceptions of the cause of identified problems and possible correction

3. Gathering records and reports from other professionals or agencies when consumers agree the data might be useful

4. Brief, highly circumscribed testing, if necessary and desired by consumers

5. Initial review of assessment findings to determine if enough information is available to proceed with client consultation

6. Holding problem-solving conference(s) with immediately concerned parties to

   - analyze problems and, in the process, again review whether other information is needed (and if so arrange to gather it)
   - arrive at an agreement about how a problem will be understood for purposes of generating alternatives
   - generate, evaluate, and make decisions about which alternatives to pursue
   - formulate plans for pursuing alternatives (designating support strategies to ensure access and follow-through)

7. Follow up via telephone or conference to evaluate the success of each pursued alternative and determine satisfaction with the process

Problem analysis and decision making can be accomplished in a session. However, if additional assessment data are needed, one or two assessment sessions and a subsequent conference are required.

In supporting the process, school staff can cultivate referral resources to maximize their responsiveness to school referrals.

NOTE: Because some people have come to overrely on experts, they may be a bit frustrated when they encounter an approach such as the one just described. They want professionals to give a battery of tests that will provide definitive answers, and they want decisions made for them. They are convinced they cannot make good decisions for themselves. These individuals often are a product of the negative side effects of professional practices that mystify consumers and make them feel totally dependent on professionals.

Monitoring and Managing Care

From the time a student is first identified as having a problem, someone must monitor and manage efforts to ensure the student gets appropriate help.

Common professional terminology designates students with problems as *cases*. Thus, processes for making certain that students connect with special assistance often are designated *case monitoring*, and efforts to coordinate and integrate interventions are designated *case management*.

Given that words profoundly shape the way people think, feel, and act, some professionals want to replace *case* with *care*. Such a move is in keeping with the view that care is a core value of helping professionals. The change also is consistent with moves to ensure schools are caring communities.

In our work, we use the term *management of care*. Involved are (1) initial monitoring, (2) ongoing management of the individual's care, and (3) management within and across systems of care. As with any intervention, the intent is to implement the work in ways that are developmentally and motivationally appropriate, as well as culturally sensitive.

1. *Initial Monitoring of Care.* Stated simply, initial monitoring of care is the process for determining whether a student is appropriately connected with special programs and services. Initial monitoring by school staff determines whether a student and his or her family are enrolled. Monitoring of care gathers information about follow-through and appropriateness.

An immediate check on referral follow-through (e.g., within 1–2 weeks) should be done to see if the student did connect effectively with help. Besides checking with the student and family, a follow-through report from those providing interventions is helpful. If there has been follow-through, initial contacts are used to evaluate whether the resource is meeting the need. The opportunity also can be used to establish communication and coordination with others involved with the student's welfare. Where follow-through has not occurred, the process can determine why and offer additional consultation.

2. *Ongoing Management of Care.* When a student is working with more than one intervener, management of care becomes a consideration. Monitoring can lead to ways to coordinate interventions, improve quality (including revising interventions as appropriate), and enhance cost-efficacy. Continuing evaluation of intervention appropriateness and effectiveness is the essence of care management.

Monitoring can use a variety of formats (e.g., written communications, phone conversations, electronic communications). All intervention monitoring and management require a system of record keeping designed to maintain an up-to-date record on the status of the student as of the last contact and remind staff when the next contact is scheduled.

If the student has not successfully connected with help or if the help isn't satisfactory, another consultation can be scheduled to determine next steps. Exhibit 39 provides a resource tool for management of care.

Exhibit 39 Ongoing Management of Care

At the core of the ongoing process of care management are the following considerations:

- Enhanced monitoring of care with a specific focus on the appropriateness of the chosen interventions
- Adequacy of client involvement
- Appropriateness of intervention planning and implementation, and progress

Such ongoing monitoring requires systems for the following:

- Tracking client involvement in interventions
- Amassing and analyzing data on intervention planning and implementation
- Amassing and analyzing progress data
- Recommending changes

Effective care management is based upon the ability to do the following:

- Monitor processes and outcomes using information systems that enable those involved with clients to regularly gather, store, and retrieve data
- Produce changes to improve quality
- Assemble a *management team* of interveners and clients and assign primary responsibility for management of care to one staff member or to several who share the work
- Assume a role that always conveys a sense of caring and a shared problem-solving orientation with families as empowered partners
- Facilitate self-determination in clients by encouraging participation in decision making and team reviews (particularly when clients are mandated or forced to enroll in treatment)
- Meet as a management team at designated review periods and whenever analysis of monitored information suggests a need for intervention changes

A few basic guidelines for primary managers of care are as follows:

- Write up analyses of monitoring findings and recommendations to share with management team.
- Immediately after a team meeting, write up and circulate changes proposed by management team and emphasize who has agreed to do which tasks by when.
- Set up a *tickler* system (e.g., a notation on a calendar) to remind you when to check on whether tasks have been accomplished.
- Follow up with team members who have not accomplished agreed-upon tasks to determine what assistance is needed.

---

3. *Systems of Care.* The concept of a *system of care* is an evolving idea that is applied in a variety of ways. While management of care is focused on a given client, the concept of systems of care emphasizes the value of coordinating, integrating,

and enhancing systems and resources. One goal is to ensure that appropriate programs are available, accessible, and adaptable to the needs of those who need help. Another is to ensure resources are used effectively and efficiently.

Enhancing system resources requires attending to various arenas and levels of potential support. A school owns and operates many programs and services. A school district has additional resources. The surrounding community has public and private sector programs and a variety of other resources that may be of assistance. City, county, and state agencies also play a role in addressing certain needs.

From its initial application, the concept of systems of care emphasized services for clients with severe and well-established problems (e.g., youngsters with serious emotional disturbance). The intent for such populations is to

- develop and provide a full array of community-based programs, including residential and nonresidential alternatives to traditional inpatient and outpatient programs (i.e., to enhance what is available and reduce overreliance on out-of-home placements and overly restrictive treatment environments);
- increase interagency collaboration in planning, developing, and carrying out programs to enhance efficacy and reduce costly redundancy;
- establish ways to adapt interventions effectively for the individuals served.

To expand these goals to encompass prevention, primary and secondary prevention programs are incorporated. As indicated in Chapter 2, we conceive three overlapping systems that encompass a continuum of caring: systems to promote health and prevent problems, intervene as early after onset of a problem as is feasible, and treat severe, pervasive, and chronic problems. The comprehensive nature of such a continuum requires concerted intervention coordination at any given time as well as over the span of time (sometimes for many years) that students and their families are assisted.

ABOUT PSYCHOLOGICAL FIRST AID

Responding to a Student in Crisis

School and community shootings, natural disasters, death of a family member or a friend, bullying—students and their families (and school staff) clearly are exposed to traumatic events. Schools must prepare to play a role in providing assistance. Psychological first aid for students, staff, and parents is as important as medical aid.

As formulated by Pynoos and Nader (1988), psychological first aid is administered during and in the immediate aftermath of a crisis. The first objective is to help individuals deal with troubling psychological reactions. Below, we highlight steps in the process, and Exhibit 40 outlines some general principles for crisis response.

First: *Manage the Situation*—A student who is upset can produce a form of *emotional contagion*. To counter this, staff must

- present a calm, reassuring demeanor;
- clarify for classmates and others that the student is upset;
- if possible, indicate why (correct rumors and distorted information);
- state what can and will be done to help the student.

Second: *Mobilize Support*—The student needs *support and guidance*. Staff can help in the following ways:

- Engage the student in a problem-solving dialogue:
  - o Normalize the reaction as much as feasible.
  - o Facilitate emotional expression (e.g., through use of empathy, warmth, and genuineness).
  - o Facilitate cognitive understanding by providing information.
  - o Facilitate personal action by the student (e.g., help the individual do something to reduce the emotional upset and minimize threats to competence, self-determination, and relatedness).
- Encourage the student's buddies to provide social support.
- Contact the student's home to discuss what's wrong and what to do.
- Refer the student to a specific counseling resource.

Third: *Follow Up*—Over the following days (sometimes longer), check on how things are progressing.

- Has the student gotten the necessary support and guidance?
- Does the student need help in connecting with a referral resource?
- Is the student feeling better? If not, what additional support is needed, and how can you help make certain that the student receives it?

Another form of *first aid* involves helping students and families connect with emergency services. This includes agencies that provide emergency food, clothing, housing, transportation, and so forth. Such basic needs constitute ongoing crises for many students and are significant mental health concerns and fundamental barriers to learning and performing and even to getting to school.

Exhibit 40   A Few General Principles Related to Responding to Crises

Immediate Response—Focused on Restoring Equilibrium

When responding, do the following:

- Be calm, direct, informative, authoritative, nurturing, and problem-solving oriented.
- Counter denial, by encouraging students to deal with facts of the event; give accurate information and explanations of what happened and what to expect—never give unrealistic or false assurances.

(Continued)

(Continued)

- Talk with students about their emotional reactions and encourage them to deal with such reactions as another facet of countering denial and other defenses that interfere with restoring equilibrium.
- Convey a sense of hope and positive expectation—that while crises change things, there are ways to deal with the impact.

Move the Student From Victim to Actor

- Plan with the student promising realistic and appropriate actions they will pursue when they leave you.
- Build on coping strategies the student has displayed.
- If feasible, involve the student in assisting with efforts to restore equilibrium.

Connect the Student With Immediate Social Support

- Find peer buddies, other staff, and family to provide immediate support, guidance, and other forms of immediate assistance.

Take Care of the Caretakers

- Be certain that support systems are in place for staff in general.
- Be certain that support (debriefing) systems are in place for all crisis response personnel.

Provide for Aftermath Interventions

- Be certain that individuals needing follow-up assistance receive it.

Before schools respond to an individual after a crisis that affects the whole school, a schoolwide response takes place. Such a response reflects emergency planning and usually prevention strategies. For example, in planning for events such as a campus shooting, schools enhance security and violence prevention. This produces a dilemma: How to make the school more secure without too much cost to a positive school climate and to the mental health of students.

One facet of this dilemma is reflected in the following request sent to our center:

I am the coordinator of all crisis work in our school district. As part of this responsibility I am charged with making sure that the school practices the district's crisis plans and procedures. We have a number of drills during our schoolyear that consist but are not limited to lock-down, lock-out, severe weather, fire, emergency evacuation, and so on. We have been doing both announced and unannounced drills to prepare students and staff. I am seeking information, research, and advice on the psychological effects, if any, these drills have on children and adolescents.

This is a true dilemma (i.e., no win-win answer is likely, only strategies to balance costs and benefits). Research on the matter is sparse. The evidence is that much more attention is paid to school safety and security (e.g., metal detectors, uniformed security officers, crisis response drills) than to minimizing negative consequences. Significant research is not available on the effectiveness and possible unintended negative effects on students and on school climate.

The dearth of research, of course, is no excuse for not considering matters such as the psychological effects of multiple emergency drills. Indeed, crisis response planners must reflect on such questions as the following:

- Do the frequent drills set a tone in the school of heightened concern about personal safety, and do they raise anxiety?
- Do frequent drills produce complacency on the part of some staff and students?
- Does the teaching staff resent the loss of time for instruction?
- Does the *excitement* of a drill disinhibit some students and result in deviant behaviors?
- Do some students view drills as an opportunity for disrupting the school day and thus initiate false fire alarms, hoax phone calls regarding bombs, and so on?

For more on this topic, see the Center's online Introductory Packet titled *Violence Prevention and Safe Schools*—available at http://smhp.psych.ucla.edu/pdfdocs/violence/violence.pdf and also the Online Clearinghouse Quick Find on the topic http://smhp.psych.ucla.edu/qf/p2108_03.htm.

ACCOUNTING FOR CULTURAL, RACIAL, AND OTHER SIGNIFICANT INDIVIDUAL AND GROUP DIFFERENCES

All schools must consider significant individual and group differences. Diversity of stakeholders is a reality at schools. This has benefits and produces problems. With respect to the latter, direct or indirect accusations such as, "You don't understand," are common and valid. Indeed, they are givens. After all, few of us fully understand complex situations or what others have experienced and are feeling.

However, accusing someone of not understanding creates barriers to working relationships. After all, the intent of such accusations is to make others uncomfortable and put them on the defensive. Avoidance of *You don't understand* accusations is one way to reduce barriers to establishing productive working relationships.

More generally, discussions of diversity and cultural competence provide a foundation for accounting for such differences. For example, a guide for enhancing cultural competence (developed by the Family Youth Services Bureau of the U.S. Department of Health and Human Services (1994) cautions readers with the following:

> Racism, bigotry, sexism, religious discrimination, homophobia, and lack of sensitivity to the needs of special populations continue to affect the lives of each new generation. Powerful leaders and organizations throughout the country continue to promote the exclusion of people who are *different*, resulting in the disabling by-products of hatred, fear, and unrealized potential. . . . We will not move toward diversity until we promote inclusion. . . . Programs will not accomplish any of (their) central missions unless . . . (their approach reflects) knowledge, sensitivity, and a willingness to learn.

The document outlines baseline assumptions that we broaden to read as follows:

- Those who work with youngsters and their families can better meet the needs of their target population by enhancing their own competence with respect to group and intragroup differences.
- Developing such competence is a dynamic, ongoing process—not a goal or outcome. That is, no single activity or event will enhance such competence. In fact, use of a single activity reinforces a false sense that the "problem is solved."
- Diversity training is widely viewed as important, but is not effective in isolation. Programs should avoid the *quick fix* theory of providing training without follow-up or more concrete management and programmatic changes.
- Hiring staff from the same background as the target population does not necessarily ensure the provision of appropriate services, especially when these personnel are not in decision-making positions *or* are not themselves appreciative of or respectful to group and intragroup differences.
- Establishing a process for enhancing a program's competence with respect to group and intragroup differences is an opportunity for positive organizational and individual growth.

In the end, of course, remember that *individual differences* are the most fundamental determinant of whether a good intervention fit and working relationship are established.

Mason, Benjamin, and Lewis (1996) outline five cultural competence values that should be reflected in staff attitude and practice and an organization's policy and structure. The emphasis is more on behavior than awareness and sensitivity. The following are the five values and the authors' description of each:

1. *Valuing Diversity*—framing cultural diversity as a strength of clients, line staff, administrative personnel, board members, and volunteers

2. *Conducting Cultural Self-Assessment*—awareness of cultural blind spots and ways in which one's values and assumptions may differ from those held by clients

3. *Understanding the Dynamics of Difference*—the ability to understand what happens when people of different cultural backgrounds interact

4. *Incorporating Cultural Knowledge*—an ongoing process

5. *Adapting to Diversity*—modifying direct interventions and the way the organization is run to reflect the contextual realities of a given catchment area and the sociopolitical forces that may have shaped those who live in the area

For more on building working relationships, see Chapter 13.

CONCLUDING COMMENTS

We conclude with three cautionary notes.

First, all who intervene with students at schools should be aware that one dictionary definition of intervention is "an interference into another's life." As is widely acknowledged, all interventions have a downside and sometimes the benefits do not outweigh the costs. For example, if not attended to properly, intervention dynamics can produce such transactions as the "Rescue Trap" (see Exhibit 41). Constant vigilance is required to avoid making students dependent, stigmatizing young people, creating self-fulfilling prophecies, and so forth.

Exhibit 41   **The Rescue Trap**

So, you want to help! That's a nice attitude, but it can sometimes lead to trouble—especially if you aren't aware of the interpersonal dynamics that can arise in helping relationships. Several concerns have been discussed in the psychotherapy literature. One that almost everyone has experienced has been described as a *rescue*.

A rescue is helping gone astray. Rescues encompass a cycle of negative interpersonal transactions that too commonly arise when one person sets out to intervene in another's life in order to help the person.

Think about a time when someone you know told you about a problem she or he was having. Because the person seemed not to know how to handle the problem, you offered some suggestions. For each idea you offered, the person had an excuse for why it wouldn't work. After a while, you started to feel frustrated and maybe even a bit angry at the person. You may have thought or said to the individual, "You don't really want to solve this problem; you just want to complain about it."

(Continued)

(Continued)

In rescue terms, you tried to help, but the person didn't work with you to solve the problem. The individual's failure to try may have frustrated you, and you felt angry and wanted to tell the person off. And that may only have been the beginning of a prolonged series of unpleasant interpersonal transactions related to the situation.

If you were ever in such a situation, you certainly experienced the price a person pays for assuming the role of rescuer. Of course, you know you didn't mean to become involved in a negative set of transactions. You wanted to help, but you didn't realize fast enough that the individual with the problem wasn't about to work with you in order to solve it. In addition, you didn't know what to do when things started going wrong with the process.

If you can't remember a time you were the rescuer, you may recall a time when someone tried to rescue you. Perhaps your parents, a teacher, or a good friend made the mistake of trying to help you when or in ways you didn't want to be helped. The person probably thought she or he was acting in your best interests, but it only made you feel upset—perhaps increased your anxiety, frustration, anger, and maybe even made you feel rather inadequate.

Rescue cycles occur frequently between teachers and students and parents and their children. Well-intentioned efforts to help usually begin to go astray because someone tries to help at a time, in a way, or toward an end the person to be helped doesn't experience as positive.

Of course, interveners are unlikely to remain victims for very long if they can help it. If they do, *burnout* may well occur.

Sometimes, after the fighting stops, the parties make up, and the intervener starts to see the other person's behavior as part of the individual's problems and tries once more to help. However, if great care is not taken, this just begins the whole cycle again.

How can the cycle be avoided or broken? One of the key ingredients in a good helping relationship is a person who wants to be helped. Thus, every intervener must be sure that those they work with are ready and willing to pursue the type of help that is being offered.

If the person is not ready and willing, interveners are left with only a few options. For one, the intervener can choose to give up trying to help. Or in cases where the individual is *forced* into doing something about the problem, the intervener can adopt a socialization strategy. Or efforts can be made to explore with the individual whether he or she wants to think about accepting some help. In effect, this last approach involves trying to establish motivational readiness.

Second, keeping up with the latest evidence about best practices is necessary in appreciating concerns about such practices and helping advance application of the science base for the field (see Chapters 4 and 14).

Finally, protecting and enhancing the mental health of all who intervene at schools requires laser-like focus (see Chapter 11). Working to help students overcome problems is a noble profession, but the volume of need in most schools is a recipe for staff burnout.

RESOURCE A

This is one of a set of self-study instruments developed by the Center as aids for surveying what a school has in place and what it may want to enhance.

A Self-Study Survey

Specialized assistance for students and their families is for the relatively few problems that cannot be handled without adding special interventions. The emphasis is on providing special services in a personalized way to assist with a broad range of needs. To begin with, social, physical, and mental health assistance available in the school and community are used. As community outreach brings in other resources, these are linked to existing activity in an integrated manner. Additional attention is paid to enhancing systems for triage, case and resource management, direct services for immediate needs, and referral for special services and special education as appropriate. Ongoing efforts are made to expand and enhance resources. While any office or room can be used, a valuable context for providing such services is a center facility, such as a family, community, health, or parent resource center.

A programmatic approach in this arena requires systems designed to provide special assistance in ways that increase the likelihood that a student will be more successful at school, while also reducing the need for teachers to seek special programs and services. The work encompasses providing all stakeholders with information clarifying available assistance and how to access help, facilitating requests for assistance, handling referrals, providing direct service, implementing case and resource management, and interfacing with community outreach to assimilate additional resources into current service delivery. It also involves ongoing analyses of requests for services as a basis for working with school colleagues to design strategies that can reduce inappropriate reliance on special assistance. Thus, major outcomes are enhanced access to special assistance as needed, indices of effectiveness, *and* the reduction of inappropriate referrals for such assistance.

Student and Family Assistance Programs and Services

Indicate all items that apply.

	Yes	More of this is needed	No	Is this something you want?

I. Providing extra support as soon as a need is recognized and doing so in the least disruptive ways

Are there classroom-based approaches to reduce the need for teachers to seek special programs and services (e.g., prereferral interventions in classrooms; problem-solving conferences with parents; open access to school, district, and community support programs—see the Survey on Classroom-Based Approaches [http://smhp .psych.ucla.edu/pdfdocs/Surveys/Set1.pdf])? ___ ___ ___ ___

II. Timely referral interventions for students and families with problems based on response to extra support

What activity is there to facilitate and evaluate requests for assistance?

A. Does the site have a directory that lists services and programs? ___ ___ ___ ___

B. Is information circulated about services and/or programs? ___ ___ ___ ___

C. Is information circulated clarifying how to make a referral? ___ ___ ___ ___

D. Is information about services, programs, and referral procedures updated periodically? ___ ___ ___ ___

E. Is a triage process used to assess

   1. specific needs? ___ ___ ___ ___

   2. priority for service? ___ ___ ___ ___

F. Are procedures in place to ensure use of prereferral interventions? ___ ___ ___ ___

G. Do inservice programs focus on teaching the staff ways to prevent unnecessary referrals? ___ ___ ___ ___

H. Other (specify) _____ ___ ___ ___ ___

III. Enhancing access to direct interventions for health, mental health, and economic assistance

A. After triage, how are referrals handled?

   1. Is detailed information provided about available services (e.g., an annotated community-resource system)? ___ ___ ___ ___

	Yes	More of this is needed	No	Is this something you want?
2. Is there a special focus on facilitating effective decision making?	____	____	____	____
3. Are students and families helped to take the necessary steps to connect with a service or program to which they have been referred?	____	____	____	____
4. Is there a process to ensure referral follow-through?	____	____	____	____

B. What types of direct interventions are provided?

1. Which medical services and programs are provided?

	Yes	More of this is needed	No	Is this something you want?
• Immunizations	____	____	____	____
• First aid and emergency care	____	____	____	____
• Crisis follow-up medical care	____	____	____	____
• Health and safety education and counseling	____	____	____	____
• Health and safety prevention programs	____	____	____	____
• Screening for vision problems	____	____	____	____
• Screening for hearing problems	____	____	____	____
• Screening for health problems (specify)	____	____	____	____
• Screening for dental problems (specify)	____	____	____	____
• Treatment of some acute problems (specify)	____	____	____	____
• Medication monitoring	____	____	____	____
• Medication administration	____	____	____	____
• Home outreach	____	____	____	____
• Other (specify) _____	____	____	____	____

2. Which psychological services and programs are provided?

	Yes	More of this is needed	No	Is this something you want?
• Psychological first aid	____	____	____	____
• Crisis follow-up counseling	____	____	____	____
• Crisis hotlines	____	____	____	____
• Conflict mediation	____	____	____	____
• Alcohol and other drug abuse programs	____	____	____	____
• Pregnancy prevention program	____	____	____	____
• Programs for pregnant and parenting students	____	____	____	____
• Gang prevention program	____	____	____	____
• Gang intervention program	____	____	____	____
• Dropout prevention program	____	____	____	____
• Physical and sexual abuse prevention and response	____	____	____	____
• Individual counseling	____	____	____	____

	Yes	More of this is needed	No	Is this something you want?
• Group counseling	___	___	___	___
• Family counseling	___	___	___	___
• Mental health education	___	___	___	___
• Home outreach	___	___	___	___
• Other (specify) _____	___	___	___	___

3. Which of the following are provided to meet basic survival needs?

• Emergency food	___	___	___	___
• Emergency clothing	___	___	___	___
• Emergency housing	___	___	___	___
• Transportation support	___	___	___	___
• Welfare services	___	___	___	___
• Language translation	___	___	___	___
• Legal aid	___	___	___	___
• Protection from physical abuse	___	___	___	___
• Protection from sexual abuse	___	___	___	___
• Child care	___	___	___	___
• Employment assistance	___	___	___	___
• Other (specify) _____	___	___	___	___

4. Which of the following special education, special eligibility, and independent study programs and services are provided?

• Early education program	___	___	___	___
• Special day classes (specify) _____	___	___	___	___
• Speech and language therapy	___	___	___	___
• Adaptive P.E.	___	___	___	___
• Occupational and physical therapy	___	___	___	___
• Special assessment	___	___	___	___
• Resource Specialist Program	___	___	___	___
• Title I	___	___	___	___
• School Readiness Language Development Program	___	___	___	___
• Other (specify) _____	___	___	___	___

5. Which of the following adult education programs are provided?

• ELL	___	___	___	___
• Citizenship classes	___	___	___	___
• Basic literacy skill	___	___	___	___
• Parenting	___	___	___	___
• Helping children do better at school	___	___	___	___
• Other (specify) _____	___	___	___	___

6. Are services and programs provided to enhance school readiness? Specify _____ ___ ___ ___ ___

	Yes	More of this is needed	No	Is this something you want?

7. Which of the following are provided to
   address attendance problems?

   - Absence follow-up ____ ____ ____ ____
   - Attendance monitoring ____ ____ ____ ____
   - First day calls ____ ____ ____ ____

8. Are discipline proceedings carried out
   regularly? ____ ____ ____ ____
9. Other? (specify) _____ ____ ____ ____ ____

IV. Care Monitoring, Management, Information Sharing, and Follow-up Assessment

A. Which of the following are used to
   manage cases and resources?

   1. Is a student information system used? ____ ____ ____ ____
   2. Is a system used to trail progress of
      students and their families? ____ ____ ____ ____
   3. Is a system used to facilitate communication
      - for case management? ____ ____ ____ ____
      - resource and system management? ____ ____ ____ ____
   4. Are there follow-up systems to determine
      - referral follow-through? ____ ____ ____ ____
      - consumer satisfaction with referrals? ____ ____ ____ ____
      - the need for more help? ____ ____ ____ ____
   5. Other? (specify) _____ ____ ____ ____ ____

B. Which of the following are used to help
   enhance the quality and quantity of
   services and programs?

   1. Is a quality improvement system used? ____ ____ ____ ____
   2. Is a mechanism used to coordinate and
      integrate services and programs? ____ ____ ____ ____
   3. Is there outreach to link up with
      community services and programs? ____ ____ ____ ____
   4. Is a mechanism used to redesign
      current activity as new collaborations
      are developed? ____ ____ ____ ____
   5. Other? (specify) _____ ____ ____ ____ ____

V. Mechanisms for *Resource* Coordination and Integration

Is there a resource-oriented mechanism
(e.g., a Learning Supports Resource Team)
that focuses on the following:

A. Coordinating and integrating resources ____ ____ ____ ____

	Yes	More of this is needed	No	Is this something you want?
B. Braiding resources	___	___	___	___
C. Pursuing economies of scale	___	___	___	___
D. Filling gaps	___	___	___	___
E. Linking with community providers (e.g., to fill gaps)	___	___	___	___
F. Is there a special facility to house student and family assistance programs and services (e.g., health center, family or parent center, counseling center)?	___	___	___	___

VI. Enhancing Stakeholder Awareness of Programs and Services

	Yes	More of this is needed	No	Is this something you want?
A. Are there *written descriptions* of available learning supports programs?	___	___	___	___
B. Are there *written descriptions* about				
1. how to make referrals?	___	___	___	___
2. the triage process?	___	___	___	___
3. the process for case monitoring and management?	___	___	___	___
4. the process for student review?	___	___	___	___
C. Are there communication processes that inform stakeholders about available learning supports programs and how to navigate the systems?	___	___	___	___

VII. Capacity Building to Enhance Student and Family Assistance

	Yes	More of this is needed	No	Is this something you want?
A. Are there programs to enhance broad stakeholder involvement in enhancing student and family assistance?	___	___	___	___
B. With respect to programs used to meet the educational needs of personnel related to student and family assistance				
1. Is there ongoing training for learning supports staff with respect to student and family assistance?	___	___	___	___
2. Is there ongoing training for others involved in enhancing student and family assistance? (e.g., teachers, administrators, volunteers)?	___	___	___	___
3. Other (specify) _____	___	___	___	___

C. Which of the following topics are covered in educating stakeholders?

	Yes	More of this is needed	No	Is this something you want?
1. Broadening understanding of causes of learning, behavior, and emotional problems	___	___	___	___
2. Broadening understanding of ways to ameliorate (prevent, correct) learning, behavior, and emotional problems	___	___	___	___
3. Developing systematic academic supports for students in need	___	___	___	___
4. What classroom teachers and the home can do to minimize the need for special interventions	___	___	___	___
5. Enhancing resource quality, availability, and scope	___	___	___	___
6. Enhancing the referral system and ensuring effective follow-through	___	___	___	___
7. Enhancing the case management system in ways that increase service efficacy	___	___	___	___
8. Other (specify) _____	___	___	___	___

D. Indicate below other things you want the school to do in providing student and family assistance.   ___   ___   ___   ___

- Indicate below other ways the school is enhancing student and family assistance.

- Other matters relevant to enhancing student and family assistance are found in the surveys on
  - Survey of Learning Supports System Status
  - Home Involvement in Schooling
  - School-Community Collaboration

RESOURCE B

Resources Developed by the UCLA Center Containing Practical Tools and Materials for Mental Health in Schools

Of the many resources on the Web site (http://smhp.psych.ucla.edu/selection.html), the following are highlighted here because they contain tools and resources specifically relevant to mental health assistance in schools.

Screening and Assessing Students: Indicators and Tools. Provides resources relevant to screening student problems; includes a perspective for understanding the screening process and aids for initial problem identification and screening. http://smhp.psych.ucla.edu/pdfdocs/assessment/assessment.pdf

School-Based Client Consultation, Referral, and Management of Care. Outlines processes related to problem identification, triage, assessment and client consultation, referral, and management of care. Provides discussion of prereferral intervention and referral as a multifaceted intervention. Examples of tools to aid in all these processes are included. http://smhp.psych.ucla.edu/pdfdocs/consultation/consultation2003.pdf

Students and Psychotropic Medication: The School's Role. Contains aids related to safeguards and provides information on the effects and monitoring of various psychopharmacological drugs used to treat child and adolescent psycho-behavioral problems. http://smhp.psych.ucla.edu/pdfdocs/psymeds/med1.pdf

School Interventions to Prevent Youth Suicide. Discusses and provides resources related to school interventions to prevent youth suicide. http://smhp.psych.ucla.edu/pdfdocs/Sampler/Suicide/suicide.pdf

Autism Spectrum Disorders and Schools. Provides those working in schools with a brief set of resources for understanding Autism Spectrum Disorders and what is done to treat them—with a special emphasis on the role of the school. http://smhp.psych.ucla.edu/pdfdocs/autism/autism.pdf

School-Based Health Centers. Information on a wide range of issues dealing with school-based health centers (e.g., general references, facts, and statistics; funding; state and national documents; guides; reports; model programs across the country). http://smhp.psych.ucla.edu/pdfdocs/Sampler/HlthCtrs.pdf

Resource Synthesis to Help Integrate Mental Health in Schools Into the Recommendations of the President's New Freedom Commission on Mental Health. This aid provides a synthesis highlighting a set of readily accessed online, noncommercial resources relevant to integrating the various agenda for mental health in schools into the Commission recommendations. In addition, a sampling of published references are listed. General resources and references are presented in Part I. Part II is organized around the Commission's goals and recommendations and presents resources that have specific relevance to each. We have tried to find and include an appropriate set of resources; obviously, we have not been exhaustive. http://smhp.psych.ucla.edu/pdfdocs/newfreedomcommisison/resourcesynthesis.pdf

Catalogue of Internet Sites Relevant to Mental Health in Schools. Contains a compilation of Internet links related to addressing barriers to student learning and MH in schools. http://smhp.psych.ucla.edu/pdfdocs/internet/catalog.pdf

Evaluation and Accountability: Related to Mental Health in Schools. Provides immediate information on a variety of resources on evaluation and accountability and how to access them. It includes resources from the clearinghouse, centers and organizations, and Internet resources on evaluation and accountability related to mental health in schools. Also listed is our consultation cadre, which is comprised of professionals who are willing to share their knowledge and expertise in their field. http://smhp.psych.ucla.edu/pdfdocs/EvalAccount/evalmh.pdf

Training Resources and Practice Notes

Assessing and Screening (Quick Training Aid)—http://www.smhp.psych.ucla.edu/pdfdocs/quicktraining/assessmentandscreening.pdf

Case Management in the School Context (Quick Training Aid)—http://www.smhp.psych.ucla.edu/pdfdocs/quicktraining/casemanagement.pdf

School Interventions to Prevent and Respond to Adolescent Affect and Mood Problems (Quick Training Aid)—http://www.smhp.psych.ucla.edu/pdfdocs/quicktraining/affect andmood.pdf

Suicide Prevention (Quick Training Aid)—http://www.smhp.psych.ucla.edu/pdfdocs/quicktraining/suicideprevention.pdf

Frequently Asked Questions About Mental Health in Schools (Info Sheet)—http://smhp.psych.ucla.edu/pdfdocs/freqaskedmh.pdf

Resources for Planning Mental Health in Schools (Info Sheets)—http://smhp.psych.ucla.edu/pdfdocs/planning.pdf

Mental Health and School Based Health Centers (Guidebook)—http://smhp.psych.ucla.edu/pdfdocs/MHSBHC/wholemhsbhc.pdf

Common Psychosocial Problems of School-Aged Youth: Developmental Variations, Problems, Disorders, and Perspectives for Prevention and Treatment (Guidebook)—http://smhp.psych.ucla.edu/pdfdocs/psysocial/entirepacket.pdf

Countering the Over-Pathologizing of Students' Feelings and Behavior: A Growing Concern Related to MH in Schools (Practice Notes)—http://smhp.psych.ucla.edu/pdfdocs/practicenotes/pathology.pdf

Developing Systems at a School for Problem Identification, Triage, Referral, and Management of Care (Practice Notes)—http://smhp.psych.ucla.edu/pdfdocs/practicenotes/developingsystems.pdf

Suicidal Crisis (Practice Notes)—http://smhp.psych.ucla.edu/pdfdocs/practicenotes/suicide.pdf

When a Student Seems Dangerous to Self or Others (Practice Notes)—http://smhp.psych.ucla.edu/pdfdocs/practicenotes/dangerous.pdf

Addressing Barriers to Learning: New Directions for Mental Health in Schools (Continuing Education Modules)—http://smhp.psych.ucla.edu/pdfdocs/contedu/conted.pdf

Addressing Barriers to Learning: A Comprehensive Approach to Mental Health in Schools (Continuing Education Modules)—http://smhp.psych.ucla.edu/pdfdocs/ceaddressing/ceforchange.pdf

Enhancing School Staff Understanding of MH and Psychosocial Concerns (Continuing Education Modules)—http://smhp.psych.ucla.edu/pdfdocs/Report/enhancingschoolstaff.pdf

Mental Health in Schools: New Roles for School Nurses (Continuing Education Modules)—http://smhp.psych.ucla.edu/pdfdocs/Nurses/unit1.pdf

About Mental Health in Schools (Introductory Packet)—http://smhp.psych.ucla.edu/pdfdocs/aboutmh/aboutmhinschools.pdf

Anxiety, Fears, Phobias, and Related Problems: Intervention and Resources for School Aged Youth (Introductory Packet)—http://smhp.psych.ucla.edu/pdfdocs/Anxiety/anxiety.pdf

Social and Interpersonal Problems Related to School Aged Youth (Introductory Packet)—http://smhp.psych.ucla.edu/pdfdocs/socialProblems/socialprobs.pdf

Affect and Mood Problems Related to School-Aged Youth (Introductory Packet)—http://smhp.psych.ucla.edu/pdfdocs/Affect/affect.pdf

Conduct and Behavior Problems in School-Aged Youth (Introductory Packet)—http://smhp.psych.ucla.edu/pdfdocs/conduct/CONDUCT.pdf

---

Quick Find Online Clearinghouse

The Center's Web site provides ready access to the online Quick Find Clearinghouse with a menu of over 130 specific topics. Among the topics covered are disaster response, classroom management, motivation (including engagement and reengagement in classroom learning), social and emotional development, specific types of student problems, and much more. Quick Find provides links directly to resources developed by the UCLA Center and to online resources across the country.

11

Focusing on the Well-Being of School Staff

The person-environment fit model of job stress holds that two kinds of fit exist between the individual and the work environment. The first involves the extent to which the person's skills and abilities match the demands and requirements of the job. The second type of fit involves the extent to which the environment provides for individual's needs. If a mismatch occurs involving either kind, the individual's well-being is threatened, and various health strains may result.

—Bunce and West (1996)

Stress is a commonplace phenomenon for almost everyone who works in school settings. Some stress comes from working with troubled and troubling youngsters. Some stems from difficult working conditions and staggering workloads. Some is the result of the frustration that arises when everyone works so hard and the results are not good enough. The many stressors, large and small, affect staff (and student) morale and mental health. In the short run, this contributes to the high rate of teacher dropout during the first three to five years on the job. Over time, stress can lead to widespread staff demoralization, exhaustion, and burnout.

Ignoring the psychological needs of staff is commonplace and a mistake (Chernis, 1995; Leiter & Maslach, 2000, 2005; Maslach, Schaufeli, & Leither, 2001; Smith & Moss, 2009; Vandenberghe & Huberman, 1999). When school personnel don't feel good about themselves, they are less likely to make students feel good about themselves.

Over the years, one of the resource packets most often downloaded from our Center Web site is *Understanding and Minimizing Staff Burnout* (Center for Mental Health in Schools, 2004c). This underscores both the need for and interest in paying greater attention to the problem. Another indicator of need comes from analyses of school improvement and staff development plans, which rarely focus sufficiently on this matter.

PERSONNEL DEVELOPMENT AND SUPPORT

The well-being of staff is a concern for planning staff development and providing daily support at a school (American Federation of Teachers, 2007; Center for Mental Health in Schools, 2008; Guarino, Santibanez, Daley, & Brewer, 2004; Hanushek, Kain, & Rivkin, 2001; National Comprehensive Center for Teacher Quality, 2007; Neville, Sherman, & Cohen, 2005). In particular, demands for high expectations and high standards must be aligned with a commitment to enhancing personnel development and support. And the focus must be on *all* personnel.

Below are five topics and some related questions that illustrate key facets of staff development and support. These are (1) recruitment, (2) preservice preparation, (3) site induction, (4) continuing professional education, and (5) retention. After briefly highlighting these and in keeping with this book's focus on mental health in schools, we zero in on continuous staff support.

Recruitment

- How can education compete better with other career options in recruiting the *best and the brightest?*
- How can a higher proportion of personnel with the greatest promise and those with proven effectiveness be attracted to the challenge of working in economically distressed locales?

Preservice Preparation and Initial Socialization

- What knowledge, skills, and attitudes should be taught to future education personnel about human growth, development, and learning; interpersonal and group relationships, dynamics, and problem solving; cultural competence and social justice; group and individual differences; intervention theory; legal, ethical, and professional concerns; and applications of advanced technology?
- What should be taught about maintaining and enhancing engagement for classroom learning?

- What should be taught about reengaging students who have become disengaged from school and classroom learning?
- What are the best ways to facilitate such preservice preparation?

Site Induction, Initial Support, and Continuing Socialization

- At work sites, what structural mechanisms and programs are needed to
  - welcome new staff, students, families, and others?
  - provide *professional* support and guidance to enable new staff to function effectively?
  - provide *personal* support and guidance?
  - ensure that socialization of education personnel includes participation in decision making and doesn't undermine idealism and new ideas and practices for advancing the field?

Continuing Professional Education, Support, and Socialization

- At work sites, what structural mechanisms and programs are needed to enhance job-related knowledge, skills, *and* attitudes
  - in a systematic manner?
  - in a personalized manner?

Retention

All of the above are relevant to retaining education personnel. In addition, questions arise about the following:

- What can be done to ensure and facilitate opportunities for career advancement?
- What else is required to retain good personnel in general and especially those working in economically distressed urban and rural locales?

As discussed in the next section, all five facets should be designed to maximize feelings of competence, self-determination, and connectedness to significant others and minimize threats to such feelings.

ABOUT SCHOOL STAFF SUPPORT

While everyone at a school site shares common stressors, those who work in underperforming schools often are overwhelmed by what they experience during a school year. Almost everyone dealing with student behavior, learning, and emotional problems over an extended period becomes fatigued (Felner et al., 2008; Payne, 2008).

Each day elementary school teachers enter a classroom to work with about 30 students. Secondary teachers multiply that by a factor of at least five. Their students bring with them a wide variety of needs. In some classrooms, many students are disengaged from the learning process. Upon entering the classroom, the teacher closes the door, and all present try to cope with each other and with the designated work. The day seldom goes smoothly, and many days are filled with conflict and failure.

For student support staff, the list of students referred for special assistance is so long that the reality is that appropriate assistance is available for only a few. Many support personnel find it virtually impossible to live up to their professional standards.

Others who work at a school, such as front office staff, are overworked, underpaid, often unappreciated, and seldom provided with inservice training. Their dissatisfaction frequently adds another layer of negativity to the school climate.

Accountability demands and daily problems produce a sense of urgency and sometimes crisis that makes the culture of schools more reactive than proactive and more remedial than preventive. The result is a structure oriented more to enhancing external control and safety than providing caring support and guidance. This translates into authoritarian demands and social control (rules, regulations, and punishment), rather than promotion of self-direction, personal responsibility, intrinsic motivation, and well-being.

Given all this, staff support is critical. Support to minimize stress and burnout resolves down to

- reducing environmental stressors,
- increasing personal capabilities,
- enhancing job supports.

Easy to say, hard to do.

Maslach et al. (2001) define burnout as "a prolonged response to chronic emotional and interpersonal stressors on the job [that] is defined by the three dimensions of exhaustion, cynicism, and inefficacy" (p. 397). They go on to state the following:

The past 25 years of research has established the complexity of the construct and places the individual stress experience within a larger organizational context of people's relation to their work. Recently, the work on burnout has expanded internationally and has led to new conceptual models. The focus on engagement, the positive antithesis of burnout, promises to yield new perspectives on interventions to alleviate burnout. The social focus of burnout, the solid research basis concerning the syndrome, and its specific ties to the work domain make a distinct and valuable contribution to people's health and well-being.

Corey (2008) notes the following:

Burnout manifests itself in many ways. Those who experience this syndrome typically find that they are tired, drained, and without enthusiasm. They talk of feeling pulled by their many projects, most of which seem to have lost meaning. They feel that what they do have to offer is either not wanted or not received; they feel unappreciated, unrecognized, and unimportant, and they go about their jobs in a mechanical and routine way. They tend not to see any concrete results of the fruits of the efforts. Often, they feel oppressed by the *system* and by institutional demands, which they contend stifle any sense of personal initiative. A real danger is that burnout syndrome can feed off itself so that practitioners feel more and more isolated. They may fail to reach out to one another and to develop a support system. Because burnout can rob us of the vitality we need personally and professionally, it is important to look at some of its causes, possible remedies, and ways of preventing it. (p. 34)

Sorry,
I'd like to help,
but my human
is down today!

Do youngsters who are *turned off* reflect instances of student burnout?

An Intrinsic Motivational Perspective

Anyone who works in schools knows about burnout. As with so many problems, if ignored, burnout takes a severe toll. The problem is talked about more often than systematic action is taken (Centers for Law and the Public's Health, 2008). Personnel who bring a mental health and motivational perspective to schools can help change the situation by enhancing understanding of causes and promoting action (Barnett & Cooper, 2009).

One way to understand the problem is in terms of three psychological needs that theorists posit as major intrinsic motivational determinants of behavior. These are the need to *feel competent*, the need to *feel self-determining*, and the need to *feel interpersonally connected*. From this perspective, burnout is one negative outcome that results when these needs are threatened and thwarted. Such needs are regularly threatened and thwarted by the prevailing culture in most schools.

Staff (and students) chronically find themselves in situations where they feel overcontrolled and less than competent. They also come to believe they have little control over long-range outcomes, and this affects their hopes for the future. A sense of alienation from other staff, students, families, and the surrounding neighborhood is all too common. Thus, not only don't they experience feelings of competence, self-determination, and positive connection with others, the reality is that such feelings are undermined.

What Needs to Change?

Minimizing burnout at a school site begins with an appreciation that causes are multifaceted and complex. Some of the problem stems from environmental stressors, and some stems from characteristics and capabilities individuals bring to the situation. Moreover, the way the environment and individual mesh is a further complication.

As with student problems, personal conditions often are the presumed cause of staff stress and burnout. This can lead to inadequate understanding of what must be done over the long run to address the matter. For example, personal *wellness* and health promotion programs and stress-reduction activities often are advocated (Centers for Law and the Public's Health, 2008). However, these individual-oriented approaches usually are an insufficient remedy. Reducing environmental stressors and enhancing job supports are more to the point, but again, by themselves these strategies are insufficient.

The solution requires reculturing schools to minimize undermining and maximize enhancement of intrinsic motivation. This requires policies and practices that ensure a regular, often a daily, emphasis on school supports that (1) promote staff and student well-being and (2) enhance how schools address barriers to teaching and learning.

RECULTURING SCHOOLS
TO PROMOTE WELL-BEING

Needed: a caring environment, effective mentoring, teaming, and other collegial supports. From an intrinsic motivational perspective, a strong collegial and social support structure and meaningful ways to participate in decision making are critical for promoting feelings of well-being at a school. As suggested in preceding chapters, key elements include well-designed and implemented programs for

- inducting newcomers into the school culture in a welcoming and socially supportive way;
- transforming working conditions by opening classroom doors and creating appropriate teams of staff and students who support, nurture, and learn from each other every day;
- transforming inservice training into personalized staff development and support from first induction into a school through ongoing capacity building;
- restructuring school governance to enable shared decision making.

Welcoming and social support. From a psychological perspective, learning and teaching at school are experienced most positively when the learner wants to learn and the teacher enjoys facilitating student learning. Each day goes best when all participants care about each other. To these ends, staff must establish a schoolwide and classroom atmosphere that is welcoming, encourages mutual support and caring, and contributes to a sense of community. A caring school develops and institutionalizes welcoming and ongoing social support programs for new staff, students, and families. Such efforts can play a key role in reducing staff burnout and benefit students in significant ways.

Opening the classroom door. New staff require a considerable amount of support and on-the-job training. All staff need to learn more about mobilizing and enabling learning in the classroom. Opening the classroom door is a key step in enhancing the learning of teachers, other staff, and students.

The crux of the matter is to ensure use of effective mentoring, teaming, and other collegial supports. This includes specialist personnel (e.g., school psychologists, counselors, special education resource teachers) who mentor and demonstrate rather than play traditional consultant roles. Specialists should be prepared to go into classrooms to model and guide teachers in the use of practices for engaging and reengaging students in learning.

In addition, teachers can do their jobs better when they integrate community resources. Anyone in the community who wants to help might make a contribution. In general, the array of people who can end the isolation of teachers in classrooms includes (1) aides and volunteers, (2) other regular and specialist teachers, (3) family members, (4) students, (5) student support staff, (6) school administrators, (7) classified staff, (8) teachers and other professionals in training, (9) school and community librarians, and more.

Personalized staff development and support. As with any learner, staff need instruction and support that is a good match for both their motivation and capabilities. This includes (1) inservice programs that account for interests, strengths, weaknesses, and limitations; (2) approaches that overcome avoidance motivation; (3) structure that provides personalized support and guidance; and (4) instruction designed to enhance and expand intrinsic motivation for learning and problem solving. Some staff also require additional, specialized support, guidance, and accommodations.

Personalized staff development and support can counter alienation and burnout. The work may encompass programs for cooperative learning, mentoring, advocacy, counseling and mediation, human relations, and conflict resolution. Regular mentoring is essential. However, learning from colleagues is not just a talking game. Good mentors model and then actively participate in making changes (e.g., demonstrating and discussing new approaches, guiding initial practice and implementation, and following-up to improve and refine). Depending on practicalities, such modeling could take place in a teacher's own classroom or be carried out in colleagues' classrooms. Some of it may take the form of team teaching. Personalized contacts increase opportunities for providing support and guidance, enhancing competence, ensuring involvement in meaningful decision making, and attaining positive social status.

Shared governance. Who is empowered to make decisions in an organization can be a contentious issue. Putting aside politics for the moment, we stress the motivational impact of not feeling empowered. A potent and negative impact on motivation occurs when staff (and students and all other stakeholders) are not involved in making major decisions that affect the quality of their lives. This argues for ensuring that personnel are provided with a variety of meaningful opportunities to shape such decisions. Participation on planning committees and teams that end up having little or no impact can contribute to burnout. Alternatively, feelings of self-determination that help counter burnout are more likely when governance structures share power across stakeholders and make room for their representatives around the decision-making table.

Mother to her son:	*Time to get up and go to school.*
Son:	*I don't want to go. It's too hard, and the kids don't like me.*
Mother:	*But you have to go—you're their teacher.*

LEARNING TO ADDRESS BARRIERS TO TEACHING AND LEARNING

As emphasized throughout this book, many students bring problems with them to school that affect their learning and perhaps interfere with the teacher's efforts to teach. In some geographic areas, potential problems stem from restricted opportunities associated with poverty and low income, difficult and diverse family circumstances, high rates of mobility, lack of English language skills, violent neighborhoods, substance abuse, inadequate health care, and lack of enrichment opportunities. Teachers must learn many ways to enable the learning of students who experience such potential barriers. Schools must develop schoolwide approaches that enable teacher effectiveness. Student support staff must work closely with teachers and with each other for mutual support.

Too many teachers know too little about how best to support and guide students who manifest commonplace behavioral, learning, and emotional problems. In saying this, we are not teacher bashing. We have the highest respect and empathy for anyone who pursues the call to work with young people. The problem is that teachers and student support staff are not being taught the fundamentals of how to help those youngsters who do not come to school each day motivationally ready and able to learn. The evidence is clear from analyses of school improvement planning. A major disconnect exists between what teachers need to learn and what they are taught about addressing student problems—and too little is being done about it. Undoubtedly, this contributes in major ways to staff burnout.

High stakes expectations, low-powered staff development. In keeping with prevailing demands for higher standards and achievement test scores, the focus of school reform and preservice teacher training is mainly on curriculum content and instruction. Analyses indicate that implicit in most instructional reforms is a presumption that students are motivationally ready and able to absorb the lesson presented. Recognition that the teacher must deal with some misbehavior and learning problems generally is treated as a separate matter calling for classroom management and some extra instruction.

For the most part, preservice teacher preparation provides little or no discussion of what to do when students are not motivationally ready and able to respond appropriately to a lesson as taught. This lapse in training is less a problem for teachers in classrooms where few students are doing poorly. In settings where large proportions are not doing well, however, and especially where many are *acting out*, teachers decry the gap in their training.

Typically, schools offer a few, relatively brief sessions on various social control techniques. Examples include eye contact, physical proximity, being alert and responding quickly before a behavior escalates, using rewards as a preventive strategy, assertive discipline, and threats and other forms of punishment. All this, of course, skirts by the matter of what is causing student misbehavior and ignores the reality that social control practices can be incompatible with enhancing student engagement with learning at school. Indeed, such practices can lead to greater student disengagement (see Chapter 9).

We hasten to stress that in highlighting the above matters, we do not mean to minimize the importance of thorough and ongoing training related to curriculum and instruction. Every teacher must have the ability and resources to bring a sound curriculum to life and apply strategies that make learning meaningful. At the same time, however, teachers and student support staff must learn how to *enable* learning by addressing interfering factors—especially factors leading to low or negative motivation for schooling.

Reculturing Classrooms

Review the preceding chapters in Part III. Think in terms of strategies to engage student interest and attention, one-to-one or small group instruction (e.g., tutoring, cooperative learning groups), enhancing protective factors, and assets building (including use of curriculum-based approaches to promote social emotional development), as well as varied forms of special assistance. All this expands definitions of good teaching to encompass practices that enable teacher effectiveness with a wide range of students. From this perspective, good teaching involves fostering a caring context for learning; it includes development of a classroom infrastructure that transforms a big classroom into a set of smaller units; it encompasses many strategies for preventing and addressing problems as soon as they arise.

CONCLUDING COMMENTS

As a 2007 report from the National Commission on Teaching and America's Future (NCTAF) indicates, "the teacher dropout problem is costing the nation billions of dollars, draining resources, diminishing teaching quality, and undermining the nation's ability to close the student achievement gap." NCTAF estimates that the national cost of public school teacher turnover could be over $7.3 billion a year.

The reasons for teachers and other staff dropping out are many. Isolation from colleagues and alienation from students and their families compound deficits in training, unrealistic demands, and relatively low salaries. Ignoring staff well-being causes programs and services to suffer and widespread personnel turnover. This translates into significant human and financial costs. Countering isolation and alienation and promoting well-being at school clearly are major agenda items for mental health in schools.

It should surprise no one that school staff might find it difficult to attend effectively to the needs of students when their own needs are ignored. Addressing staff well-being through promoting a caring, supportive, learning community at a school is basic to helping all of the school's stakeholders maintain a sense of balance, perspective, and hope.

PART IV

Policy and Systemic Change for Moving Forward

Frankly, I'm suspicious of anyone who has a strong opinion on a complicated issue.

—Scott Adams

A s stressed in Part III, a broadened view of mental health in schools empha-sizes moving student support programs and services in new directions. Specifically, the need is to develop a comprehensive approach that encompasses systematic and institutionalized interventions. The intent is to (1) enhance the role schools play in promoting healthy social and emotional development, (2) help schools respond and minimize ways they contribute to mental health and psy-chosocial problems, and (3) provide an integrated school-community system for students who require special assistance.

In this last part of the book, we turn to what must be done to move forward with this complex agenda for embedding mental health into school improvement. Moving forward requires the ability to clarify

- the case for systemic change, frame the agenda as a policy *imperative,* and enlist the support of a wide range of stakeholders;
- what is involved in *redeploying and weaving together stakeholder resources* (e.g., schools, families, neighborhoods, and institutions of higher education) to transform the currently marginalized efforts into a primary component of school improvement;

201

- the available *science-base* and the need for an *expanded accountability framework* to extend the research base for this component of school improvement;
- what is involved in making *systemic changes,* including replication and *scale-up.*

Inadequate policy support related to any of these matters decreases the likelihood of enhancing intervention effectiveness on a large scale. So while the following chapters are a step removed from the daily demands on those working in schools, they are central to the agenda of moving forward.

12

New Directions

You see things; and you say, "Why?" But I dream things that never were; and I say, "Why not?"

—George Bernard Shaw

For good reasons, a dominant emphasis in school improvement is on enhancing instruction and school management. Although issues arise about how to address these matters, the overall necessity of ensuring good instruction and good school management is inarguable.

Our concern is that improved instruction and school management alone do not appropriately address significant barriers to learning and teaching (including mental health and psychosocial concerns). As the Carnegie Council on Adolescent Development: Task Force on Education of Young Adolescents (1989) points out, "... while school systems are not responsible for meeting every need of their students, when the need directly affects learning, the school must meet the challenge."

Given the marginalized status of mental health in schools, those who want to advance the field must be prepared to make a strong case to decision makers. This chapter is devoted to underscoring why moving forward is imperative and highlighting pioneering work around the country. We also outline a few major recommendations for shifts in policy and practice.

THE IMPERATIVE

Most policy makers and administrators know that by itself good instruction delivered by highly qualified teachers cannot ensure that *all* students have an equal opportunity to succeed at school. The straightforward psychometric reality is that in schools where a large proportion of students encounter major barriers to learning, the often reported initial increases in test score averages plateau after a few years.

In general, improved instruction and school management are insufficient for

- reducing student dropout rates,
- reducing teacher dropout rates,
- reengaging students in classroom learning,
- narrowing the achievement gap,
- eliminating the plateau effect related to achievement test gains,
- reducing the list of schools designated as low performing,
- minimizing the degree to which high stakes testing takes a toll on students and schools.

The compelling reality is that too many students and too many schools continue not to do well. Thus, in terms of both enhancing equity of opportunity for students and strengthening public education, one major imperative is to move in new directions that focus directly on effectively addressing barriers and reengaging students in classroom learning. Doing so will have major implications for the mental health of children, adolescents, their families, and school personnel.

School Improvement Planning Must Do More to Address Student Supports

Over the years, we have explored and reported on the status of student supports.[1] The findings of this research underscore the imperative to move in new directions. For example, our policy and practice analyses of school improvement planning arrive at the unequivocal conclusion: *School improvement guides do not focus appropriately on addressing barriers to learning and teaching and marginalize student supports.*[2]

The Center's 2005 report titled *School Improvement Planning: What's Missing?* states the following:

> Prevailing approaches to school improvement do not encompass comprehensive, multifaceted, and integrated approaches for enabling learning through addressing barriers. This is especially unfortunate in schools where large proportions of students are not doing well. Thus, one of the poignant ironies of continuing to proceed in this way is that the aim of providing equity of opportunity for many students is undermined. Improved instruction is necessary but insufficient in many instances. Students who arrive at school on any given day with diminished motivational readiness and/or abilities need something more. That something is best addressed when school improvement planning focuses comprehensively on addressing barriers to learning and teaching.

The document concludes with the following:

The marginalized status and the associated fragmentation of efforts to address student problems are long standing and ongoing. The situation is likely to go unchanged as long as school improvement plans continue to ignore the need to restructure the work of student support professionals. Currently, most school improvement plans do not focus on using such staff to develop the type of comprehensive, multifaceted, and integrated approaches necessary to address the many overlapping barriers to learning and development.

Addressing barriers to learning and teaching must be made a high-level focus in every school improvement planning guide. To do less is to ensure too many children are left behind.

Every school improvement plan must meet this challenge by ensuring it focuses on development of a comprehensive, multifaceted, and cohesive approach to addressing barriers to learning, development, and teaching. Development of such an approach requires shifts in prevailing policy and new frameworks for practice. In addition, for significant systemic change to occur, policy and program commitments must be demonstrated through effective allocation and redeployment of resources. That is, finances, personnel, time, space, equipment, and other essential resources must be made available, organized, and used in ways that adequately operationalize policy and promising practices. This includes ensuring sufficient resources to develop an effective structural foundation for systemic changes, sustainability, and ongoing capacity building.

Some Recent Survey Findings

With these concerns in mind, note our findings from a survey of district administrators (see Exhibit 42). Almost two-thirds of the respondents were unable to designate places where school improvement planning is focused on developing a comprehensive systemic approach for addressing barriers to learning and teaching. Among those who state they are aware of such an approach, 40% indicate that the system is not well focused.

Exhibit 42	Survey of School Improvement Planning Related to Development of Comprehensive Approaches to Addressing Barriers to Learning and Teaching

A brief survey sought responses to the basic question:

- Are you aware of any school improvement planning designed to develop a comprehensive systemic approach for addressing barriers to learning and teaching? (A mapping tool was attached to clarify what constitutes a comprehensive approach.)

(Continued)

(Continued)

Respondents who replied affirmatively were asked to indicate how we could access information about the plan and also were asked to respond to two follow-up questions:

- At this stage of its development, how well does the learning support system focus on developing classroom and schoolwide interventions to both (a) enhance how students cope with barriers to learning and (b) reengage them effectively in classroom instruction?
- Is someone designated as the administrative leader to ensure development and effective implementation of a comprehensive systemic approach for addressing barriers to learning and teaching?

Of 300 responses, 289 came from district level personnel (e.g., 72 superintendents; 44 deputy, associate, or assistant superintendents; and 104 directors of student support activity).

In response to the first question, 183 (61%) indicated they *were not* aware of such planning.

The 117 who answered affirmatively gave the following ratings for how well the system focused on *both* (1) enhancing how students cope with barriers to learning and (2) reengaging them effectively in classroom instruction:

14 (12%) rated the focus as extremely high.

55 (47%) rated it as high.

40 (34%) rated it fair.

8 (7%) rated the focus as extremely low.

With respect to how we could access information about the plan, 63 of the 117 either did not respond or directed us to information not specifically relevant to the focus of the survey. Nineteen chose to send in relevant descriptions of their efforts; an additional 26 had Web sites with adequate information readily accessible online. Nine respondents indicated a comprehensive plan was just under development.

Below is a synthesis of what respondents were referencing as comprehensive. Of the responses noted above, all but a few districts appear to be referring to the limited range of programs and services usually organized as a student services or instructional support unit (often including special education). That is, only nine respondents even suggested that significant efforts were underway to rework existing approaches into a more comprehensive system for addressing barriers to learning and teaching.

Of those who sent descriptions or whose student support efforts were organized for access on the Internet, the trend was for the district to present student support services as a department with a designated director. As previously found in our analysis of district infrastructure, such departments are described in various ways. The gist is that they are overseers of the range of student services that the district establishes as systemwide and school-based interventions to meet students' academic and social needs with the intent of enabling every student to succeed at school and in the community.

The nature and scope of student services varies by district. The following list is a synthesis culled from several of the responding districts:

- Counseling and Guidance
- Psychological and Social Services (including diagnostic testing and other assessment)
- Health and Nursing Services
- Discipline Management
- Safe and Drug-Free Schools (including individual services, violence and/or bullying reduction, and drug and alcohol education)
- Student Assistance Programs
- Special Accommodations Under Section 504
- Truancy Response
- Teen Parenting
- Dropout Prevention
- Homeless Liaison
- Parent Education
- Student Transfers
- Afterschool Programs
- School-Based Health Center
- Family Resource Center (with linkages to community services)
- Family Connections

Some districts include Alternative Schools, Special Education, English Language Learners, and Diversity and Equity Programs in the student service department, but most disperse these (and many of the other activities listed above) over several divisions or departments.

A third survey question asked whether someone was designated as the administrative leader to ensure development and effective implementation of a comprehensive systemic approach for addressing barriers to learning and teaching. If so, we asked for information on how to access that person's job description.

Of the 117 who responded affirmatively, 95 (81%) indicated they had an administrative leader. However, only 70 (60%) provided information about how to access the person's job description.

Unfortunately, almost 25% did not provide information about how to access a job description. Still, a few things are evident with respect to leadership for development and effective implementation of a comprehensive systemic approach for addressing barriers to learning and teaching. For one, the descriptions provided and other readily accessible information indicate that this leadership role usually is added on to someone's existing job description. Titles listed included superintendent, administrator for a student services or instructional support unit, director for curriculum, program coordinators, and principals. A few respondents indicated that the work was assigned to multiple people and/or positions. Finally, note that almost 20% indicated no designated leader. Of these, a greater proportion indicated the work was not proceeding very well.

Our research also finds considerable variation in use of the term *comprehensive*. In general, data suggest that the term is applied liberally. At one extreme, users are denoting an extensive and/or intensive approach focused on one specific arena of activity (e.g., *We have a comprehensive program for parent involvement*). Another extreme is to denote a wide range of activity across multiple arenas, albeit not always a full spectrum of activity (e.g., *We have a comprehensive approach to providing student supports*). As applied to nonacademic barriers, *comprehensive* mainly is used to indicate attention to enhancing school safety and a supportive learning environment and pursuing mandates for parent and community involvement.

As to leadership, districts routinely divide student supports into categorical approaches reflecting funding streams and mandates with a *leader* for each. The intent is to have someone in charge and accountable. The result is district leadership pursuing overlapping functions within an organizational and operational infrastructure that marginalizes them and their work. Such leaders are poorly positioned to evolve policies and practices. On the positive side, these administrative positions could be reworked into the type of leadership necessary for developing a comprehensive system of learning supports. (See prototype job description in the Appendix.)

Finally, we find significant difficulty in publically accessing descriptions of how schools address nonacademic barriers to learning and teaching. This state of affairs is somewhat surprising given that district and school Web sites increasingly are a major communication medium. This seems yet another indication of the marginalized status of the work.

Available Evidence Underscores
Moving Forward as an *Imperative*

So given the above data and what was covered in Part I of this book, we stress that a foundation is already in place for moving the field forward. Looked at as a whole, a considerable amount of activity is taking place with substantial resources being expended. As noted, most districts offer a range of programs and services oriented to student needs and problems. Some are provided throughout a district, others are carried out at or linked to targeted schools. Some are owned and operated by schools; some are from community agencies. The interventions may be for all students in a school, for those in specified grades, for those identified as *at risk*, and/or for those in need of compensatory or special education. Many dedicated professionals are struggling to make a difference, and pockets of excellence are everywhere.

Organizationally, however, there is no system. Separate divisions deal with the same common barriers to learning, such as ineffective instruction, lack of parent involvement, violence and unsafe schools, poor support for student transitions, disabilities, and so forth. Those staffing the work commonly function in relative isolation of each other and other stakeholders, with a great deal of the work oriented to discrete problems and with an overreliance on specialized services for individuals and small groups. There is little or no coordination; attention to integration is sparse. Furthermore, an unproductive (and sometimes counterproductive) separation usually is manifested between staff focused directly on instruction and those concerned with student support. Schools confronted with a large number of students manifesting behavior, learning, and emotional problems pay dearly for this state of affairs.

Because so many programs have evolved in a piecemeal and ad hoc manner, district and school personnel often are involved in *parallel play*. This contributes to widespread counterproductive competition and wasteful redundancy. Effectiveness is compromised. So are initiatives to take projects, pilots, and demonstration programs to scale.

One response to the fragmentation is the call to enhance coordination. A more unified and cohesive approach clearly is needed. However, enhancing coordination is an insufficient strategy. The core problem that must be dealt with is that the whole enterprise devoted to addressing barriers to learning and teaching is *marginalized* in school policy, planning, and practice. This is the challenge to moving forward. Meeting the challenge is an absolute imperative given how many schools are designated as low performing, how difficult it has been to reduce dropout rates and close the achievement gap, and the continuing concerns about school safety and climate.

Meeting the challenge requires a shift in school improvement policy and practice. Such a shift must lead to rethinking how schools can more effectively use *all* support programs, resources, and personnel.

Policy makers also must expand the framework for school accountability. Prevailing accountability measures are pressuring schools to maintain a narrow focus on strategies whose face validity suggests a direct route to improving instruction. The implicit underlying assumption of most of these teaching strategies is that students are motivationally ready and able each day to benefit from the teacher's instructional efforts. This, of course, is not the case. For many students, the fact remains that a host of external interfering factors are widespread. Where schools fail to address such factors comprehensively and systemically, school improvement efforts are fundamentally flawed, and student progress and well-being pay the price.

In sum, across the country too many students are encountering barriers that prevent them from having an equal opportunity to succeed at school. Addressing such barriers requires comprehensive and systemic solutions. Unfortunately, school improvement and capacity-building efforts (including preservice and inservice staff development) generally have not dealt effectively with these realities.

> While districts are not ignoring learning, behavior, and emotional problems, available evidence indicates that most districts are continuing to plan in ways that maintain policies and practices for student support that are not effective enough. For example, all districts focus to some degree on the need for safe and drug-free schools, parent and community involvement, discipline problems, and compensatory and special education. Few, however, are developing a system to comprehensively address the many factors interfering with students having an equal opportunity to succeed at school. School improvement planners must rethink how schools can more effectively use all support programs, resources, and personnel.

EFFORTS TO MOVE IN NEW DIRECTIONS

What we find in venues across the country is that increasing numbers of stakeholders are expressing interest in moving in new directions and making systemic changes to develop comprehensive approaches. This is especially the situation every time school improvement is a major agenda item.

We regularly hear about places moving in new directions. We reach out for information, to offer support, and to compile what we learn. Examples are highlighted in *Where's It Happening? Examples of New Directions for Student Support and Lessons Learned* (available at http://smhp.psych.ucla.edu/pdfdocs/wheresithappening/overview.pdf) and in an accompanying compendium (available at http://smhp .psych.ucla.edu/summit2002/wheresithappening.htm). Such trailblazing and pioneering work provides an intriguing glimpse into the future of student support. Some have taken their first implementation steps; some are in the planning stage. A few report difficulty generating the momentum necessary to produce full-blown systemic change. All provide lessons learned.

Examples of initiatives presented in the above report that represent ambitious and comprehensive *out-of-the-box thinking* include the following:

At the state level—

- *Iowa's System of Learning Supports*—a state department of education initiative
- *Hawaii's Comprehensive Student Support System*—a statewide initiative, including state legislation
- *California's Proposed Comprehensive Pupil Learning Supports System*—proposed legislation

At the district level—

- *Berkeley (CA) School District*—a districtwide initiative in initial stages of implementation
- *New American Schools Comprehensive School Improvement, Urban Learning Center Design*—a prototype model developed as part of the New American Schools initiative, included as part of the federal initiative supporting comprehensive school reform
- *Harrisburg (PA) School District*—a districtwide initiative in planning stage
- *Multnomah (OR) Education Service District*—School Board Policy for Learning Supports

See Exhibit 43 for a brief overview of Iowa's initiative.

Exhibit 43   **Iowa: A Major Statewide Commitment**

Iowa leaders have come to recognize that meeting the challenge of enhancing achievement test scores requires not only improving teaching but also necessitates developing better ways for schools, families, and communities to facilitate learning by alleviating *barriers*, both external and internal, that can interfere with learning and teaching.

In 2003, the Department of Education established a design team, engaged national consultants and a national advisory panel, and created a stakeholder group and several workgroups to develop guiding intervention and infrastructure frameworks for Iowa's *system* of learning supports. The charge was to design a system of learning supports that is fully integrated with efforts to improve instruction and that is fully embedded into the Iowa school improvement process.

In the fall of 2004, the design for a System of Learning Supports was finalized. The design document is titled "Developing Our Youth: Fulfilling a Promise, Investing in Iowa's Future—Enhancing Iowa's Systems of Supports for Learning and Development." It has been disseminated to policy makers and leaders at state, regional, and local levels within and outside the education system who have a compelling interest in the achievement of all students and are seeking effective ways to improve student learning.

The document calls for rethinking the directions for student supports in order to reduce fragmentation in the system and increase the effectiveness and efficiency by which it operates. The intended results are for all children and youth to succeed in school, grow up healthy and socially competent, and be prepared for productive adulthood. To accomplish this, state policy emphasizes that schools and communities must work together and with their regional and state level partners and that schools and school districts need to address all aspects of students' learning, social-emotional development, and physical development.

The prototype design addresses the following:

- *Long-term results and measures* based on available data serve as leading indicators of student success in school. Additional sets of system and student performance measures reflect the intermediate and direct impact of a system of learning supports.
- *Cohesive intervention frameworks*, grounded in the agreed upon results for all children and youth in Iowa, facilitate organization of school and community resources, programs, and services into a comprehensive continuum that supports student learning and healthy development and addresses barriers to learning and teaching.
- *Infrastructure* organizes the functions and processes needed to implement a system of learning supports and connect the various system levels (local, regional, and state). The infrastructure focus is on mechanisms that permit schools and communities to make optimal use of their resources, reframe the roles of personnel, and integrate the instruction, management, and learning supports components of the educational system.
- *Supportive policies* at all levels are identified or developed to facilitate the implementation of a system of learning supports in ways that complement and are fully integrated into school-community efforts to improve teaching and learning and manage resources.
- *Capacity building* at all system levels (state, regional, and local) will (a) ensure use of definitions and guidelines that create a common language for improved communication within the educational system and with other child-serving systems and (b) enhance the knowledge, skills, and resources and tools needed to successfully implement a system of learning supports.
- *Revamp* district, school, and school-community infrastructures to weave resources together to enhance and evolve the learning supports system.
- *Pursue* school improvement and systemic change from the perspective of learning supports and the need to engage and reengage students in classroom learning.

RECOMMENDATIONS FOR SHIFTING POLICY AND PRACTICE

Fundamental changes are needed; systemic transformation is essential.

In pursuing transformation, John Maynard Keynes (1997) cautions,

The real difficulty in changing the course of any enterprise lies not in developing new ideas but in escaping old ones.

We suggest that moving forward requires escaping old ideas in addressing four key problems. First and foremost is a *policy shift*. School improvement *policies* must expand in ways that will end the marginalization of student supports.

Second, *unifying intervention frameworks must be adopted.* This encompasses a comprehensive and multifaceted continuum of interventions with the intent of guiding development of a cohesive enabling or learning supports component at every school. We take as given that moving forward requires rethinking the roles and functions of traditional support staff and compensatory education personnel (e.g., Title I staff), resource teachers who focus on prereferral interventions, and personnel who provide a variety of schoolwide programs (e.g., afterschool, safe and drug-free school programs). All address overlapping behavior, learning, and emotional concerns.

Third, *infrastructure must be reworked* at school, complex, and district levels. Changes must ensure effective leadership, redefine roles and functions to ensure development of a comprehensive system, and establish resource-oriented mechanisms.

Finally, *strategic approaches for enabling effective systemic change and scale-up* must be developed and implemented.

If the next decade is to mark a turning point in how schools and communities address the problems of children and youth, we must all join in school improvement planning to

- reframe current student support programs and services and redeploy the resources to develop a comprehensive, multifaceted, and cohesive component to enable learning;
- develop both in-classroom and schoolwide approaches—including interventions to support transitions, increase home and community connections, enhance teachers' ability to respond to common learning and behavior problems, and respond to and prevent crises.

> Addressing barriers to learning and teaching must be made an essential and high-level focus in every school improvement planning guide.
>
> To do less is to ensure too many children are left behind academically, socially, and emotionally.

Specific recommendations include the following:

1. Districts should revisit school improvement planning guides to ensure they focus on development of a comprehensive, multifaceted, and cohesive system for addressing barriers to learning and teaching and do so in ways that are fully integrated with plans for improving instruction at the school. This encompasses developing guidelines for (a) operationalizing comprehensiveness in terms of a framework that embraces a full continuum of interventions and a well conceptualized set of content arenas and (b) delineating standards and accountability indicators for each content arena.

2. Districts should designate a dedicated position for leadership of efforts to develop and implement such a comprehensive system and redesign infrastructure to ensure interventions for addressing barriers to learning and teaching are attended to as a primary and necessary component of school improvement and in ways that promote economies of scale.

3. Guidelines for school improvement planning should include an emphasis on redefining and reframing roles and functions for school-site leadership related to development and implementation of such a system.

4. Guidelines for school improvement planning should specify ways to weave school and community resources into a cohesive and integrated continuum of interventions over time.

A final recommendation is for researchers to consider the following:

Current initiatives for program evaluation and research projects should be redesigned to include a focus on amassing and expanding the research base for building and evaluating a comprehensive system for addressing barriers to learning and teaching, with a long-range emphasis on demonstrating the long-term impact of such a system on academic achievement.

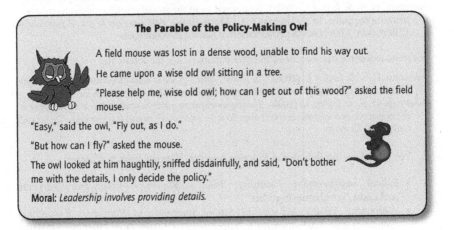

The Parable of the Policy-Making Owl

A field mouse was lost in a dense wood, unable to find his way out.

He came upon a wise old owl sitting in a tree.

"Please help me, wise old owl; how can I get out of this wood?" asked the field mouse.

"Easy," said the owl, "Fly out, as I do."

"But how can I fly?" asked the mouse.

The owl looked at him haughtily, sniffed disdainfully, and said, "Don't bother me with the details, I only decide the policy."

Moral: *Leadership involves providing details.*

NOTES

1. The following is a sample of our journal publications on student supports:

Adelman, H. S., & Taylor, L. (1997). Addressing barriers to learning: Beyond school-linked services and full service schools. *American Journal of Orthopsychiatry, 67,* 408–421.

Adelman, H. S. (1998). School counseling, psychological, and social services. In E. Marx & S. F. Wooley, with D. Northrop (Eds.), *Health is academic: A guide to coordinated school health programs.* New York: Teachers College Press.

Adelman, H. S., & Taylor, L. (1998). Reframing mental health in schools and expanding school reform. *Educational Psychologist, 33,* 135–152.

Adelman, H. S., Taylor, L., & Schnieder, M. (1999). A schoolwide component to address barriers to learning. *Reading and Writing Quarterly, 15,* 277–302.

Adelman, H. S., & Taylor, L. (2000). Moving prevention from the fringes into the fabric of school improvement. *Journal of Educational and Psychological Consultation, 11,* 7–36.

Taylor, L., & Adelman, H. S. (2000). Connecting schools, families, and communities. *Professional School Counseling, 3,* 298–307.

Adelman, H. S., & Taylor, L. (2002). Building comprehensive, multifaceted, and integrated approaches to address barriers to student learning. *Childhood Education, 78,* 261–268.

Adelman, H. S., & Taylor, L. (2002). So you want higher achievement test scores? It's time to rethink learning supports. *The State Education Standard,* Autumn, 52–56.

Adelman, H. S., & Taylor, L. (2002). School counselors and school reform: New directions. *Professional School Counseling, 5,* 235–248.

Adelman, H. S., & Taylor, L. (2003). Rethinking school psychology. *Journal of School Psychology, 41,* 83–90.

Adelman, H. S., & Taylor, L. (2006). Mapping a school's resources to improve their use in preventing and ameliorating problems. In C. Franklin, M. B. Harris, & P. Allen-Mears (Eds.), *School social work and mental health workers training and resource manual.* New York: Oxford University Press.

Adelman, H. S., & Taylor, L. (2007). Reorganizing student supports to enhance equity. In E. Lopez, G. Esquivel, & S. Nahari (Eds.), *Handbook of multicultural school psychology.*

Adelman, H. S., & Taylor, L. (2008). Best practices in the use of resource teams to enhance learning supports. In A. Thomas & J. Grimes (Eds.), *Best practices in school psychology V.* Bethesda, MD: National Association of School Psychologists.

For more extensive discussions of the above matters, see the following:

Adelman, H. S., & Taylor, L. (2006). *The school leader's guide to student learning supports: New directions for addressing barriers to learning.* Thousand Oaks, CA: Corwin.

Adelman, H. S., & Taylor, L. (2006). *The implementation guide to student learning supports in the classroom and schoolwide: New directions for addressing barriers to learning.* Thousand Oaks, CA: Corwin.

2. See the following Policy and Practice Analysis Reports from our center:

    *   *School Improvement Planning: What's Missing?*—http://smhp.psych.ucla.edu/whatsmissing.htm
    *   *Addressing What's Missing in School Improvement Planning: Expanding Standards and Accountability to Encompass an Enabling or Learning Supports Component*—http://smhp.psych.ucla.edu/pdfdocs/enabling/standards.pdf
    *   *Another Initiative? Where Does It Fit? A Unifying Framework and an Integrated Infrastructure for Schools to Address Barriers to Learning and Promote Healthy Development*—http://smhp.psych.ucla.edu/pdfdocs/infrastructure/anotherinitiative-exec.pdf
    *   *Toward a School District Infrastructure That More Effectively Addresses Barriers to Learning and Teaching*—http://smhp.psych.ucla.edu/pdfdocs//briefs/toward a school district infrastructure.pdf

13

Collaboration

Working Together to Move Forward
and Enhance Impact

It is either naive or irresponsible to ignore the connection between children's performance in school and their experiences with malnutrition, homelessness, lack of medical care, inadequate housing, racial and cultural discrimination, and other burdens.

—Harold Howe II (former Commissioner of Education),
cited in Merseth (1999)

Across the country, groups of people who often haven't worked together are combining their talents and resources to improve outcomes for children and youth. Effective collaboration to weave together the resources of schools, families, and communities is a key step in moving forward. We devote an entire chapter to the topic because all who want to advance the field need to understand what is involved in establishing and maintaining effective collaboration.

This chapter explores collaboration and particularly the formation of groups called collaboratives. The emphasis is on what makes such collaborative efforts successful and what gets in the way. The discussion is designed as an introduction to working collaboratively at various levels of intervention. Specifically, we highlight that (1) collaboration is a process for carrying out delineated functions, (2) accomplishing functions calls for dedicated mechanisms or structures, (3) data can help enhance collaboration, and (4) sustaining collaborative endeavors over time requires systemic change.

WHAT IS COLLABORATION?

Collaboratives are sprouting everywhere. Properly done, collaboration among schools, families, and communities should improve schools, strengthen families and neighborhoods, and lead to a marked reduction in young people's problems. However, collaboration that is poorly implemented can be another reform that promised a lot, did little good, and even did some harm.

Advocates for school, community, and family connections caution that some collaboratives amount to little more than groups sitting around engaging in *collabo-babble*.

Collaboratives often are established because of a desire to address a local problem or in the wake of a crisis. In the long run, however, school-family-community collaboration must be driven by a more comprehensive vision encompassing public health, public education, safe, caring, and supportive schools and neighborhoods; individual and family well-being; community development; and more.

While making informal links is relatively simple, establishing major long-term collaboration is complicated. Doing so requires vision, cohesive policy, and systemwide reforms. Complications are readily seen in efforts to develop a comprehensive approach to promoting healthy development and addressing barriers to learning and teaching. Such an approach involves much more than linking a few services, recreation, and enrichment activities to schools. Policy commitments and system changes are required to develop and evolve formal and institutionalized sharing of a wide spectrum of responsibilities and resources.

Comprehensive collaboration represents a way to weave together a critical mass of resources for moving forward. Building such collaboration encompasses strategies for developing an enlightened vision, enhancing stakeholder readiness, recruiting creative leadership, and delineating new and multifaceted roles for professionals who work in schools and communities, as well as for family and other community members who are willing to assume leadership.

Collaboratives are about building potent, synergistic, *working relationships*, not simply establishing positive personal connections. Personal relationships are helpful, but collaboratives built mainly on personal connections are vulnerable to the participant mobility that characterizes many such groups. The point is to establish stable and sustainable working relationships. This requires delineated roles, responsibilities, and an institutionalized infrastructure, including well-designed mechanisms for performing tasks, solving problems, and mediating conflict.

An optimal approach involves formally blending resources of at least one school and sometimes a group of schools or an entire school district with local family and community resources. The intent is to sustain connections over time. The range of community entities is not limited to agencies and organizations; they encompass people, businesses, community-based organizations, postsecondary institutions, religious and civic groups, programs at parks and libraries, and any other facilities that are useful for recreation, learning, enrichment, and support.

As noted, interest in connecting families, schools, and communities is growing at an exponential rate. For schools, such collaboration provides more support for schools, students, and families. For families and students, collaboration can open up school resources for expanded community use. (In poor communities, schools may be the richest resource in terms of facilities and equipment and often is the largest single employer.) For agencies, connection with schools provides better access to families and youth and an opportunity to have an impact on hard-to-reach clients.

Interest in collaboration is bolstered by the renewed concern about widespread fragmentation of school and community interventions. The hope is that coordinating and integrating resources will increase impact on *at-risk* factors and on promoting healthy development. However, collaboration can do much more than coordinate interventions and place some community services on school sites. The emphasis on coordination and colocation of services downplays the need to restructure the various education support programs and services that schools own and operate and has led some policy makers to the mistaken impression that community resources can effectively meet the needs of schools in addressing barriers to learning. In turn, this has led some legislators to view the linking of community services to schools as a way to free up the dollars underwriting school-owned services. The reality is that even when one adds together community and school assets, the total set of resources in impoverished locales is woefully inadequate. In situation after situation, as soon as the first few sites demonstrating school-community collaboration are in place, local agencies find they have stretched their resources to the limit.

Collaboratives must be open to all who are willing to contribute their talents, and all participants must share in the workload—pursuing defined roles and functions. Governance must be designed to equalize power so that decision making and accountability appropriately reflect all stakeholder groups. Leadership must include representatives from all groups.

Obviously, true collaboration involves more than meeting and talking. The point is to work together in ways that produce actions and valued results. For this to happen, collaboratives must be formed in ways that ensure productivity. This includes providing participants with the training, time, support, and authority to carry out their roles and functions. When such matters are ignored, groups find themselves meeting and meeting but going nowhere.

> It's not about collaboration, per se—it's about being effective.

WHY IS FAMILY, COMMUNITY, AND SCHOOL COLLABORATION IMPORTANT?

Schools are located in communities but often are islands with no bridges to the mainland. Families live in neighborhoods, often with little connection to each other or to the schools their children attend. Nevertheless, all these entities affect each other, for good or ill. Because of this and because they share goals related to education and socialization of the young, schools, homes, and communities must collaborate with each other if they are to minimize problems and maximize results.

Dealing with multiple, interrelated concerns, such as poverty, child development, education, mental health, violence, crime, safety, housing, and employment requires multiple and interrelated solutions. Interrelated solutions require collaboration. As Melaville and Blank (1998) sagely state,

> One of the most important, cross-cutting social policy perspectives to emerge in recent years is an awareness that no single institution can create all the conditions young people need to flourish. (p. 6)

Promoting well-being, resilience, and protective factors and empowering families, communities, and schools also requires the concerted effort of all stakeholders.

Collaboration can improve service access and provision; increase support and assistance for learning and for addressing barriers to learning; enhance opportunities for learning and development; and generate new approaches to strengthen family, school, and community. Thus, appropriate and effective collaboration and teaming are keys to promoting well-being and addressing barriers to development, learning, family well-being, and community self-sufficiency.

Schools are more effective and caring places when they are an integral and positive part of the community. This plays out as enhanced academic performance, fewer discipline problems, higher staff morale, and improved use of resources. Reciprocally, families and other community entities can enhance parenting and socialization, address psychosocial problems, and strengthen the fabric of family and community life by working collaboratively with schools.

Collaboration supports mental health in schools. For children, the most common forms of violence are physical, sexual, and psychosocial abuse experienced at school, at home, and in the neighborhood. Good data are not available on how many youngsters are affected by all the forms of violence or how many are debilitated by such experiences. But no one who works to prevent mental health problems would deny that the numbers are large. Far too many youngsters are caught up in cycles where they are the recipient or perpetrator (and sometimes both) of deviant behavior and emotional problems.

These complex problems clearly are barriers to development, learning, parenting, teaching, and socialization. The complexity precludes single-factor solutions. Mental health in schools must emphasize schoolwide prevention, corrective strategies, and emergency responses, positive school climate, promotion of healthy social and emotional development, formal connections with community services, family and community involvement, and more. School and community policy makers must collaborate to embrace comprehensive, multifaceted schoolwide and community-wide approaches. And they must do so in a way that fully integrates such approaches with school improvement efforts at every school site.

DEFINING COLLABORATION AND ITS PURPOSES

Collaboration involves more than simply working together, and a *collaborative* is more than a body to enhance cooperation and coordination. Thus, teachers who team are not a collaborative; they are a teaching team. Professionals who work as a multidisciplinary team to coordinate treatment are not a collaborative; they are a treatment team. Interagency teams established to enhance coordination and communication across agencies are not collaboratives; they are coordinating teams. Coalitions are not collaboratives; they are a form of collaboration where multiple organizations establish an *alliance* for sharing information and jointly pursuing cohesive policy advocacy and action in overlapping areas of concern.

A collaborative is a form of collaboration that involves establishing an infrastructure for *working together to accomplish specific functions* related to developing and enhancing interventions and systems in arenas where stakeholder agenda overlap.

One hallmark of authentic collaboration is a *formal agreement* among participants to establish mechanisms and processes to accomplish *mutually desired results*— usually outcomes that would be difficult to achieve by any of the stakeholders alone. Thus, while participants may have a primary affiliation elsewhere, they commit to work together under specified conditions in pursuit of a shared vision and common set of goals.

Effective collaboratives are built with vision, policy, leadership, infrastructure, and capacity building. A collaborative structure requires shared governance (power, authority, decision making, accountability) and weaving together an adequate set of resources. It also requires establishing well-defined and effective *working* relationships that enable participants to overcome individual agenda. If this cannot be accomplished, the intent of pursuing a shared agenda and achieving a collective vision is jeopardized.

Growing appreciation of human and social capital has resulted in collaboratives expanding to include a wide range of stakeholders (people, groups, formal and informal organizations). Many who at best were silent partners in the past now are finding their way to the collaborative table and becoming key players. The political realities of local control have expanded collaborative bodies to encompass local policy makers, representatives of families, nonprofessionals, and volunteers. Families, of course, have always provided a direct connection between school and community, but now they are seeking a greater decision-making role. In addition, advocates for students with special needs have opened the way for increased parent and youth participation in forums making decisions about interventions. Any effort to connect school, home, and community resources clearly must embrace a wide spectrum of stakeholders.

Effective collaboratives attempt to weave the responsibilities and resources of participating stakeholders together to create a new form of unified entity. For our purposes, any group designed to connect a school, families, and others from the surrounding neighborhood is referred to as a *school-community* collaborative. Such collaboratives may include individuals and groups focused on providing programs for education, literacy, youth development, the arts, health and human services, juvenile justice, vocational education, economic development, and more. They may include various sources of human, social, and economic capital, including teachers, student support staff, youth, families, community-based and linked organizations, such as public and private health and human service agencies, civic groups, businesses, faith-based organizations, institutions of postsecondary learning, and so forth.

In the context of a school-community collaborative, collaboration is both a desired process and an outcome. That is, the intent is to establish strong working relationships that are enduring. However, school, community, and family collaboration is not an end in itself. It is a turning point meant to enable participants to pursue increasingly potent strategies for strengthening children, families, schools, and communities.

Operationally, a collaborative is defined by its *functions*. That is, a collaborative is about accomplishing functions, not about establishing and maintaining a *collaborative* body. Major examples of functions include the following:

- Facilitating communication, cooperation, coordination, and integration
- Operationalizing the vision of stakeholders into desired functions and tasks
- Enhancing support for and developing a policy commitment to ensure necessary resources are dispensed for accomplishing desired functions
- Advocacy, analysis, priority setting, governance, planning, implementation, and evaluation related to desired functions
- Aggregating data from schools and neighborhood to analyze system needs
- Mapping, analyzing, managing, redeploying, and braiding available resources to enable accomplishment of desired functions
- Establishing leadership and institutional and operational mechanisms (e.g., infrastructure) for guiding and managing accomplishment of desired functions
- Defining and incorporating new roles and functions into job descriptions
- Building capacity for planning, implementing, and evaluating desired functions, including ongoing stakeholder development for continuous learning and renewal and for bringing new arrivals up to speed
- Defining standards and ensuring accountability
- Social marketing

Functions encompass specific tasks. Examples are mapping and analyzing resources; exploring ways to share facilities, equipment, and other resources; expanding opportunities for community service, internships, jobs, recreation, and enrichment; developing pools of nonprofessional volunteers and professional pro bono assistance; making recommendations about priorities for use of resources; raising funds and pursuing grants; and advocating for appropriate decision making.

In organizing a collaborative, the fundamental principle is *structure follows function*. Based on clear functions, a differentiated infrastructure must be developed to enable accomplishment of functions and related tasks. Minimally, the need is for infrastructure mechanisms to steer and do work on a regular basis.

Since the work almost always overlaps with that of others, a collaborative needs to establish connections with other bodies.

> It's relatively easy to establish a *collaborative* … it's turning the group into an effective mechanism and maintaining it that's hard to do.

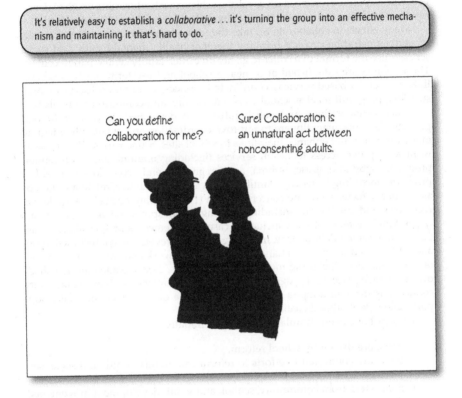

COLLABORATION

A Growing Movement Across the Country

Various levels and forms of school, community, and family collaboration are being tested, including statewide initiatives. Some cataloguing has begun, but no complete picture is available of the scope of activity. Advocacy for school-community connections comes from divergent interests.

On the community side, one major thrust has come from the push to reform community agencies, another has come from the business community, a third has come from the community school movement, and a fourth involves social activists and various community-based organizations (e.g., philanthropic foundations, the Children's Defense Fund, Communities in Schools, groups concerned with organizing communities, groups representing *minorities*). For families, connecting with schools also varies with respect to the specific groups' agenda (e.g., PTA, family organizations representing students with behavior, learning, or emotional problems). Crosscutting these sectors are initiatives to bring schools, communities, and families together to deal with a specific problem, such as raising achievement, addressing youth violence, combating substance abuse, enhancing physical and mental health, and so forth.

Many efforts to collaborate do take the form of a collaborative. For example, most demonstration projects bringing together health, mental health, and social services use the format of a *center* (e.g., health center, family center, parent center). These centers are established at or near a school and use terms such as school-linked or school-based services, coordinated services, wrap-around services, one-stop shopping, full service schools, systems of care, and community schools.[1]

When collaborations and collaboratives are developed as part of funded projects, the aims generally are to improve coordination and eventually integrate many programs and enhance their links to school sites. Scope varies. Most projects want to improve access to health services (including immunizations, prevention programs, substance abuse, asthma, and pregnancy) and access to social service programs (including foster care, family preservation, and child care). In addition or as a primary focus, some are concerned with (1) expanding afterschool academic, recreation, and enrichment, including tutoring, youth sports and clubs, art, music; (2) building systems of care, including case management and specialized assistance; (3) reducing delinquency, including truancy prevention, conflict mediation, and violence reduction; (4) enhancing transitions to work and career, and postsecondary education, including mentoring, internships, career academies, job shadowing, and job placement programs; and (5) strengthening schools and community connections through adopt-a-school programs, use of volunteers and peer supports, and neighborhood coalitions.

Projects have been stimulated by diverse initiatives:

- Some are driven by school reform.
- Some are connected to efforts to reform community health and social service agencies.
- Some stem from community, school, and youth development movements.
- A few stem from community development endeavors.

To date, only a few projects are driven by school improvement efforts. Most stem from moves to reform community health and social services with the aim of reducing redundancy and increasing access and effectiveness. These tend to focus narrowly on *services*. Projects initiated by schools often connect schools and communities to enhance school-to-career opportunities, develop pools of volunteers and mentors, and expand afterschool recreation and enrichment programs.

The community school and youth development movements have spawned school-community collaboration that go beyond a narrow service emphasis. They encourage a view of schools not only as community centers where families can access services but also as hubs for communitywide learning and activity. In doing so, they encompass concepts and practices aimed at promoting protective factors, asset-building, wellness, and empowerment. Included are efforts to establish full-fledged community schools, programs for community and social capital mobilization, and initiatives to establish community policies and structures that enhance youth support, safety, recreation, work, service, and enrichment. This work, along with adult education and training at neighborhood schools, is changing the old view that schools close when the youngsters leave. The concept of a *second shift* at a school site to respond to community needs is spreading.

School-community linkages are meant to benefit a wide range of youngsters and their families. For example, considerable attention is paid to linkages to enhance outcomes for students with emotional disturbance and their families. This population is served by classrooms, counseling, day care, and residential and hospital programs. All involved need to work together in providing services, monitoring and maintaining care, and facilitating the transitions to and from services. To address these needs, considerable investment has been made in establishing what are called *wrap-around services* and *systems of care*. The work usually is done by multidisciplinary teams, often without the support of a collaborative body. From our perspective, the work would benefit significantly from involvement with a school-community collaborative.

For various reasons, many collaboratives around the country consist mainly of professionals. Family and other citizen involvement may be limited to a few representatives of powerful organizations or to *token* participants who are needed and expected to *sign-off* on decisions.

Genuine involvement of a wide range of representative families and citizens requires a deep commitment by collaborative organizers to recruiting and building the capacity of such stakeholders so that they can competently participate as enfranchised and informed decision makers.

Collaboratives that proactively work to ensure effective participation of a broad range of stakeholders can establish a democratic base for their work and help develop a critical mass of committed participants to buffer against inevitable mobility. Such an approach not only enhances family and community involvement, it may be a key to sustaining collaborative efforts.

Exhibit 44 presents two examples of collaboratives.

Exhibit 44   Two Examples of Collaboratives

Local Management Boards—Collaboration Initiated by the Legislature Across an Entire State

In 1989, the governor of Maryland issued an executive order creating the Subcabinet for Children, Youth, and Families. In 1990, a statute was enacted requiring each local jurisdiction to establish a local governing entity now known as Local Management Boards (LMBs) (Article 49D, §11, Annotated Code of Maryland). By 1997, LMBs were operating in all 24 jurisdictions.

LMBs are the core entity established in each jurisdiction to stimulate joint action by state and local government, public and private providers, business and industry, and community residents to

(Continued)

(Continued)

build an effective system of services, supports, and opportunities that improve outcomes for children, youth, and families. An example of this process for connecting families, communities, and schools is the partnership established in Anne Arundel County created by county government in December 1993.

As described by the Anne Arundel LMB, they are a collaborative board responsible for interagency planning, goal-setting, resource allocation, developing, implementing, and monitoring interagency services to children and their families. Their mission is to enhance the well-being of all children and their families in Anne Arundel County. All of their work focuses on impacting the result of "children safe in their families and communities" with goals and priorities established by the board members through a community needs process completed in October 1997. The consortium consists of representatives of public and private agencies appointed by the Anne Arundel County Executive who serve children and families and private citizens. Membership includes Anne Arundel County Public Schools, Department of Social Services, Department of Juvenile Justice, Department of Health and Mental Health, County Mental Health Agency, Inc. (Core Service Agency), County Recreation and Parks, county government, and private citizens (e.g., private providers, advocacy groups, parents, and other consumers). Private citizens can compose up to 49% of the membership. The county executive appoints board members for a term of four years.

In pursuing their mission, they (a) foster collaboration among all public and private partners, (b) plan a wide array of services, (c) coordinate and pool resources, (d) monitor and evaluate the effectiveness of programs, and (e) provide a forum for communication and advocacy. For instance, the LMB develops community plans for providing comprehensive interagency services with guidelines established by the Subcabinet for Children, Youth, and Families. Examples of program initiatives include the following:

Early Childhood Programs

- Anne Arundel County Infants and Toddler Autism Project
- BEST (Behavioral and Emotional Support and Training Program)
- Home Connections Home Visiting Program
- Mom and Tots
- TOTs Line Live
- Arundel Child Care Connections

Juvenile Intervention Programs

- Mental Health Assessors
- ATTEND
- JIFI
- Addictions Counselor

Youth Strategies

- Youth Empowerment Services (YES)
- Combating Underage Drinking
- Keep A Clear Mind
- Teen Court

Afterschool Programs

- School Community Centers
- Youth Services Bureau
- Safe Haven
- Family Preservation Team
- Return and Diversion
- Interagency Coalition for Adolescent Pregnancy Prevention and Parenting
- Disproportionate Minority Representation
- Local Coordinating Council
- Food Link

For more information, see http://www.aacounty.org/Partnership/currentProgramsIndex.cfm

Berkeley Alliance—A Citywide Collaboration

The city of Berkeley, California, has a long tradition of valuing education, diversity, and social justice. Moreover, they believe that society is served best when public institutions, educators, and community groups work together.

To enhance their community-school-family collaboration, the city of Berkeley; the University of California, Berkeley; and the Berkeley Unified School District founded the *Berkeley Alliance* to ensure their values and beliefs are reflected in actions that serve the community. The Alliance brings policy makers, institutional leaders, and community representatives together to create solutions and citywide change and builds capacity to ensure that all Berkeley children, youth, families, and households benefit from the resources in their city.

Mission Statement: The Berkeley Alliance builds strategic community partnerships that strengthen capacity to effect change on critical issues related to social and economic equity in Berkeley.

Strategic Approach: The Alliance works to advance social and economic equity in Berkeley through three main strategies:

- Policy development and advocacy for systems change
- Building capacity of local organizations and institutions through leadership and resource development
- Convening forums for community stakeholders and institutional partners to address critical local issues

Structure: The Alliance is an independent 501(c) 3 nonprofit organization with a full-time staff based in West Berkeley, a 15-member board of directors composed of founder and community representatives, and an 11-member leadership committee representing partner institutions. Among others, the board and the leadership committee include the mayor, the school district superintendent, the university chancellor, the city manager, a city council member, and the president of the school board, agency heads, and a representative of community volunteers.

(Continued)

(Continued)

A recent, major focus has been on developing an initiative for enhancing integration of resources. The Alliance describes this as follows:

> While most Berkeley youth and children are healthy, doing well in school, and getting the support they need to become thriving adults, this is not the case for all our children. Because of socioeconomic, environmental, and other factors, there are inequities in opportunity structures in Berkeley affecting families in low-wealth communities and young people of color. These disparities can lead to lower academic performance, higher rates of special education and disciplinary referrals, and mental and physical health problems.
>
> The aim is to build on Berkeley's strong educational and social service systems and create a continuum of care that ensures the well-being of all kids and parents. Our goals are to enhance the accessibility and effectiveness of the resources already available in Berkeley, build universal learning supports to reduce educational and wellness disparities, and work with existing assets in low-wealth communities.
>
> Towards these ends, the Alliance convened the Berkeley Integrated Resources Initiative (BIRI), a major community change process that addresses a long-standing need for the city's institutions, agencies, and youth programs to change the way they work together. The goal is to address economic, social, and environmental barriers to learning and promote healthy development for children, youth, and families.

This encompasses concerns for safe schools and communities.

The vision for this communitywide policy and practice endeavor calls for the Berkeley Unified School District; the City of Berkeley; the University of California, Berkeley; and local community organizations to "work collectively and purposely to identify and weave their relevant resources to effectively address barriers to learning and promote healthy development for all Berkeley children and youth." This entails

> the strengthening of students, schools, families, and neighborhoods to foster a developmentally appropriate learning environment in which children and youth can thrive. The systemic change process emphasizes a coordinated school improvement and agency reform effort that leverages and weaves school-owned and community-owned resources in a comprehensive manner. In their work together, schools and agencies will create and provide a continuum of support for children and youth that emphasizes promoting healthy development for all, intervening early when problems arise, and providing specialized services to address critical needs.

The BIRI is guided by the Alliance leadership group, which adopts priorities and facilitates change at the policy level. A diverse Community Design Team is working to create a strategic change plan—an Agenda for Children and Youth—with a clear vision, set of outcomes, and solid recommendations for action. Workgroups such as the Schools Mental Health Partnership and the Birth-to-Five Action Team analyze specific issues, develop strategies, and make recommendations.

SOURCES: Berkeley Alliance Web site. Retrieved from www.berkeleyalliance.org and from two documents prepared by the Berkeley Integrated Resources Initiative in January 2007: (1) *Schools-Mental Health Partnership Strategic Plan* and (2) *Universal Learning Support System Assessment Report.*

SCHOOL-COMMUNITY-FAMILY COLLABORATION

State of the Art

*Much of the emerging theory and practice of family and community connections
with schools encourages a rethinking of our understanding of how children develop
and how the various people and contexts fit together to support that development.*

—Southwest Educational Development Laboratory (2001)

Schools and community entities usually function as separate agents with a few discrete linkages designed to address highly circumscribed matters. Often the links are encouraged by and/or directed at parents of school-aged children. The immediate goal of many school-family-community collaboratives is to bring the entities together to work in more cooperative ways and where feasible, to integrate resources and activities when they are dealing with overlapping concerns. More broadly, some argue the work is all about community—that families should be understood and nurtured as the heart of any community and that schools should be completely embedded and not seen as a separate agent.

As a result of the diverse agenda for collaboration, relatively little *generic* conceptual, research, and practice literature exists on school-community collaboratives. And no comprehensive catalog exists. Using the available literature and synthesizing across several arenas of work, a picture emerges related to the promise of family-community-school collaboration.

While data are sparse, a reasonable inference from available research is that school-community collaboration can be successful and cost-effective over the long run. Moreover, school-community collaborations not only have potential for improving access to and coordination of interventions, they encourage schools to open their doors and enhance opportunities for community and family involvement.

The following are highlights of the emerging promise:

1. *Strengthening Neighborhoods, Families, and Schools.* In general, those pushing for connection from the community side want to strengthen neighborhoods, families, and schools. For example, Schorr (1997) nicely describes promising community-school-family initiatives from this perspective. Her analysis concludes that a synthesis is emerging that "rejects addressing poverty, welfare, employment, education, child development, housing, and crime one at a time. It endorses the idea that the multiple and interrelated problems . . . require multiple and interrelated solutions" (p. 319).

Warren (2005) argues that for urban school reform to be successful, it must be linked to the revitalization of the surrounding communities. He categorizes current school-community collaborations as involving (1) the service approach, which he equates with the community full service schools movement; (2) the development approach seen as embodied in community sponsorship of new schools such as charter schools; and (3) the organizing approach involving direct efforts of community-organizing groups to foster collaboration with schools.

From the perspective of community organizing to transform schools, Lopez's (2003) research review concludes that a body of evidence supports the position that community organizing strengthens school reform efforts. However, she goes on to stress, "It is only one among different pathways that connects schools and low-income communities to achieve a shared vision of success for all students."

Another approach is the creation of learning communities based on the principles of parent and community involvement, collaborative governance, culturally responsive pedagogy, and advocacy-oriented assessment, which can produce outstanding results for migrant and low-income students (Reyes, Scribner, & Scribner, 1999). Also, in schools where trust is established through the daily interactions of the school community, the achievement of low-income and ethnically diverse students improves over time (Bryk & Schneider, 2002). What community organizing shares with these other approaches is the social capital that works toward the best interests of students. What makes it different is turning social capital into political capital. Community organizing focuses not only on school reform, but also on empowerment. It drives home the point that parents and communities are powerful agents of reform. Because school reform is a political issue, organizing builds the political will to ensure that poor schools gain access to the resources they need to improve the quality of education.

2. *Linking Services to Schools.* In the 1960s, concern about the fragmented way *community* health and human services are planned and implemented led to the human service integration movement, which initially sputtered but then was renewed and has grown steadily over the 1990s and into the present decade. The hope of this movement is to better meet the needs of those served and use existing resources to serve greater numbers. To these ends, considerable interest emerged for developing strong relationships between school sites and public and private community agencies.

As would be anticipated, most initial efforts focus on developing informal relationships and coordinating services. In the 1990s, a nationwide survey of school board members indicated widespread presence of school-linked programs and services in school districts (Hardiman, Curcio, & Fortune, 1998). For purposes of the survey, school-linked services were defined as "the coordinated linking of school and community resources to support the needs of school-aged children and their families" (p. 37). The researchers conclude, "The range of services provided and the variety of approaches to school-linked services are broad, reflecting the diversity of needs and resources in each community" (p. 40). They are used to varying degrees to address various educational, psychological, health, and social concerns, including substance abuse, job training, teen pregnancy, juvenile probation, child and family welfare, and housing. For example, and not surprisingly, the majority of schools report using school-linked resources as part of their efforts to deal with substance abuse; far fewer report such involvement with respect to family welfare and housing. Most of this activity reflects collaboration with agencies at local and state levels. Respondents indicate that these collaborations operate under a variety of arrangements:

> legislative mandates, state-level task forces and commissions, formal agreements with other state agencies, formal and informal agreements with local

government agencies, in-kind (nonmonetary) support of local government and nongovernment agencies, formal and informal referral network, and the school administrator's prerogative. (p. 39)

About half the respondents note that their districts have no policies governing school-linked services.

3. *Community Schools.* While the community school movement often is discussed in terms of *full-service community schools* (e.g., Dryfoos & Maguire, 2002), the movement is much more diverse than this term implies. The Coalition for Community Schools continues to survey a variety of school-community initiatives from the perspective of the community schools movement (e.g., Blank, Berg, & Melaville, 2006; Blank, Melaville, & Shah, 2004; Melaville & Blank, 1998).

In the 1998 review, the number of school-community initiatives was described as skyrocketing. Moreover, the diversity across initiatives in terms of design, management, and funding arrangements was daunting to summarize. From the perspective of the Coalition, (1) the initiatives are moving toward blended and integrated purposes and activity and (2) the activities are predominantly school-based and the education sector plays "a significant role in the creation and, particularly, management of these initiatives" (p. 100), and the trend is "toward much greater community involvement in all aspects" (p. 100) of such initiatives—especially in decision making at both the community and site levels. The Coalition also stresses, "the ability of school-community initiatives to strengthen school functioning develops incrementally" (p. 100) with the first impact seen in improved school climate.

With respect to sustainability, their findings support the need for stable leadership and long-term financing. Melaville and Blank (1998) note the following:

> The still moving field of school-community initiatives is rich in its variations. But it is a variation born in state and local inventiveness, rather than reflective of irreconcilable differences or fundamental conflict. Even though communication among school-community initiatives is neither easy nor ongoing, the findings in this study suggest they are all moving toward an interlocking set of principles. An accent on development cuts across them all. These principles demonstrate the extent to which boundaries separating major approaches to school-community initiatives have blurred and been transformed. More importantly, they point to a strong sense of direction and shared purpose within the field. With respect to evaluation of community schools, there is growing evidence that such schools contribute to enhanced family engagement with children and schools, student learning, and some neighborhood revitalization (Blank, Melaville, & Shah, 2004; Dryfoos, 2003).

4. *Parent Involvement.* The movement for parent involvement currently is motivated by the policy intent of federal education law to inform and empower parents as decision makers in their children's education. It also is bolstered by over 30 years of research indicating a significant relationship between family involvement

and student success and mental health (Christenson, Whitehouse, & VanGetson, 2008; Epstein, Coates, Salinas, & Sanders, 2002; Henderson & Mapp, 2002).

At the same time, research findings stress that the impact of family and community involvement is undercut in the absence of effective classroom and schoolwide interventions (e.g., Bryk & Schneider, 2002; EdSource, 2006).

In general, our findings are in considerable agreement with other reports (e.g., Center for Mental Health in Schools, 1997, 2005c). However, our work also stresses the limitations of prevailing collaborations. Despite their participation in collaboratives, school and community programs and services usually continue to function in relative isolation of each other and continue to focus on discrete problems and specialized services for individuals and small groups. Moreover, because the primary emphasis is on restructuring community programs and colocating some services on school sites, a new form of fragmentation is emerging as community and school professionals engage in a form of *parallel play* at school sites.

The irony is that, while collaboration is meant to reduce fragmentation (with the intent of enhancing outcomes), in many cases the problem is compounded because the initiatives mostly *link* community services to schools.[2] Too little thought is given to the importance of *connecting* community programs with existing support programs operated by the school. As a result, when community agencies colocate personnel at schools, such personnel tend to operate in relative isolation of existing school programs and services. Little attention is paid to developing effective mechanisms for coordinating complementary activity or integrating parallel efforts. Consequently, a youngster identified as at risk for bullying, dropout, and substance abuse may be involved in three counseling programs operating independently of each other.

Moreover, tension is rising between school district service personnel and their counterparts in community-based organizations. When *outside* professionals are brought in, school specialists often view it as discounting their skills and threatening their jobs. The *outsiders* often feel unappreciated and may be rather naive about the culture of schools. Conflicts arise over *turf*, use of space, confidentiality, and liability.

The situation is unlikely to improve as long as so little attention is paid to developing well-designed models to guide productive family, school, and community collaboration. Toward this end, we have begun to briefly outline key facets of collaboration.

UNDERSTANDING KEY FACETS OF COLLABORATION

Collaboration is a developing process; it must be continuously nurtured, facilitated, and supported, and special attention must be given to overcoming institutional and personal barriers.

School-community connections differ in terms of purposes and functions. They also differ in terms of a range of other dimensions. For example, they may vary in their degree of formality, time commitment, breadth of the connections, as well as the amount of systemic change required to carry out their functions and achieve their purposes.

Because collaboration can differ in so many ways, it helps to think in terms of categories of key factors relevant to such arrangements. Exhibit 45 highlights key dimensions of family-community-school collaborative arrangements. Exhibit 46 outlines a range of community resources that could be part of a collaboration.

Exhibit 45	Some Key Dimensions Relevant to Family-Community-School Collaborative Arrangements

I. Initiation

A. School led
B. Community driven

II. Nature of collaboration

A. Formal

➤ Memorandum of understanding
➤ Contract
➤ Organizational and operational mechanisms

B. Informal

➤ Verbal agreements
➤ Ad hoc arrangements

III. Focus

A. Improvement of program and service provision

➤ For enhancing case management
➤ For enhancing use of resources

B. Major systemic changes

➤ To enhance coordination
➤ For organizational restructuring
➤ For transforming system structure and functions

IV. Scope of collaboration

A. Number of programs and services involved (from just a few up to a comprehensive, multifaceted continuum)
B. Horizontal collaboration

➤ Within a school or agency
➤ Among schools or agencies

(Continued)

(Continued)

    C. Vertical collaboration

       ➢ Within a catchment area (e.g., school and community agency, family of schools, two or more agencies or other entities)

       ➢ Among different levels of jurisdictions (e.g., community, city, county, state, federal)

V. Scope of potential impact

    A. Narrow band: A small proportion of youth and families can access what they need

    B. Broad band: All can access what they need

VI. Ownership and governance of programs and services

    A. Owned and governed by school

    B. Owned and governed by community

    C. Shared ownership and governance

    D. Public-private venture—shared ownership and governance

VII. Location of programs and services

    A. Community based, school linked

    B. School based

VIII. Degree of cohesiveness among multiple interventions serving the same student and family

    A. Unconnected

    B. Communicating

    C. Cooperating

    D. Coordinated

    E. Integrated

IX. Level of systemic intervention focus

    A. Systems for promoting healthy development

    B. Systems for prevention of problems

    C. Systems for early after onset of problems

    D. Systems of care for treatment of severe, pervasive, and/or chronic problems

    E. Full continuum, including all levels

X. Arenas for collaborative activity

    A. Health (physical and mental)

    B. Education

    C. Social services

    D. Work and career

    E. Enrichment and/or recreation

    F. Juvenile justice

    G. Neighborhood and community improvement

Exhibit 46   A Range of Community Resources That Could Be Part of a Collaboration

County agencies and bodies (e.g., departments of health, mental health, children and family services, public social services, probation, sheriff, office of education, fire, service planning area councils, recreation and parks, library, courts, housing)

Municipal agencies and bodies (e.g., parks and recreation, library, police, fire, courts, civic event units)

Physical and mental health and psychosocial concerns facilities and groups (e.g., clinics, hospitals, guidance centers, Planned Parenthood, Aid to Victims, MADD, *friends of* groups; family crisis and support centers, help lines, hotlines, shelters, mediation and dispute resolution centers, private practitioners)

Mutual support and self-help groups (e.g., for almost every problem and many other activities)

Child care and preschool centers

Postsecondary education institutions for students (e.g., community colleges, state universities, public and private colleges and universities, vocational colleges; specific schools within these such as schools of law, education, nursing, dentistry)

Service agencies (e.g., PTA and/or PTSA, United Way, clothing and food pantry, Visiting Nurses Association, Cancer Society, Catholic Charities, Red Cross, Salvation Army, volunteer agencies, legal aid society)

Service clubs and philanthropic organizations (e.g., Lions Club, Rotary Club, Optimists, Assistance League, men's and women's clubs, League of Women Voters, veteran's groups, foundations)

Youth agencies and groups (e.g., Boys and Girls Clubs, YMCA and/or YWCA, scouts, 4-H, Woodcraft Rangers)

Sports, health, fitness, and outdoor groups (e.g., sports teams, athletic leagues, local gyms, conservation associations, Audubon Society)

Community-based organizations (e.g., neighborhood and homeowners' associations, Neighborhood Watch, block clubs, housing project associations, economic development groups, civic associations)

Faith community institutions (e.g., congregations and subgroups, clergy associations, interfaith hunger coalition)

Legal assistance groups (e.g., public counsel, schools of law)

Ethnic associations (e.g., Committee for Armenian Students in Public Schools, Korean Youth Center, United Cambodian Community, African American, Latino, Asian Pacific, Native American organizations)

Special interest associations and clubs (e.g., Future Scientists and Engineers of America, pet owner and other animal-oriented groups)

(Continued)

(Continued)

Artists and cultural institutions (e.g., museums, art galleries, zoo, theater groups, motion picture studios, TV and radio stations, writers' organizations, instrumental and/or choral, drawing and/or painting, technology-based arts, literary clubs, collector's groups)

Businesses, corporations, unions (e.g., neighborhood business associations, chambers of commerce, local shops, restaurants, banks, AAA, Teamsters, school employee unions)

Media (e.g., newspapers, TV and radio, local access cable)

Family members, local residents, senior citizens groups

BARRIERS TO COLLABORATION

Barriers to collaboration arise from a variety of institutional and personal factors. Institutional barriers to family-community-school collaboration stem from the degree to which the work is marginalized. For the most part, existing policy, accountability, leadership, budget, space, time schedules, and capacity-building agenda do not support collaboration. Nonsupport may simply take the form of benign neglect. Occasionally, nonsupport takes the ugly form of forces at work trying to actively undermine collaboration. More often, it stems from a lack of understanding, commitment, and/or capability related to establishing and maintaining a potent infrastructure for working together and for sharing resources.

For instance, problems arise in bringing schools and community agencies to the same table because of differences in organizational mission, functions, cultures, bureaucracies, and accountabilities. Considerable effort is required to teach and learn from each other about these matters. When families are at the table, power differentials are common, especially when low-income families are involved and are confronted with credentialed and titled professionals.

Examples of institutional barriers include the following:

- Policies that mandate collaboration but do not enable the process (e.g., a failure to reconcile differences among participants with respect to the outcomes for which they are accountable; inadequate provision for braiding funds across agencies and categorical programs)
- Policies for collaboration that do not provide adequate resources and time for leadership and stakeholder training and for overcoming barriers to collaboration
- Leadership that does not establish an effective infrastructure, especially mechanisms for steering and accomplishing work and/or tasks on a regular, ongoing basis
- Differences in the conditions and incentives associated with participation, such as the fact that meetings usually are set during the work day, which means community agency and school personnel are paid participants, while family members are expected to volunteer their time

Collaboration also suffers from resource deprivation. Collaboratives usually have to piece together a core operational budget with little direct funding and sparse in-kind contributions. Overlapping arenas of concern, such as safe schools and neighborhoods, provide opportunities to braid separate funding streams together. Extramural grants provide opportunities to supplement the budget. Note, however, that funding for projects can be counterproductive if the project distracts the collaborative from vigorously pursuing its vision in a cohesive manner.

Also, note that confidentiality is a major collaboration concern and can be an institutional barrier. The concern has both ethical and legal facets. All who collaborate must value privacy concerns and be aware of legal requirements to protect privacy. At the same time, certain professionals have the legal responsibility to report endangering and illegal acts. Such reporting requirements naturally raise concerns about confidentiality and privacy protections. At the same time, in working collaboratively, agencies and schools must share information.

The dilemma is clear. On the one hand, care must be taken to avoid undermining privacy (e.g., confidentiality and privileged communication); on the other hand, appropriate information should be available to enable schools and agencies and other collaborative members to work together effectively. The temptation is to resolve the dilemma by asserting that all information should be confidential and privileged. Such a position, however, ignores the fact that failure to share germane information can seriously hamper efforts to help. For this reason, concerns about privacy must be balanced with developing a process to facilitate appropriate sharing of information. This is an example of an area where a collaborative can make a significant contribution. (See the Center's Online Clearinghouse on the topic of "Confidentiality" for information on the various matters related to this ethical and legal concern—http://smhp.psych.ucla.edu/qf/confid.htm)

On a personal level, barriers mostly stem from practical deterrents, negative attitudes, and deficiencies of knowledge and skill. These vary for different stakeholders but often include problems related to work schedules, transportation, child care, communication skills, understanding of differences in organizational culture, accommodations for language and cultural differences, and so forth.

Other barriers arise because of inadequate attention to factors associated with systemic change. Sufficient resources and time must be redeployed so participants can learn and carry out new functions effectively. When newcomers join, well-designed procedures must be in place to bring them up to speed.

Working collaboratively requires overcoming the barriers. This is easier to do when all stakeholders are committed to learning how to do so. It means moving beyond naming problems to careful analysis of why the problem has arisen and then moving on to creative problem solving.

When collaboratives are not well conceived and carefully developed, they generate additional barriers to their success. In too many instances, so-called collaborations amount to little more than bringing community agency staff onto school campuses (i.e., colocating services). Services

(Continued)

(Continued)

continue to function in relative isolation from each other and professionals' *parallel play*. Too little thought is given to the importance of meshing (as opposed to simply linking) community services and programs with existing school-owned and operated activity. The result is that a small number of youngsters are provided services that they might otherwise not receive, but little connection is made with families and school staff and programs. Moreover, when *outside* professionals are brought into schools, district personnel may view the move as discounting their skills and threatening their jobs. On the other side, the *outsiders* often feel unappreciated. Conflicts arise over *turf*, use of space, confidentiality, and liability.

OVERCOMING BARRIERS RELATED TO DIFFERENCES

Participants in a collaborative must be sensitive to a variety of human and institutional differences and learn strategies for dealing with them. These include differences in sociocultural and economic background, current lifestyles, primary language spoken, ethnicity, gender, and motivation. In addition, there are differences related to power, status, and orientation.

Workshops and presentations often are used to teach cultural awareness. However, only so much can be learned in such sessions, and in a community of many cultures, the amount to learn is staggering. Also, note the potential danger of prejudgments based on apparent cultural awareness. Language skills and cultural awareness are helpful, so is not rushing to judgment.

On an organizational level, the cultures of schools and community agencies and organizations differ greatly. School professionals usually do not understand the culture of community agencies; agency personnel are rather naive about the culture of schools.

As part of a working relationship, differences can be complementary and helpful—as when staff from different disciplines work with and learn from each other. Differences become a barrier to working relationships when negative attitudes are allowed to prevail and engender conflict and poor communication.

For example, an individual who has been treated unfairly, been discriminated against, been deprived of opportunity and status at school, on the job, and in society may use whatever means available to seek redress and sometimes to strike back. Such an individual may promote conflict in hopes of correcting power imbalances or at least to call attention to a problem.

In general, differences in status, ethnicity, power, orientation, and so forth can cause one or more persons to enter the situation with negative (including competitive) feelings. Often, power differentials are so institutionalized that individual action has little impact. Fighting an institution is hard and frustrating. Much easier and immediately satisfying is fighting with other individuals one sees as representing that institution. However, when this occurs in situations where individuals are supposed to work together, those with negative feelings may act and say things in ways that produce significant barriers to establishing a working relationship. Often, the underlying message is "You don't understand," or worse yet, "You probably don't want to understand," or even worse, "You are my enemy."

It is unfortunate when barriers arise among those we are trying to help; it is a travesty when such barriers interfere with helpers working together effectively. Conflicts among collaborative members detract from accomplishing goals and contribute in a major way to burnout.

No easy solutions are available for overcoming deeply embedded negative attitudes. A first step certainly is to understand that the nature of the problem is not differences per se but negative perceptions stemming from the politics and psychology of the situation. It is these perceptions that lead to (1) prejudgments that a person is bad because of an observed difference and (2) the view that little can be gained from working with that person. Thus, minimally, the task of overcoming negative attitudes interfering with a particular working relationship involves finding ways to counter negative prejudgments (e.g., to establish the credibility of those who have been prejudged) and demonstrate something of value can be gained from working together.

To be effective in working with others, one needs to build a positive working relationship around the tasks at hand. Ingredients include the following:

- Encouraging all participants to defer negative judgments about those with whom they will be working
- Enhancing expectations that working together will be productive, with particular emphasis on establishing the value added by each participant in pursuing mutually desired outcomes
- Ensuring appropriate time for making connections
- Establishing an infrastructure that provides support and guidance for effective task accomplishment
- Providing active, task-oriented meeting facilitation that minimizes ego-oriented behavior
- Ensuring regular celebration of positive outcomes that result from working together

 The process also requires taking time to ensure all participants understand that building relationships and effective communication requires the willingness and ability to do the following:

- Convey empathy and warmth (e.g., to communicate understanding and appreciation of what others are thinking and feeling and to transmit a sense of liking)
- Convey genuine regard and respect (e.g., to transmit real interest and interact in a way that enables others to maintain a feeling of integrity and personal control)

- Talk with, not at, others (e.g., listen actively and be carful not to be judgmental; avoid prying, share experiences as appropriate and needed)

BUILDING AND MAINTAINING EFFECTIVE COLLABORATIVES

We don't accomplish anything in this world alone . . . and whatever happens is the result of the whole tapestry of one's life and all the weavings of individual threads from one to another that creates something.

—Sandra Day O'Connor

Policy makers and other leaders must establish a foundation for building collaborative bridges connecting school, family, and community. Then, policy must be translated into authentic agreements to build bridges spanning schools, families, and communities. Although all this takes considerable time and other resources, the importance of building such bridges cannot be overemphasized. To a great extent, failure to establish and successfully maintain effective collaborations is attributable to the absence of high-level and long-term policy support to align diverse agenda (Bodily, Chun, Ikemoto, & Stockly, 2004). For example, the primary agenda of community agencies in working with schools usually is to increase access to clients; this is a marginal item in the school accountability agenda for raising test scores and closing the achievement gap. Effective collaboration depends on delineating a greater overlap in what the agency and school can contribute to each other's mission in order to elevate the work to a high priority.

When all major parties have a high-level commitment to collaboration, the next step is to develop their ability to facilitate the significant systemic changes required. Leaders must have both a vision for change and an understanding of how to develop and institutionalize an effective collaborative infrastructure. Tasks include the following:

- Modifying existing governance. Over time, the aim is shared decision making involving school and community agency staff, families, students, and other community representatives. This involves equalizing power and sharing leadership so that decision making appropriately reflects and accounts for all stakeholder groups.
- Assigning high-level leadership to facilitate systemic changes and build and maintain family-community-school connections.
- Establishing and institutionalizing mechanisms for analyzing, planning, coordinating, integrating, monitoring, evaluating, and strengthening collaborative efforts.

Evidence of appropriate policy support and stakeholder commitment to collaboration is seen in funding for *capacity building* to (1) accomplish desired system changes and (2) ensure the collaborative operates effectively over time. Accomplishing systemic changes requires establishing temporary facilitative mechanisms and providing incentives, supports, and training to enhance commitment to and capacity for needed changes. Ensuring effective collaboration requires institutionalized mechanisms, long-term capacity building, and ongoing support (Adelman & Taylor, 2003a).

Three matters warrant special discussion here: (1) taking time to create readiness, commitment, and capacity for working collaboratively; (2) building from localities outward; and (3) ensuring an effective infrastructure is established for carrying out planned functions.

1. Creating Readiness for Collaboration and New Ways of Doing Business—Too often, insufficient time is allowed to establish initial readiness and commitment. Some points to consider include the following:

Matching motivation and capabilities. Among the most fundamental errors related to collaboratives is the tendency to set actions into motion without taking sufficient time to lay the foundation for change and the ongoing work. Success in establishing an effective collaborative depends on stakeholders' motivation and capability. Success is most likely when high levels of positive energy are mobilized and appropriately directed over extended periods of time. Thus, one of the first concerns is how to mobilize and direct the energy of a critical mass of participants to ensure readiness and commitment. This calls for strategies that establish and maintain an effective match with the motivation and capabilities of involved parties.

Readiness is an everyday concern. Initially and over time, sufficient time *must* be devoted to creating the motivational readiness of key stakeholders and building their capacity and skills. The initial focus is on communicating basic information about the work and doing so in ways that clarify that the benefits of collaboration outweigh costs. Communication strategies must be personalized, accessible, and build consensus and commitment. Capacity building spans four stages: orientation, foundation building, capacity building, and continuing education.

Over time, the complexity of collaboration requires close monitoring of mechanisms and immediate follow-up to address problems. In particular, it means providing continuous, personalized guidance and support to enhance knowledge and skills and counter anxiety, frustration, and other stressors. To these ends, adequate resource support must be provided (time, space, materials, equipment) and opportunities must be available for increasing ability and generating a sense of renewed mission. Participant turnover must be addressed by welcoming and orienting new members.

A note of caution. In marketing new ideas, the temptation is to accentuate their promising attributes and minimize complications. For instance, in negotiating agreements for school connections, school policy makers frequently are asked simply to sign a memorandum of understanding, rather than involving them in processes that lead to a comprehensive, informed commitment. Sometimes they agree mainly to obtain extra resources; sometimes they are motivated by the desire for their constituents to see them doing *something* to improve the school. Insufficient commitment leads to premature implementation, resulting in the form rather than the substance of change.

2. Building From Localities Outward—Collaborations can be organized by any group of stakeholders. Connecting the resources of families and the community through collaboration with schools is necessary for developing comprehensive, multifaceted programs and services.

An effective school-community-family collaboration must coalesce at the local level. Thus, a school and its surrounding community are a reasonable focal point around which to build an infrastructure. Primary emphasis on this level meshes nicely with contemporary restructuring views that stress increased school-based and neighborhood control.

To maintain the focus on evolving a comprehensive system of intervention that plays out in an effective manner in *every locality*, we conceive the process from the local level outward. In practice, of course, collaboration may begin at any level. From a local perspective, the initial focus is on mechanisms at the school-neighborhood level. Subsequently, mechanisms are conceived that enable several school-neighborhood collaboratives to work together for increased efficiency, effectiveness, and economies of scale (e.g., connecting a complex or *family* of schools, such as a high school and its feeder schools). Then, systemwide mechanisms can be (re)designed to provide support for the work of each locality.

3. Mechanisms—School-community-family collaborations require development of a well-conceived organizational and operational infrastructure that is appropriately sanctioned and endorsed by governing bodies (see Exhibit 47). Infrastructure mechanisms provide oversight, leadership, capacity building, and ongoing development and support. Tasks include (1) decision making about priorities and resource allocation; (2) systematic planning, implementation, maintenance and evaluation; (3) enhancing and redeploying existing resources and pursuing new ones; and (4) nurturing the collaborative. At each level, such tasks require pursuing an assertive agenda.

At the most basic level, infrastructure connects families and community resources with one school. At the next level, collaborative connections may encompass a family of schools and/or may coalesce several collaboratives. Such connections facilitate coordination and sharing to minimize redundancy and deploy and pool resources to increase equity, efficiency, and effectiveness and achieve economies of scale. Many natural connections exist in catchment areas serving a high school and its feeder schools. Because adjoining localities have common concerns, they usually have programmatic activity that can use the same resources. Some school districts and agencies already pull together several geographically related clusters to combine and integrate personnel and programs.

Systemwide (e.g., district, city, county) mechanisms can be designed to provide support for what each locality is trying to develop. At this level, the need is for policy, guidance, leadership, and assistance to ensure localities can establish and maintain collaboration and steer the work toward successful accomplishment of desired goals. Development of systemwide mechanisms should reflect a clear conception of how each supports local activity. Key at this level is leadership with responsibility and accountability for maintaining the vision, developing strategic plans, supporting capacity building, and ensuring coordination and integration of activity among

Exhibit 47   Basic Facets of a Comprehensive Collaborative Infrastructure[a]

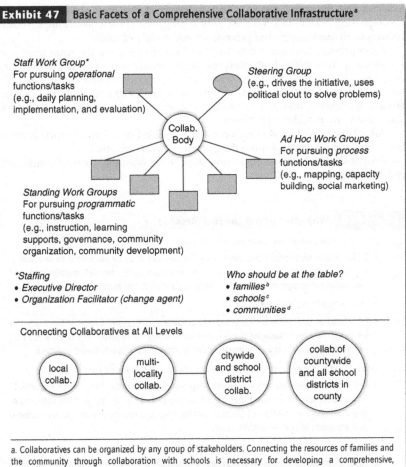

*Staff Work Group**
For pursuing *operational*
functions/tasks
(e.g., daily planning,
implementation, and evaluation)

Steering Group
(e.g., drives the initiative, uses
political clout to solve problems)

Collab.
Body

Ad Hoc Work Groups
For pursuing *process*
functions/tasks
(e.g., mapping, capacity
building, social marketing)

Standing Work Groups
For pursuing *programmatic*
functions/tasks
(e.g., instruction, learning
supports, governance, community
organization, community development)

*Staffing
• *Executive Director*
• *Organization Facilitator (change agent)*

Who should be at the table?
• *families*[b]
• *schools*[c]
• *communities*[d]

Connecting Collaboratives at All Levels

local
collab.

multi-
locality
collab.

citywide
and school
district
collab.

collab.of
countywide
and all school
districts in
county

a. Collaboratives can be organized by any group of stakeholders. Connecting the resources of families and the community through collaboration with schools is necessary for developing a comprehensive, multifaceted system of interventions. Efficiencies and economies of scale are achieved by connecting a complex (or *family*) of schools. Conceptually, think in terms of building from the local outward, but in practice, the process of establishing the initial collaboration may begin at any level.

b. *Families*. Ensure all types of families are represented (not just advocates for organized family groups). The aim is to mobilize all the human and social capital represented by family members and other residence caretakers (e.g., foster homes, shelters).

c. *Schools*. This encompasses all institutionalized entities that are responsible for formal education (e.g., from preK through higher education). The aim is to draw on their resources.

d. *Communities*. This encompasses all the other resources (public and private money, facilities, human and social capital) that can be brought to the table at each level (see Exhibit 46). As the collaborative develops, additional steps must be taken to outreach to disenfranchised groups.

localities and the entire system. Other functions at this level include evaluation, encompassing determination of the equity in program delivery, quality improvement reviews of all mechanisms and procedures, and review of results.

All collaboratives need a core team to steer the process. The team must consist of competent individuals who are highly motivated—not just initially but over time. The complexity of collaboration requires providing continuous, personalized guidance and support to enhance knowledge and skills and counter anxiety, frustration, and other stressors. This entails close monitoring and *immediate* follow-up to address problems.

All collaboratives need effective work or task groups. Thus, particular attention must be paid to developing the capacity of such groups.

Exhibit 48 demonstrates some first steps in establishing a school-community collaborative.

Exhibit 48   What Are Some of the First Steps?

1. *Adopting a comprehensive vision for the collaborative*
   - Collaborative leadership builds consensus that the aim of those involved is to help weave together community and school resources to develop a comprehensive, multifaceted, and integrated continuum of interventions so that no child is left behind

2. *Writing a "brief" to clarify the vision*
   - Collaborative establishes a writing team to prepare a *white paper,* Executive Summary and set of *talking points* clarifying the vision by delineating the rationale and frameworks that will guide development of a comprehensive, multifaceted, and integrated approach

3. *Establishing a steering committee to move the initiative forward and monitor process*
   - Collaborative identifies and empowers a representative subgroup that will be responsible and accountable for ensuring that the vision (*big picture*) is not lost and the momentum of the initiative is maintained through establishing and monitoring ad hoc work groups that are asked to pursue specific tasks

4. *Starting a process for translating the vision into policy*
   - Steering committee establishes a work group to prepare a campaign geared to key local and state school and agency policy makers that focuses on (a) establishing a policy framework for the development of a comprehensive, multifaceted, and integrated approach and (b) ensuring that such policy has a high enough level of priority to end the current marginalized status such efforts have at schools and in communities

5. *Developing a five-year strategic plan*
   - Steering committee establishes a work group to draft a five-year strategic plan that delineates (a) the development of a comprehensive, multifaceted, and integrated approach and (b) the steps to take in accomplishing the required systemic changes. (The strategic plan will cover such matters as formulation of basic agreements about policy, resources, and practices; assignment of committed leadership; change agents to facilitate systemic changes; infrastructure redesign; enhancement of infrastructure mechanisms; resource mapping, analysis, and redeployment; capacity building; standards, evaluation, quality improvement, and accountability; social marketing.)

- Steering committee circulates draft of plan (a) to elicit suggested revisions from key stakeholders and (b) as part of a process for building consensus and developing readiness for proceeding with its implementation
- Work group makes relevant revisions based on suggestions

6. *Moving the strategic plan to implementation*
   - Steering committee ensures that key stakeholders finalize and approve strategic plan
   - Steering committee submits plan on behalf of key stakeholders to school and agency decision makers to formulate formal agreements (e.g., memoranda of understanding [MOUs], contracts) for start-up, initial implementation, and ongoing revisions that can ensure institutionalization and periodic renewal of a comprehensive, multifaceted, and integrated approach
   - Steering committee establishes work group to develop action plan for start-up and initial implementation (The action plan will identify general functions and key tasks to be accomplished, necessary systemic changes, and how to get from here to there in terms of who carries out specific tasks, how, by when, who monitors, and so forth.)

GETTING FROM HERE TO THERE

Because building and maintaining effective collaboratives requires systemic changes, the process of getting from here to there is complex. The process often requires knowledge and skills not currently part of the professional preparation of those called on to act as change agents. For example, few school or agency professionals assigned to make major reforms are taught how to create the necessary motivational readiness among a critical mass of stakeholders or how to develop and institutionalize the mechanisms required for effective collaboration.

The literature on systemic change clarifies the value of (1) a high level of policy and leadership commitment that is translated into an inspiring vision and appropriate resources (leadership, space, budget, time); (2) incentives for change, such as intrinsically valued outcomes, expectations for success, recognitions, rewards; (3) procedural options that reflect stakeholder strengths and from which those expected to implement change can select options they see as workable; (4) a willingness to establish an infrastructure and processes that facilitate efforts to change, such as a governance mechanism that adopts strategies for improving organizational health; (5) use of change agents who are perceived as pragmatic (e.g., as maintaining ideals while embracing practical solutions); (6) accomplishing change in stages and with realistic timelines; (7) providing feedback on progress; and (8) taking steps to institutionalize support mechanisms that maintain and evolve changes and generate periodic renewal. An understanding of concepts espoused by community psychologists such as empowering settings and enhancing a sense of community also can make a critical difference. Such concepts stress the value of open, welcoming, inclusive, democratic, and supportive processes.

Substantive change is most likely when high levels of positive energy among stakeholders are mobilized and appropriately directed over extended periods of time. Thus, one of the first concerns is how to mobilize and direct the energy of a critical mass of participants to ensure readiness and commitment and build *authentic* agreements. The next concerns are capacity building and ensuring appropriate supports are in place during each phase of the change process.

Change evolves slowly in the organizational and familial cultures represented in a collaborative. Early in the process the emphasis is on creating an official and psychological climate for change, including overcoming institutionalized resistance, negative attitudes, and barriers to change. New attitudes, new working relationships, new skills all must be engendered, and negative reactions and dynamics related to change must be addressed. Creating this readiness involves tasks designed to produce fundamental changes in the culture that characterizes schools and community agencies, while accommodating cultural differences among families. One of these tasks is building *authentic* agreements.

Agreements require ongoing modifications that account for the intricacies and unanticipated problems that characterize efforts to introduce major innovations into complex systems. Informed commitment is strengthened and operationalized through negotiating and renegotiating formal agreements among various stakeholders. Policy statements articulate the commitment and provide for resources. Memoranda of understanding and contracts specify agreements about such matters as funding sources, resource appropriations, personnel functions, incentives, and safeguards for risk taking, stakeholder development, immediate and long-term commitments and timelines, accountability procedures, and so forth. Authentic agreements ensure a common vision, valuing, and attention to relationship building; clarification of mutual expectations and benefits; and provision for rapid renegotiation of initial agreements.

There is much more to discuss about systemic change. We go into greater detail in Chapter 15.

A Note of Caution. Without careful planning, implementation, and capacity building, collaboration rarely lives up to initial hopes. For example, formal arrangements for working together often take the form of committees and meetings. To be effective, such sessions require thoughtful and skillful facilitation. Even when they begin with great enthusiasm, poorly facilitated working sessions quickly degenerate into another meeting, more talk but little action, another burden, and a waste of time. This is particularly likely to happen when the emphasis is mainly on the unfocused mandate to *collaborate* rather than on moving a valued vision and mission forward through productive working relationships.

Most of us know the difficulties involved in working effectively with a group. We all can point to the many committees and teams that drained our time and energy to little avail. Obviously true, collaboration involves more than meeting and talking. The point is to work in ways that lead to actions that produce results. For this to happen, steps must be taken to ensure that committees, councils, and teams are formed in ways that maximize productivity. Such steps include providing training, time, support, and authority to carry out roles and functions. When such matters are ignored, groups find themselves meeting but going nowhere. Exhibit 49 offers some guidelines for planning and facilitating effective meetings.

| **Exhibit 49** | Planning and Facilitating Effective Meetings |

Forming a working group

- There should be a clear statement about the group's mission.
- Be certain that members agree to pursue the stated mission and, for the most part, share a vision.
- Pick someone who the group will respect and who either already has good facilitation skills or will commit to learning those that are needed.
- Provide training for members so they understand their role in keeping a meeting on track and turning talk into effective action.
- Designate processes (a) for sending members information before a meeting regarding what is to be accomplished, specific agenda items, and individual assignments and (b) for maintaining and circulating a record of decisions and planned actions (what, who, when).

Meeting format

- Be certain a written agenda is used that states the purpose of the meeting, specific topics, and desired outcomes for the session.
- Begin the meeting by reviewing purpose, topics, desired outcomes, and so forth. Until the group is functioning well, it may be necessary to review meeting ground rules.
- Facilitate the involvement of all members, and do so in ways that encourage them to focus specifically on the task. The facilitator remains neutral in discussion of issues.
- Try to maintain a comfortable pace (neither too rushed, nor too slow; try to start on time and end on time, but don't be a slave to the clock).
- Periodically, review what has been accomplished and move on to the next item.
- Leave time to sum up and celebrate accomplishment of outcomes and end by enumerating specific follow-up activity (what, who, when). End with a plan for the next meeting (date, time, tentative agenda). For a series of meetings, set the dates well in advance so members can plan their calendars.

Some group dynamics to anticipate

- Hidden Agendas—All members should agree to help keep hidden agendas in check and, when such items cannot be avoided, facilitate the rapid presentation of a point and indicate where the concern needs to be redirected.

(Continued)

(Continued)

- A Need for Validation—When members make the same point over and over, it usually indicates they feel an important point is not being validated. To counter such disruptive repetition, account for the item in a visible way so that members feel their contributions have been acknowledged. When the item warrants discussion at a later time, assign it to a future agenda.
- Members Are at an Impasse—Two major reasons groups get stuck are (a) some new ideas are needed to "get out of a box" and (b) differences in perspective need to be aired and resolved. The former problem usually can be dealt with through brainstorming or by bringing in someone with new ideas to offer; to deal with conflicts that arise over process, content, and power relationships employ problem-solving and conflict management strategies (e.g., accommodation, negotiation, mediation).
- Interpersonal Conflict and Inappropriate Competition—These problems may be corrected by repeatedly bringing the focus back to the goal—improving outcomes for students and families; when this doesn't work, restructuring group membership may be necessary.
- Ain't It Awful!—Daily frustrations experienced by staff often lead them to turn meetings into gripe sessions. Outside team members (parents, agency staff, business and/or university partners) can influence school staff to exhibit their best behavior.

Making meetings work

A good meeting is task focused and ensures that tasks are accomplished in ways with the following characteristics:
- Are efficient and effective
- Reflect common concerns and priorities
- Are implemented in an open, noncritical, nonthreatening manner
- Turn complaints into problems that are analyzed in ways that lead to plans for practical solutions
- Feel productive (produces a sense of accomplishment and of appreciation)

About building relationships and communicating effectively

- Convey empathy and warmth (e.g., this involves working to understand and appreciate what others are thinking and feeling and transmitting a sense of liking them)
- Convey genuine regard and respect (e.g., this involves transmitting real interest and interacting in ways that enable others to maintain a feeling of integrity and personal control)
- Talk with, not at, others—active listening and dialogue (e.g., this involves being a good listener, not being judgmental, not prying, and being willing to share experiences as appropriate)

CONCLUDING COMMENTS

The success of collaboration in enhancing school, family, and community connections is first and foremost in the hands of policy makers. For increased connections to be more than another desired but underachieved aim, policy makers must support development of comprehensive and multifaceted school-community collaboratives and not primarily focus on linking community services to schools. The latter emphasis downplays the role of existing school and other community and family resources, perpetuates an orientation that overemphasizes individually prescribed services, results in fragmented interventions, and undervalues the human and social capital indigenous to every neighborhood.

More specifically, policy must do the following:

- Move existing *governance* toward shared decision making and appropriate degrees of local control and private sector involvement—a key facet of this is guaranteeing roles and providing incentives, supports, and training for effective involvement of line staff, families, students, and other community members.
- Create *change teams and change agents* to carry out the daily activities of systemic change related to building support and redesigning processes to initiate, establish, and maintain changes over time.
- Delineate high-level *leadership assignments* and underwrite *leadership and/or management training* about vision for change, how to effect such changes, how to institutionalize the changes, and generate ongoing renewal.
- Establish institutionalized *mechanisms to manage and enhance resources* for family-school-community connections and related systems (focusing on analyzing, planning, coordinating, integrating, monitoring, evaluating, and strengthening ongoing efforts).
- Provide adequate funds for *capacity building* related to both accomplishing desired system changes and enhancing intervention quality over time—a key facet of this is a major investment in staff recruitment and development using well-designed, and technologically sophisticated strategies for dealing with the problems of frequent turnover and diffusing information updates; another facet is an investment in technical assistance at all levels and for all aspects and stages of the work.
- Use a sophisticated approach to *accountability* that initially emphasizes data that can help develop effective collaboration in providing interventions and a results-oriented focus on short-term benchmarks that evolves into evaluation of long-range indicators of impact. (As soon as feasible, move to technologically sophisticated and integrated management information systems.)

The many steps and tasks described throughout this chapter are not a straightforward sequential process. The work is entangled with myriad political and bureaucratic difficulties and underwritten with sparse resources. The process calls for a high degree of commitment and relentlessness of effort. What makes it all worthwhile is that collaboration enables stakeholders to build the comprehensive system of interventions needed to make a significant impact in strengthening youngsters, their families, schools, and neighborhoods.

NOTES

1. In practice, the terms *school-linked* and *school-based* encompass two separate dimensions: (a) where programs and/or services are *located* and (b) who *owns* them. Taken literally, school-based should indicate activity carried out on a campus, and school-linked should refer to off-campus activity with formal connections to a school site. In either case, services may be owned by schools or a community-based organization or in some cases may be co-owned. As commonly used, the term school-linked refers to community owned on- and off-campus services and is strongly associated with the notion of coordinated services.

2. As the notion of school-community collaboration spreads, the terms *services* and *programs* are used interchangeably and the adjective *comprehensive* often is appended. The tendency to refer to all interventions as services is a problem. Addressing a full range of factors affecting young people's development and learning requires going beyond *services* to utilize an extensive continuum of programmatic interventions. Services themselves should be differentiated to distinguish between narrow-band, personal and/or clinical services and broad-band, public health and social services. Furthermore, although services can be provided as part of a program, not all are. For example, counseling to ameliorate a mental health problem can be offered on an ad hoc basis or may be one element of a multifaceted program to facilitate healthy social and emotional development. Pervasive and severe psychosocial problems, such as gang violence, delinquency, substance abuse, teen pregnancy, and physical and sexual abuse require multifaceted, programmatic interventions. Besides providing services to correct existing problems, such interventions encompass primary prevention (e.g., public health programs that target groups seen as *at risk*) and a broad range of open enrollment didactic, enrichment, and recreation programs. Differentiating services and programs and taking greater care when using the term comprehensive can help mediate against tendencies to limit the range of interventions and underscores the breadth of activity requiring coordination and integration.

14

Show Us the Data

Using and Extending the Research Base

The science base for intervention is an essential building block. However, we must extend it, and we must be careful that we don't limit progress while we do so.

Commonly heard these days is the following shibboleth:

In God we trust; from all others demand data.

Increasingly, policy makers and others who make decisions are demanding the following:

Show me the data!

All professional interveners need data to enhance the quality of their efforts and to monitor their outcomes in ways that promote appropriate accountability. This is especially the case for those who work with youngsters who manifest behavior, learning, and emotional problems. Sound planning, implementation, accountability, and advancement of the field necessitate amassing and analyzing information and gathering appropriate evaluative data. In addition, the field is at a point in time when policy intensively emphasizes showing an evidence base for all interventions.

With respect to mental health in schools, the policy demand for an evidence base has produced somewhat of a catch-22. Any proposal focused on strengthening student supports is consistently met with demands from policy makers for data showing that the additional effort will improve student achievement. The reality is that relevant data stem from the broader agenda for addressing barriers interfering with achievement; evidence specific to mental health in schools is sparse. Because of the limited data on the direct and immediate relationship, many districts shy away from emphasizing mental health in schools, per se. This makes generating better impact data difficult.

Nevertheless, in moving forward, the field can draw on an existing research base. This chapter begins by briefly referencing that research. Then, we focus on concerns about and frameworks for extending the base of evidence. In doing so, we stress the need to expand the framework for current school accountability and explore the value of program evaluation as a tool for advancing the field.

A USABLE RESEARCH BASE

Throughout this book, we have stressed the conceptual base for developing a comprehensive focus on addressing barriers to student learning and promoting healthy development—including a broad emphasis on mental health. Elsewhere, we review the extensive body of literature supporting the conceptual base. That review includes the research presented in Chapter 13 on school, family, and community collaboration. Other *formal* studies have focused on specific interventions. Exhibit 50 references lists highlighting such research.

| **Exhibit 50** | **Annotated Lists of Empirically Supported and/or Evidence-Based Interventions for School-Aged Children and Adolescents** |

The following table provides a list of lists with indications of what each covers, how it was developed, what it contains, and how to access it.

I. Universal Focus on Promoting Healthy Development

A. *Safe and Sound. An Educational Leader's Guide to Evidence-Based Social and Emotional Learning Programs.* (2002). The Collaborative for Academic, Social, and Emotional Learning (CASEL).

   1. *How it was developed:* Contacts with researchers and literature search yielded 250 programs for screening; 81 programs were identified that met the criteria of being a multiyear program with at least eight lessons in one program year, designed for regular education classrooms, and nationally available.

   2. *What the list contains:* Descriptions (purpose, features, results) of the 81 programs.

3. *How to access:* CASEL
   (www.casel.org)

B. *Positive Youth Development in the United States: Research Findings on Evaluations of Positive Youth Development Programs* (2002). Social Development Research Group, University of Washington.

1. *How it was developed:* 77 programs that sought to achieve positive youth development objectives were reviewed. Criteria used: research designs employed control or comparison group and had measured youth behavior outcomes.

2. *What the list contains:* 25 programs designated as effective based on available evidence.

3. *How to access:* Available at http://aspe.hhs.gov/hsp/Positive YouthDev99/index.htm

II. Prevention of Problems; Promotion of Protective Factors

A. *Blueprints for Violence Prevention* (1998). Center for the Study and Prevention of Violence.

1. *How it was developed:* Review of over 450 delinquency, drug, and violence prevention programs based on a criteria of a strong research design, evidence of significant deterrence effects, multiple site replication, sustained effects.

2. *What the list contains:* 11 model programs and 21 promising programs.

3. *How to access:* Center for the Study and Prevention of Violence (www.colorado.edu/cspv/publicati ons/otherblueprints.html)

B. *Exemplary Substance Abuse and Mental Health Programs* (SAMHSA).

1. *How it was developed:* These science-based programs underwent an expert consensus review of published and unpublished materials on eight criteria (e.g., theory, fidelity, evaluation, sampling, attrition, outcome measures, missing data, outcome data, analysis, threats to validity, integrity, utility, replications, dissemination, cultural and/or age appropriateness). The reviews have grouped programs as *models, effective,* and *promising* programs.

2. *What the list contains:* Prevention programs that may be adapted and replicated by communities.

3. *How to access:* SAMHSA's National Registry of Evidence-based Programs and Practices (http://nrepp.samhsa.gov)

C. *Preventing Drug Use Among Children & Adolescents. Research Based Guide* (1997). National Institute on Drug Abuse (NIDA).

1. *How it was developed:* NIDA and the scientists who conducted the research developed research protocols. Each was tested in a family, school, and/or community setting for a reasonable period with positive results.

2. *What the list contains:* 10 programs that are universal, selective, or indicated.

3. *How to access:* NIDA (www.nida.nih .gov/prevention/prevopen.html)

D. *Safe, Disciplined, and Drug-Free Schools Expert Panel Exemplary Programs* (2001). U.S. Department of Education Safe and Drug-Free Schools.

(Continued)

(Continued)

1. *How it was developed:* Review of 132 programs submitted to the panel. Each program reviewed in terms of quality, usefulness to others, and educational significance.
2. *What the list contains:* Nine exemplary and 33 promising programs focusing on violence, alcohol, tobacco, and drug prevention.
3. *How to access:* U.S. Department of Education (www.ed.gov/ offices/OERI/ORAD/KAD/ expert_panel/drug-free.html)

III. Early Intervention: Targeted Focus on Specific Problems or At-Risk Groups

A. *The Prevention of Mental Disorders in School-Aged Children: Current State of the Field* (2001). Prevention Research Center for the Promotion of Human Development, Pennsylvania State University.

1. *How it was developed:* Review of scores of primary prevention programs to identify those with quasi-experimental or randomized trials and been found to reduce symptoms of psycho-pathology or factors commonly associated with an increased risk for later mental disorders.
2. *What the list contains:* 34 universal and targeted interventions that have demonstrated positive outcomes under rigorous evaluation and the common characteristics of these programs.
3. *How to access:* Online journal *Prevention & Treatment* (http:// content.apa.org/journals/pre/4/1/1)

IV. Treatment for Problems

A. *American Psychological Association's Society for Clinical Child and*

Adolescent Psychology, Committee on Evidence-Based Practice List.

1. *How it was developed:* Committee reviews outcome studies to determine how well a study conforms to the guidelines of the Task Force on Promotion and Dissemination of Psychological Procedures (1996).
2. *What it contains:* Reviews of the following:

➤ Depression (dysthymia)— *Analyses indicate only practice meets criteria for "well-established treatment"(best supported) and two practices meet one criteria for "probably efficacious" (promising).*

➤ Conduct and/or oppositional problems—*Two meet criteria for well established treatments: videotape modeling parent training programs (Webster-Stratton) and parent training program based on Living With Children (Patterson and Guillion). Ten practices identified as probably efficacious.*

➤ ADHD—*Behavioral parent training, behavioral interventions in the classroom, and stimulant medication meet criteria for well established treatments. Two others meet criteria for probably efficacious.*

➤ Anxiety disorders—*For phobias, participant modeling and reinforced practice are well established; filmed modeling, live modeling, and cognitive behavioral interventions that use self-instruction training are probably efficacious. For anxiety disorders, cognitive-behavioral procedures with and without family anxiety management, modeling, in vivo exposure, relaxation training, and reinforced practice are listed as probably efficacious.*

➤ Caution: *Reviewers stress the importance of devising developmentally and culturally sensitive interventions targeted to the unique needs of each child; a need for research informed by clinical practice.*

3. *How to access:*
www.effectivechildtherapy.com

V. Review, Consensus Statements, and Compendia of Evidence-Based Treatments

A. *School-Based Prevention Programs for Children and Adolescents* (1995). J. A. Durlak. Thousand Oaks, CA: Sage. Reports results from 130 controlled outcome studies that support "a secondary prevention model emphasizing timely intervention for subclinical problems detected early.... In general, best results are obtained for cognitive-behavioral and behavioral treatments and interventions targeting externalizing problems."

B. *Mental Health and Mass Violence.* Evidence-based early psychological intervention for victims and survivors of mass violence. A workshop to reach consensus on best practices (U.S. Departments of Health and Human Services, Defense, Veterans Affairs, Justice, and American Red Cross). Available at www.nimh.nih. gov/health/publications/massviolence.pdf

C. *Society of Pediatric Psychology,* Division 54, American Psychological Association, *Journal of Pediatric Psychology.* Articles on empirically supported treatments in pediatric psychology related to obesity, feeding problems, headaches, pain, bedtime refusal, enuresis, encopresis, and symptoms of asthma, diabetes, and cancer.

D. *Preventing Crime: What Works, What Doesn't, What's Promising. A Report to the United States Congress* (1997) by L. W. Sherman, Denise Gottfredson, et al. Washington, DC: U.S. Department of Justice. Reviews programs funded by the OJP for crime, delinquency and substance use (www.ncjrs.org/pdffiles/171676.pdf). Also see Denise Gottfredson's book: *Schools and Delinquency* (2001). New York: Cambridge University Press.

E. *School Violence Prevention Initiative Matrix of Evidence-Based Prevention Interventions* (1999). Center for Mental Health Services, SAMHSA. Synthesis of several lists cited above to highlight examples of programs that meet some criteria for a designation of evidence based for violence prevention and substance abuse prevention (i.e., synthesizes lists from the Center for the Study and Prevention of Violence, Center for Substance Abuse Prevention, Communities that Care, Department of Education, Department of Justice, Health Resources and Services Administration, National Association of School Psychologists).

F. *What Works Clearinghouse.* Collects, screens, and identifies studies of effectiveness of educational interventions (programs, products, practices, and policies) (http://ies.ed.gov/ncee/wwc/).

Because of the fragmented nature of the research base, findings are best appreciated in terms of the whole being greater than the sum of the parts, and implications are best derived from the total theoretical and empirical picture. When such a broad perspective is adopted, schools have a significant science base to draw upon in understanding the value of mental health in schools. Reports suggest positive outcomes for school and society associated with a wide range of interventions. Examples include better school attendance, fewer behavior problems, improved interpersonal skills, enhanced achievement, and increased bonding at school and at home.

Moreover, many *natural* experiments underscore the promise of ensuring that all youngsters have access to a broad spectrum of interventions. These natural societal experiments play out in every school and neighborhood where families are affluent enough to purchase the additional programs and services they feel will maximize their youngsters' well-being. Those who can afford such interventions clearly understand their value. It will surprise no one that most indicators of well-being, including higher achievement test scores, are correlated with socioeconomic status. Societal inequities are well documented and underscore the need for a broad approach to mental health in schools as one facet of establishing equity of opportunity.

Taken as a whole, the research base indicates a promising range of activity that can enable students to learn and teachers to teach (Center for Mental Health in Schools, 2000b, 2004a). The findings also underscore that addressing behavior, learning, and emotional problems one at a time is unwise because the problems are interrelated and require multifaceted and cohesive solutions. In all, the literature offers support for a comprehensive, multifaceted, and cohesive approach.

EXPANDING THE ACCOUNTABILITY FRAMEWORK FOR SCHOOLS

Accountability has extraordinary power to reshape schools—for good or bad. Systems are driven by what is measured for purposes of accountability. This is particularly so when the systems are the focus of major reform.

The Problem

Under reform conditions, policy makers often use a quick and easy recipe. This leads to measures that hold program administrators and staff accountable for specific, short-term results. Little thought is given to the negative effects that overemphasizing quick outcomes can have on achieving desired long-term results.

Current school accountability is a good example of the problem. The situation is one where there is increasing accountability demand focusing on narrow outcome indicators. School personnel are quick to learn what will and will not be evaluated. Slowly but surely, greater emphasis is placed on teaching what will be measured. Over time, what is measured increasingly is viewed as the most important outcome. Because only so much time is available at school, other educational concerns are de-emphasized and even dropped.

What's wrong with that? Nothing—if what is evaluated reflects all the important things we want youngsters to learn in school. This, of course, is not the case.

Current accountability pressures reflect values and biases that are reshaping the entire nature and scope of schooling. As everyone involved in school improvement knows, the only measures that really count are achievement test scores. These scores drive school accountability. What the tests measure has become the be-all and end-all of decision making. This produces a growing disconnect between the direction in which many policy makers and school reformers are leading the public and the realities of what it takes to improve academic performance and student well-being for *all* students in a school district.

The disconnect is especially evident in typical schools enrolling students from *low-wealth* families. Such families and those who work in schools serving them have a clear appreciation of many barriers that must be addressed so students can benefit from the teacher's efforts to teach. These stakeholders stress that major academic improvements are unlikely until comprehensive and multifaceted approaches for addressing the barriers are developed and pursued effectively.

At the same time, anyone who looks will find no direct accountability for addressing barriers to learning and teaching. Ironically, the lack of an accountability focus on these matters contributes to devaluing of and justifying cuts in student and learning supports.

Thus, rather than building the type of system that can produce improved academic performance, prevailing accountability measures pressure schools to pursue mainly a direct and ineffective route to improving instruction. The implicit underlying assumption of the direct route is that all students are motivationally ready and able each day to benefit from the teacher's instruction. The reality, of course, is that in many schools, the *majority* does not fit this picture and are not benefiting from promising instructional improvements. The results of persevering in this direction are continuing low test scores and an ongoing widespread achievement gap.

Logically, major systemic efforts should address interfering factors. However, current accountability pressures override the logic and result in marginalizing almost every initiative not viewed as a direct and quick path to higher achievement test scores. The irony is that such policy not only works against what must be done, it works against gathering evidence on the necessity and effectiveness of directly and comprehensively addressing barriers to learning.

An Expanded Framework

In moving forward, an expanded framework for school accountability is needed. Exhibit 51 highlights such a framework.

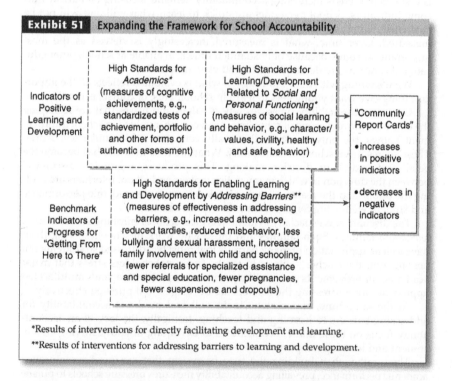

Exhibit 51 Expanding the Framework for School Accountability

Indicators of Positive Learning and Development

High Standards for *Academics** (measures of cognitive achievements, e.g., standardized tests of achievement, portfolio and other forms of authentic assessment)

High Standards for Learning/Development Related to *Social and Personal Functioning** (measures of social learning and behavior, e.g., character/ values, civility, healthy and safe behavior)

Benchmark Indicators of Progress for "Getting From Here to There"

High Standards for Enabling Learning and Development by *Addressing Barriers*** (measures of effectiveness in addressing barriers, e.g., increased attendance, reduced tardies, reduced misbehavior, less bullying and sexual harassment, increased family involvement with child and schooling, fewer referrals for specialized assistance and special education, fewer pregnancies, fewer suspensions and dropouts)

"Community Report Cards"

• increases in positive indicators

• decreases in negative indicators

*Results of interventions for directly facilitating development and learning.

**Results of interventions for addressing barriers to learning and development.

We view the expanded framework as a move toward what has been called *intelligent accountability*. As illustrated, the intent is not to deflect from the laser-like focus on accountability for meeting high standards related to academics. The debate will continue as to how best to measure academic outcomes, but clearly, schools must demonstrate they effectively teach academics.

Schools also are expected, however, to pursue high standards in promoting positive social and personal functioning, including enhancing civility, teaching safe and healthy behavior, and some form of *character education*. Every school we visit has specific goals related to this facet of student development and learning. But schools currently are not held accountable for goals in this arena. That is, no systematic evaluation or reporting of the work is done. As would be expected, then, schools direct few resources and too little attention to these unmeasured concerns. Yet society wants schools to attend to these matters, and most professionals understand that personal and social functioning is integrally tied to academic performance. From this perspective, not holding schools accountable for improving students' social and personal functioning is self-defeating.

For schools where a large proportion of students are not doing well, not attending to benchmark indicators of progress in addressing barriers to learning also is self-defeating. Schools cannot teach children who are not in class. Therefore, increasing attendance always is an expectation (and an important budget consideration). Other basic indicators of school improvement and precursors of enhanced academic performance are reducing tardiness and problem behaviors, reducing suspension and dropout rates, and abating the large number of inappropriate referrals for special education. Given this, the progress of school staff in addressing such problems should be measured and treated as a significant aspect of school accountability.

School outcomes, of course, are influenced by the well-being of the families and the neighborhoods in which they operate. Therefore, performance of any school should be judged within the context of the current status of indicators of community well-being, such as economic, social, and health measures. When those indicators are not improving or are declining, schools find it difficult to make progress. Judging school performance out of context is patently unfair.

In summary, an expanded accountability framework is needed to encourage and support movement toward a broad approach to mental health in schools. Because the broader approach recognizes the interconnectedness of neighborhood, family, school, and student factors, changes in all are a relevant focus of data gathering. We are reminded of Ulric Neisser's dictum: *Changing the individual while leaving the world alone is a dubious proposition.* Exhibit 52 presents a range of indicators on which an expanded accountability framework focuses measurement.

Exhibit 52   Indicators for a Broad Accountability Framework

Students

- Increased knowledge, skills, and attitudes to enhance
  - acceptance of responsibility (including attending, following directions and agreed upon rules and laws),
  - self-esteem and integrity,

(Continued)

(Continued)

- o social and working relationships,
- o self-evaluation and self-direction and regulation,
- o physical functioning,
- o health maintenance,
- o safe behavior.

- Reduced barriers to school attendance and functioning by addressing problems related to
  - o health,
  - o lack of adequate clothing,
  - o dysfunctional families,
  - o lack of home support for student improvement,
  - o physical and sexual abuse,
  - o substance abuse,
  - o gang involvement,
  - o pregnant and parenting minors,
  - o dropouts,
  - o need for compensatory learning strategies.

Families and Communities

- Increased social and emotional support for families
- Increased family access to special assistance
- Increased family ability to reduce child risk factors that can be barriers to learning
- Increased bilingual ability and literacy of parents
- Increased family ability to support schooling
- Increased positive attitudes about schooling
- Increased home (family and parent) participation at school
- Enhanced positive attitudes toward school and community
- Increased community participation in school activities
- Increased perception of the school as a hub of community activities
- Increased partnerships designed to enhance education and service availability in community
- Enhanced coordination and collaboration between community agencies and school programs and services
- Enhanced focus on agency outreach to meet family needs
- Increased psychological sense of community

Programs and Systems

- Enhanced processes by which staff and families learn about available programs and services and how to access those they need
- Increased coordination among services and programs
- Increases in the degree to which staff work collaboratively and programmatically
- Increased services and programs at school site
- Increased amounts of school, family, and community collaboration
- Increases in quality of services and programs because of improved systems for requesting, accessing, and managing assistance for students and families (including overcoming inappropriate barriers to confidentiality)
- Establishment of a long-term financial base

RESULTS AND BEYOND

A Framework for Program Evaluation

Evaluation practiced at the highest level of the state-of-the-art is one means of speeding up the processes that contribute to human and social progress.

—Rossi, Freeman, and Wright (1979)

Whatever the focus of accountability, the prevailing cry is for specific *outcome* evidence and for cost containment. Although understandable in light of the unfulfilled promise of so many programs and the insatiable demands on limited public finances, a narrow *results* emphasis ignores the state of the art related to comprehensive, complex interventions. To move the field forward, policy and practice need to go beyond simply calling for data on results and pay greater attention to evaluation research methodology.

Intervention evaluation can aid efforts to (1) *make decisions* about whether to undertake, continue, modify, or stop an intervention and (2) *advance knowledge* about interventions in ways that can enhance understanding of and improve practices, training, and theory. Evaluation methodology is basic to assessing intervention efficiency, effectiveness, and impact.

Two unfounded presumptions are at the core of most results-oriented intervention evaluations in education and psychology. One premise is that an intervention in widespread use is at a relatively evolved stage of development and therefore warrants the cost of *summative* evaluation. The other supposition is that major conceptual and methodological problems associated with evaluating intervention are resolved. The truth is that interventions are frequently introduced prior to adequate development with a view to evolving them based on what is learned each day. Moreover, many well-institutionalized approaches remain relatively underfunded and underdeveloped. As to evaluation methodology, every review of the literature outlines major unresolved concerns. Given this state of affairs, evaluations done to meet accountability demands often are unreasonable and chronically reflect a naive view of research and theory.

Overemphasis on immediate evaluation of the efficacy of underdeveloped interventions draws resources and attention away from the type of intensive research programs necessary for advancing intervention knowledge and practice. Cost-effective outcomes cannot be achieved in the absence of intervention development and research. *Premature* efforts to carry out comprehensive summative evaluations clearly are not cost-effective. Consequently, policies mandating naive accountability run the risk of generating evaluative practices that are neither cost-effective nor wise. Moving forward requires understanding evaluation and using the methodology to advance the field.

Evaluation involves determining the worth or value of something (Stake, 1967, 1976). For purposes of this discussion, evaluation is defined as a systematic process designed to describe and judge the overall impact and value of an intervention for purposes of making decisions and advancing knowledge.

More specifically, the objectives are to do the following:

1. *Describe* and *judge* an intervention's (a) rationale, including assumptions and intentions, and (b) standards for making judgments

2. *Describe* and *judge* an intervention's (a) actual activity, including intended and unintended procedures and outcomes, and (b) costs (financial, negative effects)

3. *Make decisions* about continuing, modifying, or stopping an intervention for an individual or for all those enrolled in a program

4. *Advance knowledge* about interventions to improve (a) practices, (b) training, (c) theory, and (d) policy.

The information needed to meet these purposes comes from comprehensive evaluations that include both immediate and long-term program data. The full range of data that might be gathered is suggested by the particular evaluation framework adopted.

A framework formulated by Robert Stake provides a specific example of the type of models used by evaluators concerned not just about results but also understanding factors that influence outcomes. Stake's framework offers a graphic and comprehensive picture of various facets of evaluation and how they relate to each other (see Exhibit 53).

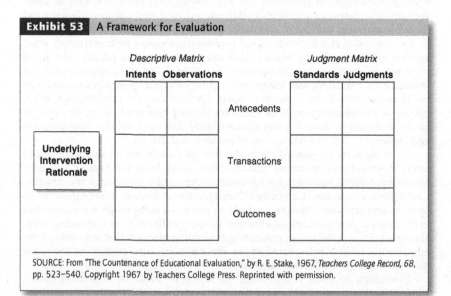

Exhibit 53   A Framework for Evaluation

SOURCE: From "The Countenance of Educational Evaluation," by R. E. Stake, 1967, *Teachers College Record, 68*, pp. 523–540. Copyright 1967 by Teachers College Press. Reprinted with permission.

In brief, Stake emphasizes, "the two basic acts of evaluation" are description and judgment. Descriptions take the form of data gathered by formal or informal means. Judgments are interpretive conclusions about the meaning of the data such as whether a procedure is good or bad, a student is above or below norm, a behavior is pathological or not. In practice, judgments are used for purposes of decision making. When it comes to deciding specifically what to describe and judge, evaluators often are guided by their understanding of decisions to be made at the conclusion of the evaluation.

Stake stresses that proper program evaluation requires data and criteria for analyzing the degree to which

- conditions anticipated prior to the program (antecedents), planned procedures (transactions), and intended outcomes are consistent with the program rationale and are logical in relation to each other;
- intended antecedents, transactions, and outcomes actually occur.

In general, the types of data Stake's framework calls for can provide a wealth of information for use in describing and judging programs and making decisions about ways to improve them. As such, the data are useful not only for purposes of accountability, but to help build the research base. The data also can be used for purposes of *social marketing* (see Exhibit 54).

Exhibit 54   Using Data for Social Marketing

The mass communication and advertising industries use fundamentally the same approaches in developing media programs and marketing products; commercial and industrial corporations evaluate the procedures they use in selecting and promoting employees and organizing their work forces; political candidates develop their campaigns by evaluating the voter appeal of different strategies . . . administrators in both the public and private sectors are continually assessing clerical, fiscal, and interpersonal practices of their organizations. The distinction between these uses of evaluation lies primarily in the intent of the effort to be evaluated . . . to benefit the human condition . . . [or] for other purposes, such as increasing profits or amassing influence and power.

—Rossi and Freeman (1989)

Social marketing is a valuable tool for fostering a critical mass of stakeholder support for new directions to improve schools. Particularly important to effective marketing of change is the inclusion of the evidence base for moving in new directions.

Social marketing draws on concepts developed for commercial marketing. But in the context of school and community change, the emphasis is not on selling products. The intent is to build consensus for ideas and new directions that can strengthen youngsters, families, schools, and neighborhoods. Social marketing is about creating readiness for change and influencing action by key stakeholders.

(Continued)

(Continued)

- To achieve these aims, basic information must be communicated to key stakeholders. Strategies must be used to help them understand the need for what is proposed and that benefits will outweigh costs.
- The strategies used must be personalized and accessible to the subgroups of stakeholders (e.g., must be *enticing*, emphasize that costs are reasonable, and engage them in processes that build consensus and commitment).

One caution: Beware of thinking of social marketing as just an event. Because stakeholders and systems are continuously changing, social marketing is an ongoing process. The temptation is to plan a *big day* to bring people together to inform, share, involve, and celebrate. This can be a good thing if this is one facet of a carefully thought out strategic plan. It can be counterproductive as a one-shot activity that drains resources and energy and leads to a belief that *We did our social marketing.*

Systematic evaluation planning requires decisions about (1) the focus of evaluation (e.g., person or environment, immediate objectives vs. long-range aims); (2) whose perspective is to determine the evaluation focus, methods, and standards used (e.g., the client, intervener, program underwriter); and (3) the best way to proceed in gathering, analyzing, and interpreting information (e.g., specific measures, design). In making such decisions, concerns arise because what can be evaluated is far less than what a program may intend to accomplish. Furthermore, inappropriate bias and vested interests shape evaluation planning and implementation, thereby influencing whether a program is seen as good or bad.

Finally, remember that all aspects of evaluation have the potential to produce negative effects. For instance, over time, what is evaluated can reduce and reshape a program's intended aims. On a personal level, evaluation can lead to invasion of privacy and an undermining of the ability of those evaluated to self-evaluate.

In sum, evaluations of whether an intervention is any good must first address the question: *Is what it is trying to accomplish appropriate?* The frame of reference for such evaluations may be the intervention rationale or what others think the program should be doing or both. After judging the appropriateness of what is wanted or expected, a program's intended breadth of focus should guide efforts to evaluate effectiveness. Because not everything is measurable in a technically sophisticated way, some things will be poorly measured or simply reviewed informally. Obviously, this is less than satisfactory. Still, from a rational perspective, continued emphasis on the entire gamut of what is intended is better than limiting the process to what can be measured readily or to meeting naive accountability demands.

CONCLUDING COMMENTS

*Today's enthusiastic embrace of data has waltzed us directly from a petulant resis-
tance to performance measures to a reflexive and unsophisticated reliance on a few
simple metrics. . . . The result has been a nifty pirouette from one troubling mind-
set to another; with nary a misstep, we have pivoted from the "old stupid" to the
"new stupid."*

—Frederick Hess (2008)

Gathering good evaluative data is a key to designing a promising future.
Evaluation methodology can improve programs, protect consumers, and
advance knowledge. The work, however, is difficult and involves tasks many
would prefer to avoid.

Professionals clearly must work on improving their practices. The need to
improve evaluation methodology is equally clear. Because evaluations can as easily
reshape programs in negative as in positive directions, methodology must be
improved and accountability pressures must not inappropriately narrow the focus.

Care also is needed as the push for using evidence-based practices increases.
The danger is that resources will be redeployed in ways that favor the current
evidence base—no matter what its deficits. This will narrow options for dealing
with learning, behavior, and emotional problems (see Chapter 4). The likelihood
also is that efforts to deal with complex problems in a comprehensive, multifaceted way will be further undermined.

Finding out if a program is any good is a necessity. But in doing so, it is wise
to recognize that evaluation is not simply a technical process. Evaluation involves
decisions about what and how to measure. It involves decisions about what standards to use in making judgments. These decisions are based in great part on values and beliefs.

Limited knowledge, bias, vested interests, and ethical issues are constantly influencing descriptive and judgmental processes and shaping conclusions at the end of an evaluation. While researchers build a better evidence base over the next 20 years, rational judgments must temper the zeal to prematurely claim scientific validation. Everyone concerned about learning, behavior, and emotional problems must increase the efforts to bolster both the scientific and rational bases for enhancing learning supports.

As Dennie Wolf, director of the Opportunity and Accountability Initiative at the Annenberg Institute for School Reform, notes,

> Clearly, we know how to raise standards. However, we are less clear on how to support students in rising to meet those standards.

Then, she asks,

> Having invested heavily in *raising* both the standards and the stakes, what investment are we willing to make to support students in *rising* to meet those standards?

Ultimately, the answer to that question will affect not only individuals with learning, behavior, and emotional problems but the entire society.

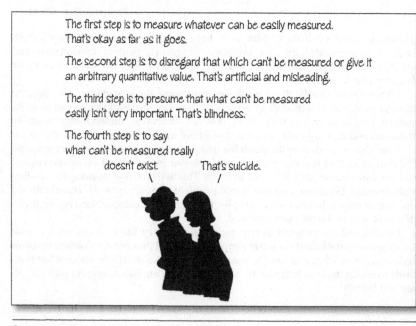

The first step is to measure whatever can be easily measured. That's okay as far as it goes.

The second step is to disregard that which can't be measured or give it an arbitrary quantitative value. That's artificial and misleading.

The third step is to presume that what can't be measured easily isn't very important. That's blindness.

The fourth step is to say what can't be measured really doesn't exist. That's suicide.

Statement attributed to Yankelovich

15

Addressing Systemic Change

The real difficulty in changing the course of any enterprise lies not in developing new ideas but in escaping old ones.

—John Maynard Keynes

Comprehensive school improvements require significant systemic change. As indicated in Chapter 13, our analyses of school improvement planning guides indicate a lack of concern for developing a comprehensive system for addressing psychosocial and mental health concerns. Another striking finding is the widespread failure to plan ways to accomplish desired improvements. Without sophisticated strategic planning for systemic change, schools and districts are unlikely to succeed in moving from where they are to where they want to go.

Moving forward requires understanding the process of systemic change. Success also is built on an appropriate science base, leadership, and adequate resources to facilitate capacity building. With all this in mind, we frame and outline some basic considerations related to planning systemic change.

SCHOOL IMPROVEMENT, PROJECTS, AND SYSTEMIC CHANGE

Despite the nationwide emphasis on mental health in schools and school improvement, the complexities of accomplishing desired systemic changes are given short shrift in policy, research, training, and practice (Adelman & Taylor, 2007a, 2007b; Green & Glasgow, 2006). This is not surprising given that programs to prepare leaders pay so little attention to the processes and problems of systemic change and scale-up (Duffy, 2005; Elmore, 2003, 2004; Fullan, 2005; Glennan, Bodilly, Galegher, & Kerr, 2004; Hargreaves & Fink, 2000; Thomas, 2002).

At this point, we should clarify use of the term *systemic change* in the context of this book. Our focus is on district and school organization and operations and the networks that shape decision making about fundamental changes and their implementation. From this perspective, systemic change involves modifications that amount to a cultural shift in institutionalized values (i.e., reculturalization). For interventionists, the problem is that the greater the distance and dissonance between the current culture of schools and intended school improvements, the greater the difficulty in successfully accomplishing major systemic changes.

Moving forward begins with well-conceived, designed, and implemented prototype innovations. Prototypes for advancing mental health in schools usually are developed and initially implemented as a pilot demonstration at one or more schools. This is particularly the case when the demonstration is funded as a project.

Pilot and project mentality can hamper systemic change. A common tendency of those involved in projects or piloting a new school program is to think of it as time limited. Other school stakeholders also tend to perceive the work as temporary (e.g., "It will end when the grant runs out," or "I've seen so many reforms come and go; this too shall pass."). The history of education is strewn with valuable innovations that were not sustained. Naturally, financial considerations play a role in failures to sustain and replicate, but a widespread *project mentality* also is culpable.

Moving forward with mental health in schools requires much more than implementing a few demonstrations. Any improvement in schooling is only as good as a district's ability to develop and institutionalize it equitably in all its schools. This process often is called diffusion, replication, roll out, or scale-up. The frequent failure to sustain innovations and take them to scale in school districts has increased interest in understanding systemic change as a central concern in school improvement.

FRAMING SYSTEMIC CHANGE CONSIDERATIONS

Our interest in systemic change has evolved over many years of implementing demonstrations and working to institutionalize and diffuse them on a large scale (Adelman & Taylor, 1997b, 2003b, 2006a, 2006d; Taylor, Nelson, & Adelman, 1999). By now, we are fully convinced that advancing the field requires escaping *project mentality* (sometimes referred to as *projectitis*) and becoming sophisticated about facilitating systemic change. Fullan (2005) stresses that what is needed is leadership that "motivates people to take on the complexities and anxieties of difficult change" (p. 104). We would add that such leadership also must develop a refined understanding of how to facilitate systemic change.

In struggling to make sense of systemic change processes, we find it useful to outline major elements, phases, steps, and tasks. We highlight some of this here to convey the nature and scope of what school improvement planners need to address in strategic ways.

Exhibit 55 suggests how major elements involved in designing school improvements are logically connected to considerations about systemic change. That is, the same elements used to frame key intervention concerns apply to systemic change and are intimately linked to the other.

The elements are conceived as encompassing the

- vision, aims, and underlying rationale for what follows;
- resources needed to do the work;
- general functions, major tasks, activities, and phases that must be pursued;
- infrastructure and strategies needed to carry out the functions, tasks, and activities;
- positive and negative results that emerge.

Strategic planning for systemic change in schools and districts should account for each of these elements. The process starts with a clear sense of a prototype. Then, planning delineates how the school will accomplish major changes. At the district level, strategic planning clarifies how the district will facilitate replication and scale-up of prototype practices. (See Adelman & Taylor, 2007b for a discussion of each of the above elements.)

Exhibit 55	Linking Logic Models for Designing School Improvement and Systemic Change

Key considerations with respect to both (1) desired school improvements and (2) *getting from here to there* (e.g., systemic changes):

- What are the vision, long-term aims, and underlying rationale?
- What are the existing resources that might be (re)deployed and woven together to make good progress toward the vision?
- What general functions, major tasks, activities, and phases need to be implemented?
- What infrastructure and strategies are needed to carry out the functions, tasks, and activities?
- What short-term indicators will be used as process benchmarks, what intermediate outcomes will indicate progress toward long-range aims, and how will negative outcomes be identified?

(Continued)

(Continued)

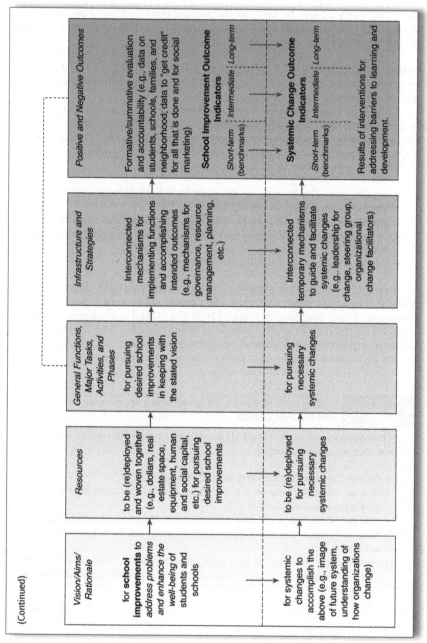

Exhibit 56 briefly highlights key considerations related to planning, implementing, sustaining, and going to scale, including the four phases of the change process. (Here too see Adelman & Taylor, 2007b for a discussion of each cell in the matrix.)

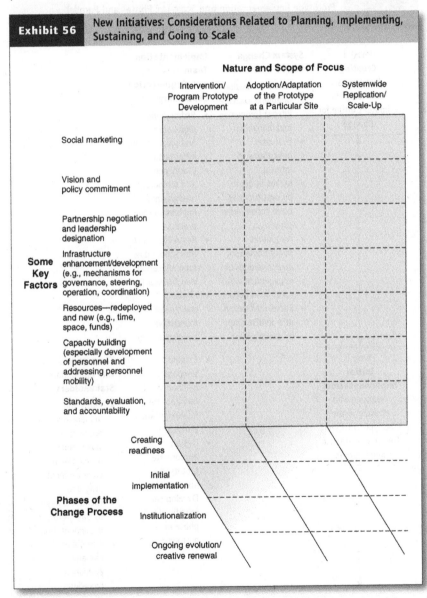

Exhibit 56 New Initiatives: Considerations Related to Planning, Implementing, Sustaining, and Going to Scale

Nature and Scope of Focus

Intervention/Program Prototype Development — Adoption/Adaptation of the Prototype at a Particular Site — Systemwide Replication/Scale-Up

Some Key Factors

- Social marketing
- Vision and policy commitment
- Partnership negotiation and leadership designation
- Infrastructure enhancement/development (e.g., mechanisms for governance, steering, operation, coordination)
- Resources—redeployed and new (e.g., time, space, funds)
- Capacity building (especially development of personnel and addressing personnel mobility)
- Standards, evaluation, and accountability

Phases of the Change Process

- Creating readiness
- Initial implementation
- Institutionalization
- Ongoing evolution/creative renewal

Exhibit 57 highlights a set of parallel and linked tasks related to each of the four phases.

Exhibit 57	Prototype Implementation and Scale-Up: Phases and Parallel and Linked Tasks

Phase I
Creating Readiness: Enhancing the Climate/Culture for Change

System Change Staff

- Disseminates the prototype to create interest (promotion and marketing)
- Evaluates indications of interest
- Makes in-depth presentations to build stakeholder consensus
- Negotiates a policy framework and conditions of engagement with sanctioned bodies
- Elicits ratification and sponsorship by stakeholders

Implementation Team works at site with **Organization Leadership** to

- Redesign the organizational and programmatic infrastructure
- Clarify need to add temporary mechanisms for the implementation process
- Restructure time (the school day, time allocation over the year)
- Conduct stakeholder foundation-building activity

Phase II
Initial Implementation: Adapting and Phasing in the Prototype With Well-Designed Guidance and Support

- Establish temporary mechanisms to facilitate the implementation process
- Design appropriate prototype adaptations
- Develop site-specific plan to phase in prototype

Team works at site with appropriate **Stakeholders**

- Plans and implements ongoing stakeholder development/ empowerment programs
- Facilitates day-by-day prototype implementation
- Establishes formative evaluation procedures

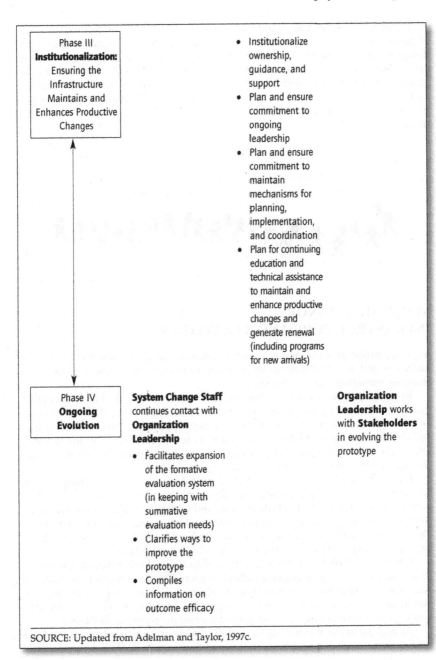

Phase III
Institutionalization:
Ensuring the
Infrastructure
Maintains and
Enhances Productive
Changes

- Institutionalize ownership, guidance, and support
- Plan and ensure commitment to ongoing leadership
- Plan and ensure commitment to maintain mechanisms for planning, implementation, and coordination
- Plan for continuing education and technical assistance to maintain and enhance productive changes and generate renewal (including programs for new arrivals)

Phase IV
**Ongoing
Evolution**

System Change Staff
continues contact with
**Organization
Leadership**

- Facilitates expansion of the formative evaluation system (in keeping with summative evaluation needs)
- Clarifies ways to improve the prototype
- Compiles information on outcome efficacy

**Organization
Leadership** works
with **Stakeholders**
in evolving the
prototype

SOURCE: Updated from Adelman and Taylor, 1997c.

Exhibits 55, 56, and 57 outline fundamental matters for policy makers and planners to address in order to ensure that effective systemic changes are designed, implemented, sustained, and taken to scale. In our experience, the prevailing tendency is to give such matters short shrift. This tendency results in failure to create sufficient readiness for change, develop an effective organizational and operational infrastructure, and strategically plan for start-up and phase-in. Failure to address such fundamentals is a recipe for early innovative implosion.

It is only those who don't care about where they end up who can afford not to be involved in which way they are going.

SYSTEMIC CHANGE INFRASTRUCTURE AND STRATEGIES

Implementation and scaling-up of major systemic changes requires *administrative leadership* and the addition of *temporary infrastructure mechanisms* to facilitate changes, including capacity building.

In general, existing infrastructure mechanisms must be modified in ways that guarantee new policy directions are translated into appropriate daily operations. Well-designed mechanisms ensure local ownership, a critical mass of committed stakeholders, processes that overcome barriers to stakeholders working together effectively, and strategies that mobilize and maintain proactive effort so that changes are implemented with renewal over time.

Rarely do we find situations where a well-designed systemic change infrastructure is in place. More characteristically, ad hoc mechanisms are set in motion with personnel who have too little training and without adequate formative evaluation. Structures, such as teams and collaboratives, commonly operate without clear understanding of functions and major tasks. This, of course, defies the basic organizational principle that structure should follow function.

Effective and linked administrative leadership *at every level* are keys to the success of any systemic change initiative in school districts. Everyone needs to be aware of who is leading and who is accountable for planned changes. Such leaders must be specifically trained to guide systemic change. They must be sitting at key decision-making tables when budget and other fundamental decisions are discussed.

As highlighted in Exhibits 55, 56, and 57, the general functions and major tasks related to sustainability and large-scale replication require dedicated change agent mechanisms that are fully integrated into the infrastructure for school improvement at each school site, for a complex or *family* of schools, and at the district level. Thus, a significant portion of the resources for systemic change must be used to design and implement the set of integrated mechanisms that constitute the temporary, but necessary, infrastructure for steering, facilitating, and evaluating the change process itself.

Mechanisms for System Change

At school and district levels, it helps to think in terms of four key *temporary* systemic change mechanisms. These are (1) a site-based *steering* mechanism to guide and support systemic change activity; (2) a *change agent* who works with the change team and has full-time responsibility for the daily tasks involved in creating readiness and the initial implementation of desired changes; (3) a *change team* (consisting of key stakeholders) that has responsibility for coalition building, implementing the strategic plan, and maintaining daily oversight (including problem solving, conflict resolution, and so forth); and (4) *mentors* and *coaches* who model and teach specific elements of new approaches.

Below, we offer a few introductory points about each of these.

1. *Steering the change process.* A steering mechanism is a key facet of a systemic change infrastructure. Such a mechanism can be a designated individual or a small committee or team. The oversight functions of such a mechanism include ensuring that personnel assigned to facilitate changes (a) maintain a big picture perspective, (b) make appropriate movement toward long-term goals, and (c) have sufficient support and guidance. Where changes are underway at several levels, an interactive interface is needed among separate steering mechanisms. And of course, a regular, interactive interface is needed between steering and organizational governance mechanisms.

A team of *champions* who agree to steer the process is preferable. Such a team provides a broad-based and potent mechanism for guiding change. Steering groups should not be too large. For example, at a school level, membership should include a few well-connected champions and the key change agents (e.g., the administrative leader and other system change staff) who have responsibility for implementing school improvements. To work against the perception of being a closed, elite group, *focus groups* can be hosted to elicit input and feedback, provide information, and problem solve. Those doing the steering must be well versed with respect to what is planned, and they should be highly motivated not just to help get things underway but also to ensure sustainability.

2. *Change agent.* A well-trained change agent is invaluable for facilitating the process of getting from here to there. Such a professional ensures that tasks and concerns are addressed expeditiously. The first focus is on ensuring that capacity is built to accomplish the desired systemic changes. This begins by ensuring an adequate policy and leadership base for implementation is in place. Then, the emphasis is on helping form, train, guide, and support a change *team*, monitor progress, and solve problems.

3. *Change team.* Such a team (which includes various work groups) consists of personnel representing specific programs, administrators, union reps, and staff and other stakeholders who the change agent trains to help facilitate changes. A range of representation enables a blending of agents for change who have responsibility and accountability for addressing the daily concerns. Team functions include helping to create readiness, build coalitions, implement strategic plans, maintain daily oversight, solve problems, resolve stakeholder conflicts, and so forth. After the initial implementation stage, the team works to ensure that functions for maintenance and renewal are adopted by the institutionalized mechanisms.

4. *Mentors and coaches.* During initial implementation, the need for mentors and coaches is acute. Inevitably new ideas, roles, and functions require a variety of stakeholder development activities, including demonstrations of new program elements and infrastructure mechanisms. The designated change agent is among the first providing mentorship. The change team helps identify mentors who have relevant expertise. A regularly accessible cadre of district mentors and coaches is an indispensable resource in responding to stakeholders' calls for help. For some types of change, specially contracted coaches may be needed.

A Bit More About the Functions of a Change Agent and Team

A change agent's core functions require an individual whose background and training have prepared her or him to understand the following:

- The specific systemic changes (content and processes) to be accomplished (In this respect, a change agent must have an understanding of the fundamental concerns underlying the need for change.)
- How to work on changes with different groups of stakeholders

As can be seen in Exhibit 58, the main work revolves around planning and facilitating the following:

- Infrastructure development, maintenance, action, mechanism liaison and interface, and priority setting
- Stakeholder development (coaching—with an emphasis on creating readiness both in terms of motivation and skills; team building; providing technical assistance; organizing basic *cross-disciplinary training*)
- Communication (visibility), resource mapping, analyses, coordination, and integration
- Formative evaluation and rapid problem solving
- Ongoing support

In general, with the change agent initially taking the lead, members of the change team (and its work groups) are catalysts and managers of change. As such, they must ensure the *big picture* is implemented in ways that are true to the vision and compatible with the local culture. The work requires team members

| **Exhibit 58** | Examples of Task Activity for a Change Agent |

1. Infrastructure tasks

  A. Works with governing agents to further clarify and negotiate agreements concerning the following:

    ➢ *Policy changes*

    ➢ *Participating personnel (including administrators authorized to take the lead for systemic changes)*

    ➢ *Time, space, and budget commitments*

  B. Identifies several representatives of stakeholder groups who agree to lead the change team

  C. Helps leaders to identify members for change, program, and work teams and prepare them to carry out functions

2. Stakeholder development

  A. Provides general orientations for governing agents

  B. Provides leadership coaching for site leaders responsible for systemic change

  C. Coaches members of change and work teams

3. Communication (visibility), coordination, and integration

With a view to rectifying problems, monitors to determine whether

  A. information on new directions (including leadership and team functions and membership) has been written up and circulated

  B. leaders and team members are effectively handling priority tasks

  C. change, program, and work teams are effective

  D. communication to and among stakeholders is effective

  E. systems are in place to identify problems related to functioning of infrastructure and communication mechanisms

4. Formative evaluation and rapid problem solving

  A. Works with leaders and team members to develop procedures for formative evaluation and processes that ensure rapid problem solving

  B. Checks regularly on the effectiveness of formative evaluation and rapid problem solving

5. Ongoing support

  A. Offers ongoing coaching on an *on-call* basis

  B. At appropriate points in time, reviews progress and long-range planning, and if necessary, explores ways to improve

  C. Helps participants identify sources for continuing capacity building

who are committed each day to ensuring effective replication and have enough time and ability to attend to details.

Team members help develop linkages among resources, facilitate redesign of regular structural mechanisms, and establish other temporary mechanisms. They also are problem solvers—not only responding as problems arise but also designing strategies to counter anticipated barriers to change, such as negative reactions and dynamics, common factors interfering with working relationships, and system deficiencies. All systemic change benefits when the process enhances empowerment, a sense of community, and general readiness and commitment to new approaches.

As indicated in Exhibit 57, at the district level, the daily operational infrastructure for systemic change calls for a *system change staff*. They provide a necessary organizational base and skilled personnel for diffusing improvements into a school and across a district. Change agents play a key role in rotating among schools to guide the change process. In addition, special *coaches* or mentors can be brought in whenever a specialist is needed to assist in replicating a specific type of improvement. After the initial implementation stage, the change staff works to ensure that functions for maintenance and renewal are adopted by the institutionalized mechanisms.

Once systemic changes have been accomplished effectively, all temporary mechanisms are phased out—with any new roles and functions assimilated into the ongoing operational infrastructure.

> Some years ago, as part of a federal dropout prevention initiative, we developed a change agent position called an Organization Facilitator to aid with major restructuring (Adelman & Taylor, 1997a, 1997b, 1997c; Center for Mental Health in Schools, 2000a, 2001a, 2001b; Taylor, Nelson, & Adelman, 1999). This form of specially trained change agent embodies the expertise to help school sites and complexes substantively implement and institutionalize school improvements. Such an individual provides a change agent for one school or a group of schools. A cadre of such professionals can facilitate change across an entire district. The work can range from facilitating a few key changes to full-scale restructuring.

Strategic Approach for Facilitating Systemic Change

Besides conceptual work, our involvement at state, regional, and local levels requires us to develop a strategic approach for facilitating systemic changes. In doing so, we draw on available literature (see those cited in the Center resources listed at the end of the chapter) and lessons learned in the field. For illustrative purposes, some beginning steps are discussed below.

As we noted already, any move toward substantive systemic change should begin with activity designed to create readiness by enhancing a climate for change. Steps include the following:

- Articulation of a clear, shared vision for the changes (e.g., building interest and consensus; introducing basic concepts to relevant groups of stakeholders)
- Mobilizing interest, consensus, and support among key stakeholders (e.g., identifying champions and other individuals who are committed to the

changes; planning and implementing a *social marketing* strategy to mobilize a critical mass of stakeholder support; planning and implementing strategies to obtain the support of key policy makers, such as administrators and school boards)

- Clarifying feasibility (e.g., how changes can be accomplished; who will lead; what mechanisms can be used to steer and underwrite the change process)
- Ensuring a major policy commitment from all participating stakeholders (e.g., establishing a policy framework that recognizes the importance of the work)
- Negotiating agreements with decision makers and implementers (e.g., about role responsibilities; about how accountability for commitments will be ensured)

This is followed by processes for

- enhancing and/or developing an infrastructure based on a clear articulation of basic functions (e.g., mechanisms for governance and priority setting, steering, operations, resource mapping and coordination).

Pursuing the work requires special attention to the problem of the match between intervention and those who are to change and

- ensuring strong facilitation related to all mechanisms;
- redeploying resources and establishing new ones;
- building capacity (especially personnel development and strategies for addressing personnel and other stakeholder mobility);
- establishing standards, evaluation processes, and accountability procedures.

Because substantive change requires stakeholder readiness and ongoing motivation and capability, key tasks include monitoring these matters and maintaining an ongoing emphasis on social marketing and capacity building.

Systemic changes are not easily accomplished. The process is not a straightforward sequential or linear one. Major institutional changes confront a myriad of political, bureaucratic, and economic difficulties. The many steps and tasks described above clearly call for a high degree of commitment and relentlessness of effort. Moreover, time frames for building capacity to accomplish desired institutional changes must be realistic. Those interested in generating systemic changes must be opportunistic.

A Few Comments About Systemic Change Practices at Schools

Although many of the above points seem self-evident, their profound implications for enhancing mental health in schools and for school improvement in general are widely ignored. As a result, it is no surprise when improvements are not effectively implemented and when so many are not sustained and replicated.

For example, think about the first phase of facilitating systemic change. New collaborative arrangements must be established, and authority (power) redistributed. Key stakeholders and their leadership must understand and commit. School improvement policy and program commitments must be demonstrated through strategic planning and effective allocation and redeployment of resources to facilitate organizational and operational changes at school, complex, and district levels. That is, finances, personnel, time, space, equipment, and other necessary resources must be made available, organized, and used in ways that adequately facilitate the work. Appropriate incentives and safeguards for personnel must be in place as they become enmeshed in the complexities of systemic change.

Moreover, reforms and major school improvements obviously require ensuring that those who carry out necessary functions have adequate training, resources, and support over time. This includes ensuring sufficient resources for scale-up, sustainability, and ongoing capacity building.

An understanding of concepts espoused by community psychologists such as empowering settings and enhancing a sense of community also is useful. A growing body of work suggests that the success of a variety of initiatives depends on interventions that can empower stakeholders and enhance their sense of community (Beeker, Guenther-Grey, & Raj, 1998; Trickett, 2002). However, the proper design of such interventions requires understanding that empowerment is a multifaceted concept. As noted earlier, in discussing power, theoreticians distinguish *power over* from *power to* and *power from*. Power over involves explicit or implicit dominance over others and events; power to is seen as increased opportunities to act; power from implies ability to resist the power of others (Riger, 1993).

Enhancing a sense of community involves ongoing attention to daily experiences. With respect to sustaining initiatives, stakeholders must experience initiative in ways that make them feel they are valued members who are contributing to a collective identity, destiny, and vision. Their work together must be facilitated in ways that enhance feelings of competence, self-determination, and connectedness with and commitment to each other (Deci & Ryan, 1985). As Tom Vander Ark wisely notes, "Effective practices typically evolve over a long period in high-functioning, fully engaged systems" (Vander Ark, 2002).

Projects as Catalysts for Systemic Change

Most demonstration projects and initiatives can be catalysts for systemic change. More to the point, the case frequently is that such projects *must* produce systemic changes or much of what they have developed is not sustained.

Federally funded projects, such as those established through the Safe Schools/Healthy Students initiative and the Integration of Schools and Mental Health Systems, illustrate both the need and opportunity for being a catalytic force. These types of projects are funded with the aim of coalescing school and community collaboration and have a strong focus on enhancing mental health in schools. When such projects enter their final period of federal support, folks usually scramble to find another grant to sustain threatened functions. A few realize that sustainability should not be thought about in terms of hopefully finding more grant money. Rather, they understand the necessity of taking steps from the project's onset to move policy in ways that can sustain the work. Moreover, they understand the importance of embedding changes into a school improvement context.

With specific respect to projects that include new mental health activity, district policy makers and planners generally are pleased by the added resources a project brings. However, they continue to view the new activity as an add-on and seldom integrate it into school improvement planning. This contributes to the fragmentation and marginalization that characterizes mental health in schools and works against sustaining the effort after the project ends.

To counter all this, project staff must approach their special funding as an opportunity to leverage systemic changes. This means negotiating ways into decision making, capacity building, and operational infrastructures. Being at decision-making tables enables direct and ongoing discussion about sustainability and even about replicating the work on a large scale.

However, to be successful at the table, project staff must also embed the work into the broader context of school improvement planning. For example, mental health activity can be presented as an integral part of the type of comprehensive enabling (or learning supports) component described in this book, and such a component can be braided into other school improvement initiatives.

By moving into a catalytic role, project personnel position themselves as a potent force for systemic change. In the process, however, they must not lose sight of a basic reality: *Schools are unlikely to invest and embrace substantive change unless it significantly enhances their capability to meet current accountability indicators.*

CONCLUDING COMMENTS

As Seymour Sarason (1971) stressed a long time ago:

> Good ideas and missionary zeal are sometimes enough to change the thinking of individuals; they are rarely, if ever, effective in changing complicated organizations (like the school) with traditions, dynamics, and goals of their own. (p. 213)

As we have highlighted in this chapter, those who set out to enhance mental health in schools across a district are confronted with two enormous tasks. The first is to develop prototypes; the second involves large-scale replication. One without the other is insufficient. Yet considerably more attention is paid to developing and validating prototypes than to delineating and testing systemic change processes required for sustainability, replication, and scale-up.

We need not belabor all this. Our main intent in including this chapter is to generate greater appreciation for and more attention to the problems of systemic change. Moving forward for mental health in schools requires substantive systemic change. Lack of attention to this reality hampers the field's advancement.

A Few Other Related Center Documents and Publications

Systemic Change for School Improvement: Designing, Implementing, and Sustaining Prototypes and Going to Scale. Available at http://smhp.psych.ucla.edu/pdfdocs/systemic/systemicreport.pdf

Toward a Scale-Up Model for Replicating New Approaches to Schooling. Available at http://smhp.psych.ucla.edu/publications/06%20toward%20a%20scale%20up%20model%20for%20replicating%20new%20approaches.pdf

Scaling-Up Reforms Across A School District. Available at http://smhp.psych.ucla.edu/publications/21%20scalingup%20reforms%20across%20a%20school.pdf

Organization Facilitators: A Change Agent for Systemic School and Community Changes. Available at http://smhp.psych.ucla.edu/pdfdocs/Report/orgfacrep.pdf

On Sustainability of Project Innovations as Systemic Change. Available at http://smhp.psych.ucla.edu/publications/45%20on%20sustainability%20of%20project%20innovations%20as%20systemic%20change.pdf

Systemic Change for School Improvement. (2007). *Journal of Educational and Psychological Consultation, 17,* 55–77. Available on request.

New Initiatives: Considerations Related to Planning, Implementing, Sustaining, and Going to Scale. Available at http://smhp.psych.ucla.edu/pdfdocs/briefs/sustainbrief.pdf

Sustaining School and Community Efforts to Enhance Outcomes for Children and Youth: A Guidebook and Tool Kit. Available at http://smhp.psych.ucla.edu/pdfdocs/sustaining.pdf

Getting From Here to There: A Guidebook for the Enabling Component. Available at http://smhp.psych.ucla.edu/pdfdocs/enabling/gettingfromhere.pdf

Diffusion of Innovations and Science-Based Practices to Address Barriers to Learning and Improve Schools: A Series of Information Resources on Enabling System Change. Available at http://smhp.psych.ucla.edu. As of 2009, this developing series includes the following:

- Brief Overview of Major Concepts From E. M. Rogers' Work on Diffusion of Innovations
- Brief Overview of Malcolm Gladwell's Concept of the Tipping Point
- Some Key Terms Related to Enabling System Change
- Systemic Change for School Improvement
- Change Agent Mechanisms for School Improvement: Infrastructure Not Individuals
- System Change and Empirically Supported Practices: The Implementation Problem
- Policy Implications for Advancing Systemic Change for School Improvement
- Some Key References Related to Enabling System Change

Call to Action

Moving Forward

eaders concerned with advancing mental health in school need to focus on
much more than just increasing clinical services. This is a message long con-
veyed by those who stress that mental *health* is about much more than mental *illness*. Concern for mental health encompasses promoting youth development,
wellness, social and emotional learning, and fostering the emergence of caring,
supportive, nurturing, and just environments.

In the abstract, most stakeholders support all efforts to advance the mental
health field. When it comes to formulating policy, however, competition arises
related to priorities. Advocates for those with serious and chronic personal problems know that not enough services are available and accessible, especially for
low-income families. So these advocates mainly support expansion of specialized clinical services. This makes other mental health concerns, such as promotion of mental health and primary prevention, secondary agenda items in the
competition for sparse resources.

One poignant irony in all this is that advocacy for specialized clinical services has contributed not only to increasing the number of students identified
as having diagnosable problems but also to assigning formal diagnostic labels
to many students manifesting commonplace behavior, learning, and emotional
problems. In the last decade, the number diagnosed as attention deficit
hyperactivity disorder (ADHD), learning disabled (LD), and clinically
depressed has escalated exponentially. How many are misdiagnosed is anyone's guess. However, the probability is that many misdiagnosed students are
consuming specialized resources needed for those with severe and chronic
problems. And the demand for specialized services outstrips supply to an
alarming degree.

Continuing along this path is untenable.

NEEDED: WIDESPREAD ACKNOWLEDGMENT OF THE ZERO SUM GAME

A zero sum game is a situation or interaction in which one participant's gains result only from another's equivalent losses. In trying to make the world a better place for children and adolescents, many advocates feel they must focus strategically and laserlike on one concern because resources are sparse and distributed politically. Thus, they enter into a zero sum game.

The continuing tendency of many advocates for mental health in schools is to compete in this way even though it pits the needs and interests of some youngsters against the needs and interests of others. And too often, it generates counterproductive relationships among school staff and between school and community professionals, with the situation at times exacerbated by narrow pursuit of specific professional guild interests.

Inevitably, some advocacy is necessary for specific groups of children and adolescents. Given current policy inequities, however, those doing the advocacy can only hope for small zero sum successes. With respect to mental health in schools, usually this means immediate specialized help for a few more students but at a cost for others that is seldom articulated.

NEEDED: A NEW ADVOCACY COALITION FOR THE FEW *AND* THE MANY

The mission of schools calls for ensuring that *all* students have an equal opportunity to succeed at school and beyond. Therefore, advocacy for mental health in schools must address the needs and interests of all students. And given that the responsibility for student progress rests so greatly on the shoulders of the adults who teach and those who provide student and school support, advocacy for mental health in schools must encompass a focus on the well-being of staff as well as students.

Anyone who has done a substantive analysis of what schools do to address psychosocial and mental health concerns can articulate a host of deficiencies. Adequate data are available to make the case for systemic changes. The problem is agreeing on an agenda.

Those who view mental health in schools through the lens of providing as many specialized clinical services as possible point to the number who are not served and then advocate for more services. A different agenda surfaces when the situation is viewed by those concerned mainly with classroom management and school discipline interventions. And still other agenda arise when the concerns are promoting youth development, wellness, social and emotional learning, and fostering the emergence of a caring, supportive, and nurturing climate throughout a school.

The different agenda produce ongoing advocacy for a variety of initiatives, such as Positive Behavior Support; Coordinated School Health; Community

Schools; Safe Schools/Healthy Students; Response to Intervention; Early Intervening; social and emotional learning; character education; projects to ameliorate bullying, violence, substance abuse, pregnancy, and dropouts; efforts to enhance school connectedness and student reengagement; and many more. Each initiative focuses on a defined concern; each has a political constituency and a silo of economic support; each has established a niche. And each contributes to the piecemeal, ad hoc, and often simplistic approaches that characterize efforts to address multifaceted problems.

Given that many problems experienced by students arise from the same underlying causes, it makes sense not to consider each separately. Indeed, various policy and practice analyses indicate that it is unwise to do so. The complexity of factors interfering with learning and teaching underscore the need to coalesce efforts to address the variety of factors that interfere with a school accomplishing its mission. Such an agenda embeds the focus on those needing specialized assistance within the broader school improvement agenda for addressing barriers to learning, development, and teaching.

STUDENT SUPPORT PROFESSIONALS

Time to Awaken the Sleeping Giant

Our center's policy and program analyses make it clear that student support personnel are not appropriately accounted for in school improvement planning and implementation. In all likelihood, this is the result of the absence of such professionals from the tables where school improvement plans and decisions are made. This is the case for those who are employed by schools and those from the community who colocate at schools.

We have come to think of the collective mass of student support professionals as a sleeping giant. And our reading of literature and politics suggests that sleeping giants often are at risk. Before it is too late, such professionals must become more proactive in school improvement planning. In doing so, they must find their way to planning and decision-making tables; they must come with sophisticated and detailed analyses of how the school is and is not addressing barriers to learning and teaching; they must be prepared to articulate ways for a school to develop a comprehensive system to address such barriers.

Also, in coming to the table, student support personnel must place less emphasis on intervention ownership and more on accomplishing desired outcomes through flexible and expanded roles and functions. Such a stance recognizes the underlying commonalities among a variety of school concerns and intervention strategies. It requires delineating generic functions for all student support professionals to play a role in developing a comprehensive system of learning supports as a prime component of school improvement, and it embeds their specialized functions into that context.

With all this in mind, pre-inservice and inservice programs that prepare student support professionals and the associations and guilds representing such professionals must accelerate work on defining expanded roles and functions. This will lead to increased attention to cross-disciplinary training and inter-professional education and fundamental changes in the professional preparation, credentialing, and licensing of those who work in and with schools.

THE AIM IS TO TRANSFORM HOW SCHOOLS ADDRESS BARRIERS TO LEARNING, DEVELOPMENT, AND TEACHING

Schools must fundamentally *transform* the ways in which they address barriers to learning, development, and teaching. Such a transformation is essential to enhancing achievement for all, closing the achievement gap, reducing dropouts, and increasing the opportunity for schools to be valued as treasures in their neighborhood.

For some time, we have suggested that such transformation requires reform initiatives that confront four fundamental and interrelated considerations. The need is to do the following:

1. *Expand policy*—broadening policy for school improvement to fully integrate, as primary and essential, a comprehensive, multifaceted, and cohesive system for addressing barriers to learning and teaching, with school safety embedded in natural and authentic ways

2. *Reframe interventions in classrooms and schoolwide*—unifying the fragmented interventions used to address barriers to learning and teaching and promote healthy development under a framework that can guide development of a comprehensive system at every school

3. *Reconceive infrastructure*—reworking the operational and organizational infrastructure for a school, a family of schools, the district, and for school-family-community collaboration with a view to weaving resources together to develop a comprehensive system

4. *Rethink the implementation problem*—framing the phases and tasks involved in "getting from here to there" in terms of widespread diffusion of innovations in organized settings that have well-established institutional cultures and systems.

As these four considerations underscore, enabling all students to have an equal opportunity to succeed at school requires moving significantly beyond prevailing thinking and school improvement tinkering.

The next decade must mark a turning point for how schools, families, and communities address the problems of children and youth. In particular, the focus must be on initiatives to transform how schools work to prevent and ameliorate the many problems experienced by too many students. The call is for redesigning student and learning supports to meet the needs of all students. To borrow a phrase from John Dewey, any other agenda for public schools is "narrow and unlovely."

WHERE TO BEGIN

A good starting place is to revise policy that perpetuates narrow-focused, categorical approaches. Current policy is a grossly inadequate response to the many complex factors that interfere with positive development, learning, and teaching. Such policy promotes an orientation that overemphasizes individually prescribed treatment services to the detriment of prevention programs, results in marginalized and fragmented interventions, and undervalues the human and social capital indigenous to every neighborhood. School improvement policy must be expanded to support development of the type of comprehensive, multifaceted, and cohesive approach that can effectively address barriers to learning and teaching. To do less is to make value statements such as, "We want all children to succeed," simply rhetorical pronouncements.

Given sparse school resources, moves toward transformation must be accomplished by rethinking and redeploying how existing resources are used and by taking advantage of the natural opportunities at schools for countering problems and promoting personal and social growth. Staff and students need to feel positive about themselves and what they are doing if they are to cope with challenges proactively and effectively. Every school needs to commit to fostering staff and student strengths and creating an atmosphere that encourages mutual support, caring, and sense of community. For example, a welcoming induction and ongoing social support are critical elements both in creating a positive sense of community and in facilitating staff and student school adjustment and performance. Schoolwide strategies for welcoming and supporting staff, students, and families at school *every day* are part of creating a safe and healthy school—one where staff, students, and families interact positively and identify with the school and its goals.

We must and we can move forward.

Appendix

Leadership at a School Site for an Enabling or Learning Supports Component

JOB DESCRIPTIONS

Available at http://smhp.psych.ucla.edu/pdfdocs/studentsupport/toolkit/aidd.pdf

Given that an Enabling or Learning Supports Component is one of three primary and essential components of a comprehensive school reform model, it is imperative to have designated administrative and staff leadership. These may be specified as the Enabling or Learning Supports Component's:

- *Administrative Lead*—may be an assistant principal, dean, or other leader who regularly sits at administrative and decision making *tables*
- *Staff Lead for Daily Operations*—may be a support service staff member (e.g., a school psychologist, social worker, counselor nurse), a program coordinator, a teacher with special interest in this area

These leaders, along with other key staff, embody the vision for the Enabling or Learning Supports Component. Their job descriptions should delineate specific functions related to their roles, responsibilities, and accountabilities.

The major functions for these lead personnel involve the following spheres of activity with respect to addressing barriers to student learning and promoting healthy development:

I. **Enhancing interventions and related systems within the school**

- Coordination and integration of programs, services, and systems
- Development of programs, services, and systems

II. Enhancing school-community linkages and partnerships through coordination and integration of school-community resources and systems

III. Capacity building (including stakeholder development)

Administrative Lead for an Enabling or Learning Supports Component

For the Enabling or Learning Supports Component to be, in fact, one of three primary and essential components in school improvement, it is imperative to have an administrative leader who spends at least 50% of each day pursuing functions relevant to the component. This leader must ensure that the school's governance and advisory bodies and staff have an appropriate appreciation of the component and account for it in all planning and decision making.

Examples of Specific Job Duties

- Represents the Enabling or Learning Supports Component at the decision-making and administrative tables to address policy implementation, budget allocations, operational planning, infrastructure development and maintenance, interface with instruction and governance, information management, development of an effective communication system, development of an effective system for evaluation and accountability with an emphasis on positive accomplishments and quality improvement
- Provides support, guidance, visibility, public relations, and advocacy for the component at the school and in the community (e.g., maintaining a high level of interest, support, and involvement with respect to the component)
- Ensures effective communication, coordination, and integration among those involved with the component and among the three components (i.e., the Enabling and Learning Supports Component, the Instructional Component, and the Management and Governance Component
- Leads the Component Steering Committee that reviews, guides, and monitors progress and long-range plans, problem solves, and acts as a catalyst to keep the component linked to the Instruction and Management and Governance Components
- Participates on the Learning Supports Resource Team to facilitate progress related to plans and priorities for the component
- Mentors and helps restructure the roles and functions of key Learning Supports staff (e.g., pupil services personnel and others whose roles and functions fall within the arenas of the component); in particular, helps redefine traditional pupil-service professionals' roles and functions in ways that enables them to contribute to all six arenas of the component
- Anticipates and identifies problems and provides rapid problem solving (including a focus on morale)

- Identifies capacity-building impact and future needs related to the component (e.g., status of stakeholder development and particularly inservice staff development) and takes steps to ensure that plans are made to meet needs and that an appropriate amount of capacity building is devoted to the component
- Meets with the staff lead for daily Learning Supports operations on a regular basis to review progress related to the components and to discuss and advocate for ways to enhance progress

Staff Lead for Daily Operations of
an Enabling or Learning Supports Component

The staff lead works under the direct supervision of the school's administrative lead for the component. The job entails working with staff and community resources to develop, over time, a full array of programs and services to address barriers to student learning and promote healthy development by melding school, community, and home resources together. Moreover, it involves doing so in a way that ensures programs are fully integrated with each other and with the Instructional and Management and Governance Components at the school.

The essence of the staff lead's day-by-day functions is to be responsible and accountable for ongoing progress in developing a comprehensive, multifaceted, and integrated approach to addressing barriers to student learning and promoting healthy development. This encompasses systems related to (1) a full continuum of interventions ranging from primary prevention through early intervention to treatment of serious problems and (2) programs and services in all content arenas of an Enabling or Learning Supports Component. (Note: The arenas have been delineated as follows: (a) enhancing regular classroom strategies to enable learning, (b) providing support for the many transitions experienced by students and families, (c) increasing home and school connections, (d) responding to and preventing crises, (e) facilitating student and family access to effective services and special assistance as needed, and (f) expanding community involvement and support.)

Examples of Specific Job Duties

- Has daily responsibility to advance the agenda for the component, carries out daily tasks involved in enhancing the component, ensures that system and program activity is operating effectively, provides daily problem solving related to systems and programs
- Organizes and coaches the Learning Supports Resource Team and its various work groups
- Monitors progress related to plans and priorities formulated for the component
- Monitors current component programs to ensure they are functioning well and takes steps to improve their functioning and ongoing development (e.g., ensuring program availability, access, and effectiveness)

- Participates in the Leadership Group to contribute to efforts for reviewing, guiding, and monitoring progress and long-range plans, problem solving, and effectively linking with the Instructional and Management and Governance Components
- Provides support, guidance, visibility, public relations, and advocacy for the component at the school and in the community (e.g., maintaining a high level of interest, support, and involvement with respect to the component)
- Supports capacity building for all stakeholders (staff, family members, community members)
- Ensures all new students, families, and staff are provided with a welcome and orientation to the school and the activities related to addressing barriers to learning and promoting healthy development
- Coordinates activity taking place in the Family Center (where one is in operation)
- Ensures effective communication, coordination, and integration among those involved with the component and with the Instructional and Management and Governance Components
- Anticipates and identifies problems and provides rapid problem solving (including a focus on morale)
- Acts as the liaison between the school and other entities (e.g., community resources) that work with the site related to enabling activity
- Ensures that the activities of other entities (e.g., community resources) that work with the site related to addressing barriers to learning and promoting healthy development operate under the umbrella of the component and are well coordinated and integrated with daily activities
- Meets with the administrative lead for the component on a regular basis to discuss and advocate for ways to enhance progress

---

Examples of Generic Criteria for Evaluating Performance for This Position

I. Related to interventions to enhance systems within schools

A. Coordinates and integrates programs, services, and systems (e.g., demonstrates the ability to plan, implement, and evaluate mechanisms for collaborating with colleagues to ensure activities are carried out in the most equitable and cost-effective manner consistent with legal and ethical standards for practice—examples of mechanisms include case-oriented teams; resource-oriented teams; consultation, coaching and mentoring mechanisms; triage, referral, and care monitoring systems; crisis teams)

B. Facilitates development of programs, services, and systems (e.g., demonstrates the ability to enhance development of a comprehensive, multifaceted, and integrated continuum of interventions for equitably addressing barriers to learning and promoting healthy development; works

(Continued)

(Continued)

effectively to bring others together to improve existing interventions and to fill gaps related to needed prevention programs, early-after-onset interventions, and specialized assistance for students and families)

II. Related to interventions to enhance school-community linkages and partnerships

Coordinates and integrates school-community resources and systems (e.g., demonstrates the ability to plan, implement, and evaluate mechanisms for collaborating with community entities; facilitates weaving together of school and community resources and systems to enhance current activity; enhances development of a comprehensive, multifaceted, and integrated continuum of interventions for a diverse range of students and their families)

III. Related to capacity building

Supervises professionals in training; facilitates welcoming, orientation, and induction of new staff, families, and students; represents component in planning arenas where budget, space, and other capacity-building matters are decided (e.g., demonstrates the ability to coach, mentor, and supervise professionals in training; provides orientation to the Learning Support component for newly hired personnel; ensures effective support for transitions of all newcomers)

References

Adelman, H. S. (1995a). Clinical psychology: Beyond psychopathology and clinical interventions. *Clinical Psychology, Science and Practice, 2,* 28–44.

Adelman, H. S. (1995b). Education reform: Broadening the focus. *Psychological Science, 6,* 61–62.

Adelman, H. S. (1996a). Restructuring education support services and integrating community resources: Beyond the full service school model. *School Psychology Review, 25,* 431–445.

Adelman, H. S. (l996b). *Restructuring support services: Toward a comprehensive approach.* Kent, OH: American School Health Association.

Adelman, H. S., & Taylor, L. (1993). *Learning problems and learning disabilities: Moving forward.* Pacific Grove, CA: Brooks/Cole.

Adelman, H. S., & Taylor, L. (1994). *On understanding intervention in psychology and education.* Westport, CT: Praeger.

Adelman, H. S., & Taylor, L. (1997a). Addressing barriers to learning: Beyond school-linked services and full service schools. *American Journal of Orthopsychiatry, 67,* 408–421.

Adelman, H. S., & Taylor, L. (1997b). Restructuring education support services and integrating community resources: Beyond the full-service school model. *School Psychology Review, 25,* 431–445.

Adelman, H. S., & Taylor, L. (1997c). Toward a scale-up model for replicating new approaches to schooling. *Journal of Educational and Psychological Consultation, 8,* 197–230.

Adelman, H. S., & Taylor, L. (1998). Reframing mental health in schools and expanding school reform. *Educational Psychologist, 33,* 135–152.

Adelman, H. S., & Taylor, L. (2000a). Looking at school health and school reform policy through the lens of addressing barriers to learning. *Children's Services: Social Policy, Research, and Practice, 3,* 117–132.

Adelman, H. S., & Taylor, L. (2000b). Promoting mental health in schools in the midst of school reform. *Journal of School Health, 70,* 171–178.

Adelman, H. S., & Taylor, L. (2000c). Shaping the future of mental health in schools. *Psychology in the Schools, 37,* 49–60.

Adelman, H. S., & Taylor, L. (2002). Building comprehensive, multifaceted, and integrated approaches to address barriers to student learning. *Childhood Education, 78,* 261–268.

Adelman, H. S., & Taylor, L. (2003a). Creating school and community partnerships for substance abuse prevention programs. *Journal of Primary Prevention, 23,* 331–369.

Adelman, H. S., & Taylor, L. (2003b). On sustainability of project innovations as systemic change. *Journal of Educational and Psychological Consultation, 14,* 1–26.

Several hundred references to published works of direct relevance to mental health in schools are provided on the Center's Web site—see http://smhp.psych.ucla.edu/qf/references.htm

In addition, see many other special reports, briefs, and materials developed by Adelman and Taylor and their staff at the national Center for Mental Health in Schools (operating under the auspices of the School Mental Health Project at UCLA). Go to http://smhp.psych.ucla.edu and click on Resources and Materials.

Adelman, H. S., & Taylor, L. (2003c). Toward a comprehensive policy vision for mental health in schools. In M. Weist, S. Evans, & N. Lever (Eds.), *Handbook of school mental health programs*. New York: Kluwer.

Adelman, H. S., & Taylor, L. (2006a). *The implementation guide to student learning supports in the classroom and schoolwide: New directions for addressing barriers to learning*. Thousand Oaks, CA: Corwin.

Adelman, H. S., & Taylor, L. (2006b). Mapping a school's resources to improve their use in preventing and ameliorating problems. In C. Franklin, M. B. Harris, & P. Allen-Mears (Eds.), *School social work and mental health workers training and resource manual*. New York: Oxford University Press.

Adelman, H. S., & Taylor, L. (2006c). Mental health in schools and public health. *Public Health Reports, 121,* 294–298.

Adelman, H. S., & Taylor, L. (2006d). *The school leaders guide to student learning supports: New directions for addressing barriers to learning*. Thousand Oaks, CA: Corwin.

Adelman, H. S., & Taylor, L. (2007a). School improvement: A systemic view of what's missing and what to do about it. In B. Despres (Ed.), *Systems thinkers in action: A field guide for effective change leadership in education*. Rowman & Littlefield Education.

Adelman, H. S., & Taylor, L. (2007b). Systemic change for school improvement. *Journal of Educational and Psychological Consultation, 17,* 55–77.

Adelman, H. S., & Taylor, L. (2008). Schoolwide approaches to addressing barriers to learning and teaching. In J. Cummings & E. Doll (Eds.), *Transforming school mental health services: Population-based approaches to promoting the competency and wellness of children*. Thousand Oaks, CA: Corwin.

Adelman, H. S., & Taylor, L. (2009). Ending the marginalization of mental health in schools: A comprehensive approach. In R. Christner & R. Mennuti (Eds.), *School-based mental health: A practitioner's guide to comparative practices*. New York: Routledge.

American Federation of Teachers. (2007). *Meeting the challenge: Recruiting and retaining teachers in hard-to-staff schools*. Washington, DC: Author. Retrieved July 2008, from http://www.aft.org/pubs-reports/downloads/teachers/h2s.pdf

American Psychiatric Association. (1994). *Diagnostic and statistical manual of mental disorders* (4th ed.). Washington, DC: Author.

American Youth Policy Forum. (2000). *High schools of the millennium report*. Washington, DC: Author.

Anglin, T. M. (2003). Mental health in school: Program of the federal government. In M. Weist, S. Evans, & N. Lever (Eds.), *Handbook of school mental health programs: Advancing practice and research*. Norwell, MA: Kluwer Academic Publishers.

Association for Supervision and Curriculum Development. (2000, October). *SmartBrief*. Available at http://www.ascd.org/

Association for Supervision and Curriculum Development. (2007). "New compact" to educate the whole child. *Education Update, 49.* Retrieved from http://www.ascd.org/learningcompact

Atkins, M. S., Graczyk, P. A., Frazier, S. L., & Abdul-Adil, J. (2003). Toward a new model of promoting urban children's mental health: Accessible, effective, and sustainable school-based mental health services. *School Psychology Review, 32,* 503–514.

Barnett, J. E., & Cooper, N. (2009). Creating a culture of self-care. *Clinical Psychology: Science and Practice, 16,* 16–20.

Baumgartner, L. (1946). Some phases of school health services. *American Journal of Public Health, 36,* 629–635.

Bear, G. G. (1995). Best practices in school discipline. In A. Thomas & J. Grimes (Eds.), *Best practices in school psychology III*. Washington, DC: National Association of School Psychologists.

Bear, G. G. (2008). Schoolwide approaches to behavior problems. In B. Doll & J. A. Cummings (Eds.), *Transforming school mental health services*. Thousand Oaks, CA: Corwin.

Beeker, C., Guenther-Grey, C., & Raj, A. (1998). Community empowerment paradigm drift and the primary prevention of HIV/AIDS. *Social Science Medicine, 46,* 831–842.

Benedict, R. (1934). *Patterns of culture*. Boston: Houghton Mifflin.

Blank, M., Berg, A., & Melaville, A. (2006). *Community-based learning*. Washington, DC: Coalition for Community Schools.

Blank, M. J., Melaville, A., & Shah, B. P. (2004). *Making the difference: Research and practice in community schools.* Washington, DC: Coalition for Community Schools. Retrieved July 17, 2006, from http://www.communityschools.org/CCSFullReport.pdf

Bodilly, S., Chun, J., Ikemoto, G., & Stockly, S. (2004). *Challenges and potential of a collaborative approach to education reform.* Santa Monica, CA: RAND. Available at http://www.rand.org/pubs/monographs/MG216

Brener, N. D., Weist, M., Adelman, H., Taylor, L., & Vernon-Smiley, M. (2007). Mental health and social services: Results from the School Health Policies and Programs Study 2006. *Journal of School health, 77,* 486–499. Retrieved from http://www.ashaweb.org/files/public/JOSH_1007/josh77_8_brener_p486.pdf

Brooks-Gunn, J., & Duncan, G. J. (1997). The effects of poverty on children. *The Future of Children, 7,* 55–71.

Brophy, J. (2004). *Motivating students to learn* (2nd ed.). Mahwah, NJ: Lawrence Erlbaum.

Bryk, A. S., & Schneider, B. L. (2002). *Trust in schools: A core resource for improvement.* New York: Russell Sage Foundation.

Bunce, D., & West, M. A. (1996). Stress management and innovation interventions at work. *Human Relations, 49,* 209–231.

Burns, B. J., Costello, E. J., Angold, A., Tweed., D., Stangl, D., Farmer, E., & Erkanli, A. (1995). Children's mental health service use across service sectors. *Health Affairs, 14,* 147–159.

Califano, J. (1977). School health message. *Journal of School Health, 47,* 395–396.

Caplan, P. J., & Cosgrove, L. (Eds.). (2004). *Bias in psychiatric diagnosis. How perspectives and politics replace science in mental health.* Lanham, MD: Rowman & Littlefield.

Carlson, C., Paavola, J., & Talley, R. (1995). Historical, current, and future models of schools as health care delivery settings. *School Psychology Quarterly, 10,* 184–202.

Carnegie Council on Adolescent Development: Task Force on Education of Young Adolescents. (1989). *Turning points: Preparing American youth for the 21st century.* Washington, DC: Author.

Catalano, R. F., Berglund, M. L., Ryan, J. A. M., Lonczak, H. S., & Hawkins, J. D. (2004). Positive youth development in the United States: Research findings on evaluations of positive youth development programs. *The ANNALS of the American Academy of Political and Social Science, 591,* 98–124.

Center for Mental Health in Schools. (1996). *Policies and practices for addressing barriers to learning: Current status and new directions.* Los Angeles: Author. Available at http://smhp.psych.ucla.edu/pdfdocs/newdirections/policiesfull.pdf

Center for Mental Health in Schools. (1997). *Addressing barriers to student learning: Closing gaps in school/community policy and practice.* Los Angeles: Author. Available at http://smhp.psych.ucla.edu/pdfdocs/barriers/closinggaps.pdf

Center for Mental Health in Schools. (2000a). *Organization facilitators: A change agent for systemic school and community changes.* Los Angeles: Author. Available at http://smhp.psych.ucla.edu/pdfdocs/Report/orgfacrep.pdf

Center for Mental Health in Schools. (2000b). *A sampling of outcome findings from interventions relevant to addressing barriers to learning.* Los Angeles: Author. Available at http://smhp.psych.ucla.edu/pdfdocs/Sampler/Outcome/outcome.pdf

Center for Mental Health in Schools. (2001a). *Enhancing classroom approaches for addressing barriers to learning: Classroom-focused enabling.* Los Angeles: Author. Available at http://smhp.psych.ucla.edu/pdfdocs/contedu/cfe.pdf

Center for Mental Health in Schools. (2001b). *Sustaining school-community partnerships to enhance outcomes for children and youth: A guidebook and tool kit.* Los Angeles: Author. Available at http://smhp.psych.ucla.edu/pdfdocs/sustaining.pdf

Center for Mental Health in Schools. (2002). *Report from the leadership summit on student support staff: Moving in new directions through school improvement—a call to action.* Los Angeles: Author. Available at http://smhp.psych.ucla.edu/summit2002/calltoactionreport.pdf

Center for Mental Health in Schools. (2003a). *Leadership training: Moving in new directions for student support.* Los Angeles: Author. Available at http://smhp.psych.ucla.edu/pdfdocs/contedu/movinginnewdirections.pdf

Center for Mental Health in Schools. (2003b). *Youngsters' mental health and psychosocial problems: What are the data?* Los Angeles, CA: Author. Available at http://smhp.psych.ucla.edu/pdfdocs/prevalence/youthMH.pdf

Center for Mental Health in Schools. (2004a). *Addressing barriers to student learning & promoting healthy development: A usable research-base.* Los Angeles: Author. Available at http://smhp.psych.ucla.edu/pdfdocs/briefs/BarriersBrief.pdf

Center for Mental Health in Schools. (2004b). *Integrating agendas for mental health in schools into the recommendations of the President's New Freedom Commission on Mental Health.* Los Angeles: Author. Available at http://smhp.psych.ucla.edu/pdfdocs/newfreedomcommisison/newfreedbrief.pdf

Center for Mental Health in Schools. (2004c). *Understanding and minimizing staff burnout.* Los Angeles: Author. Available at http://smhp.psych.ucla.edu/pdfdocs/Burnout/burn1.pdf

Center for Mental Health in Schools. (2005a). *Addressing what's missing in school improvement planning: Expanding standards and accountability to encompass an enabling or learning supports component.* Los Angeles: Author.

Center for Mental Health in Schools. (2005b). *Another initiative? Where does it fit? A unifying framework and an integrated infrastructure for schools to address barriers to learning and promote healthy development.* Los Angeles: Author. Available at http://smhp.psych.ucla.edu/pdfdocs/infrastructure/anotherinitiative-exec.pdf

Center for Mental Health in Schools. (2005c). School-community partnerships: A guide (Rev.). Los Angeles: Author. http://smhp.psych.ucla.edu/pdfdocs/guides/schoolcomm.pdf

Center for Mental Health in Schools. (2005d). *School improvement planning: What's missing?* Los Angeles: Author. Available at http://smhp.psych.ucla.edu/whatsmissing.htm

Center for Mental Health in Schools. (2007a). The current status of mental health in schools: A policy and practice analysis. Los Angeles: Author. Available at http://smhp.psych.ucla.edu/pdfdocs/currentstatusmh/Report.pdf

Center for Mental Health in Schools. (2007b). *Where's it happening? Examples of new directions for student support & lessons learned.* Los Angeles: Author. Available at http://smhp.psych.ucla.edu/summit2002/wheresithappening.htm

Center for Mental Health in Schools. (2008). Preparing all education personnel to address barriers to learning & teaching. Los Angeles: Author. Available at http://smhp.psych.ucla.edu/pdfdocs/preparingall.pdf

Center for the Future of Children. (1992). *The future of children: School-linked services.* 2. Los Altos, CA: David and Lucille Packard Foundation.

Centers for Disease Control and Prevention. (2005). *Mental health in the United States: Health care and well being of children with chronic emotional, behavioral, or developmental problems—United States, 2001.* Washington, DC: U.S. Government Printing Office. Available at http://www.cdc.gov/mmwr/preview/mmwrhtml/mm5439a3.htm

Centers for Disease Control and Prevention. (2007). *School health policies and program study.* Available at http://www.cdc.gov/Features/SchoolHealth/

Centers for Law and the Public's Health. (2008). A CDC review of school laws and policies concerning child and adolescent health. *Journal of School Health, 78,* February issue. Available at http://www.ashaweb.org/i4a/pages/index.cfm?pageid=3341#school_laws_and_policies

Charcot, J. M. (1857). *De l'expectoration en medicine. Charcot-Leyden crystals.* Available at http://www.whonamedit.com

Chernis, C. (1995). *Beyond burnout: Helping teachers, nurses, therapists, and lawyers recover from stress and disillusionment.* New York: Routledge.

Christenson, S. L., Whitehouse, E. M., & VanGetson, G. R. (2008). Partnering with families to enhance students' mental health. In B. Doll & J. A. Cummings (Eds.), *Transforming school mental health services.* Thousand Oaks, CA: Corwin.

Christner, R. & Mennuti, R. (Eds.). (2009). *School-based mental health: A practitioner's guide to comparative practices.* New York: Routledge.

Collaboration for Academic, Social, and Emotional Learning. (2003). *Safe and sound: An educational leader's guide to evidence-based social and emotional learning (SEL) programs.* Chicago: Author

Corey, G. (2008). *Theory and practice of counseling and psychotherapy.* Pacific Grove, CA: Brooks/Cole.

Cullen, J. B. (1999). *The impact of fiscal incentives on student disability rates.* National Bureau of Economic Research, Working Paper 7173. Available at http://www.nber.org/papers/w7173

Deci, E. L., & Ryan, R. M. (1985). *Intrinsic motivation and self-determination in human behavior.* New York: Plenum.

Deci, E. L., & Ryan, R. M. (Eds.). (2002). *Handbook of self-determination research.* Rochester, NY: University of Rochester Press.

Dishion, T. J., & Dodge, K. A. (2005). Peer contagion in interventions for children and adolescents: Moving towards an understanding of the ecology and dynamics of change. *Journal of Abnormal Child Psychology, 33*, 395–400.

Doll, B., & Cummings, J. A. (2008). Why population-based services are essential for school mental health, and how to make them happen at your school. In B. Doll & J. A. Cummings (Eds.), *Transforming school mental health services.* Thousand Oaks, CA: Corwin.

Dryfoos, J., & Maguire, S. (2002). *Inside full service community schools.* Thousand Oaks, CA: Corwin.

Dryfoos, J. G. (1990). *Adolescents at risk: Prevalence and incidence.* New York: Oxford University Press.

Dryfoos, J. G. (1994). *Full-service schools.* San Francisco: Jossey-Bass.

Dryfoos, J. G. (2003). *Evaluation of community schools: Findings to date.* Retrieved July 1, 2007, from http://www.communityschools.org/Resources/evalcontents.html

Duffy, F. M. (2005). *Power, politics, and ethics: Dynamic leadership for whole-system change in school districts.* Lanham, MD: Rowman & Littlefield Education.

Dynarski, M., Clarke, L., Cobb, B., Finn, J., Rumberger, R., & Smink, J. (2008). *Dropout prevention: A practice guide.* Washington, DC: USDOE. http://ies.ed.gov/ncee/wwc/pdf/practiceguides/dp_pg_090308.pdf

EdSource. (2006, June). *Similar students, different results: Why do some schools do better?* Mountain View, CA: Author. Retrieved July 1, 2007, from http://www.edsource.org/pdf/simstusumm06.pdf

Elias, M. J., & Barbarasch, B. (2009). Fostering social competence in schools. In R. Christner & R. Mennuti (Eds.), *School-based mental health: A practitioner's guide to comparative practices.* New York: Routledge.

Elias, M. J., Zins, J. E., Graczyk, P. A., & Weissberg, R. P. (2003). Implementation, sustainability, and scaling up of social-emotional and academic innovations in public schools. *School Psychology Review 32*, 303–319.

Elmore, R. F. (2003). *Knowing the right thing to do: School improvement and performance-based accountability.* Washington, DC: NGA Center for Best Practices. Available at http://www.nga.org/cda/files/0803knowing.pdf

Elmore, R. F. (2004). *School reform from the inside out: Policy, practice, and performance.* Cambridge, MA: Harvard Educational Publishing Group.

Epstein, J. L., Coates, L., Salinas, K. C., & Sanders, M. G. (2002). *School, family, and community partnerships: Your handbook for action* (2nd ed.). Thousand Oaks, CA: Corwin.

Felner, R. D., Seitsinger, A. M., Brand, S., Burns, A., & Bolton, N. (2008). Creating small learning communities: Lessons from the Project on High Performing Learning Communities about "what works" in creating productive, developmentally enhancing, learning contexts. *Educational Psychologist, 42*, 209–221.

Flaherty, L. T., Weist, M. D., & Warner, B. S. (1996). School-based mental health services in the United States: History, current models, and needs. *Community Mental Health Journal, 25*, 341–352.

Forum on Child and Family Statistics. (2007). *America's children: Key national indicators of well-being.* Washington, DC: Federal Interagency Forum on Child and Family Statistics. Available at http://www.childstats.gov/americaschildren/

Foster, S., Rollefson, M., Doksum, T., Noonan, D., Robinson, G. & Teich, J. (2005). *School mental health services in the United States, 2002–2003.* DHHS Pub. No. (SMA) 05-4068. Rockville, MD: Center for Mental Health Services, Substance Abuse and Mental Health Services Administration. Available at http://www.mentalhealth.samhsa.gov/publications/allpubs/sma05-4068/

Fraser, B. J. (1998). Classroom environment instruments: Development, validity, and applications. *Learning Environments Research, 1*, 7–33.

Fredricks, J. A., Blumenfeld, P. C., & Paris, A. H. (2004). School engagement: Potential of the concept, state of the evidence. *Review of Educational Research, 74,* 59–109.

Freiberg, H. J. (Ed.). (1999). *School climate: Measuring, improving, and sustaining healthy learning environments.* London: Falmer Press.

Fullan, M. G. (2005). *Leadership & sustainability: System thinkers in action.* Thousand Oaks, CA: Corwin.

Garbarino, J. (1995). *Raising children in a socially toxic environment.* San Francisco: Jossey-Bass.

Glennan, T. K., Bodilly, S. J., Galegher, J., & Kerr, K. A. (Eds.). (2004). *Expanding the reach of education reforms: Perspectives from leaders in the scale-up of educational interventions.* Santa Monica, CA: RAND.

Graczyk, P. A., Domitrovich, C. E., & Zins, J. E. (2003). Facilitating the implementation of evidence-based prevention and mental health promotion efforts in schools. In M. D. Weist, S. W. Evans, & N. A. Lever (Eds.), *Handbook of school mental health: Advancing practice and research.* New York: Kluwer Academic/Plenum Publishers.

Gray, G., Young, I., & Barnekow, V. (2006). *Developing a health-promoting school.* Available at http://www.euro.who.int/document/e90053.pdf

Green, L. W., & Glasgow, R. E. (2006). Evaluating the relevance, generalizability, and applicability of research. *Evaluation and the Health Professions, 29,* 126–153.

Greenberg, M. T., Domitrovich, C., Bumbarger, B. (1999). *Preventing mental disorder in school-aged children: A review of the effectiveness of prevention programs.* Report submitted to The Center for Mental Health Services (SAMHSA), Prevention Research Center, Pennsylvania State University. Available at http://www.psu.edu/dept/prevention/

Greenberg, M. T., Weissberg, R. P., O'Brien, M. U., Zins, J. E., Fredericks, L., Resnik, H., & Elias, M. J. (2003). School-based prevention: promoting positive social development through social and emotional learning. *American Psychologist, 58*(6/7), 466–474.

Greene, J. P., & Forster, G. (2002). *Effects of funding incentives on special education enrollment.* Manhattan Institute for Policy Research. Available at http://www.manhattan-institute .org/html/cr_32.htm

Guarino, C., Santibanez, L., Daley, G., & Brewer, D. (2004). A review of the research literature on teacher recruitment and retention. Prepared by RAND for the Education Commission of the States. Santa Monica, CA: RAND. Retrieved July 17, 2008, from http://rand.org/pubs/technical_reports/TR164/index.html

Hanushek, E. A., Kain, J. F., & Rivkin, S. G. (2001). *Why public schools lose teachers.* Cambridge, MA: National Bureau of Economic Research.

Hardiman, P. M., Curcio, J. L., & Fortune, J. C. (1998). School-linked services. *The American School Board Journal, 185,* 37–40.

Hargreaves, A. (1994). *Changing teachers, changing times: Teachers' work and culture in the postmodern age.* New York: Teachers College Press.

Hargreaves, A., & Fink, D. (2000). The three dimensions of reform. *Educational Leadership, 57,* 30–34.

Hawkins, J. D., Kosterman, R., Catalano, R. F., Hill, K. G., & Abbott, R. D. (2008). Effects of social development intervention in childhood 15 years later. *Archives of Pediatric Adolescent Medicine, 162,* 1133–1141.

Henderson, A. T., & Mapp, K. L. (2002). *A new wave of evidence: The impact of school, family, and community connections on student achievement.* Austin, TX: Southwest Educational Development Laboratory, National Center for Family & Community Connections with Schools.

Hess, F. (2008). Data: Now what? *Educational Leadership, 66.* Special Issue. Available at http://www.ascd.org

Hobbs, N. (1975). *The futures of children.* San Francisco: Jossey-Bass.

Hodgkinson, H. (2008). *Demographic trends and the federal role in education.* Paper commissioned by the Center on Education Policy. Washington, DC. Available at http://www.cep-dc.org/_data/n_0001/resources/live/RethinkingFederalRole/Demographic.pdf

Hoffman, D. M. (2009). Reflecting on social emotional learning: A critical perspective on trends in the United States. *Review of Educational Research, 79,* 533–556.

Holt, J. (1989). *Learning all the time.* Reading, MA: Da Capo Press.

Hyman, I., Flanagan, D., & Smith, K. (1982). Discipline in the schools. In C. R. Reynolds & T. B. Gutkin (Eds.), *The handbook of school psychology* (pp. 454–480). New York: Wiley.

IDEA Partnership. (2005). *Overview 2005—Shared agenda: A cross-state community of practice on school behavioral health.* Alexandria, VA: National Association of State Directors of Special Education. Retrieved from http://www.ideainfo.org

Institute of Medicine. (1994). *Reducing risks for mental disorders: Frontiers for preventive intervention research.* Washington, DC: National Academy of Sciences.

Jané-Llopis, E., & Barry, M. M. (2005). What makes mental health promotion effective? *Promotion and Education,* Supplement 2, 47–55.

Keynes, J. M. (1997). *The general theory of employment, interest, and money.* Amherst, NY: Prometheus Books.

Knitzer, J., Steinberg, Z., & Fleisch, B. (1990). *At the schoolhouse door: An examination of programs and policies for children with behavioral and emotional problems.* New York: Bank Street College of Education.

Knoff, H. M. (1987). School-based interventions for discipline problems. In C. A. Maher & J. E. Zins (Eds.), *Psychoeducational interventions in the schools* (pp. 118–140). New York: Pergamon.

Kohn, A. (1999). Constant frustration and occasional violence. The legacy of American high schools. *American School Board Journal.* Available at http://www.alfiekohn.org/teaching/cfaov.htm

Kutash, K., Duchnowski, A. J., & Lynn, N. (2006). *School-based mental health: An empirical guide for decision-makers.* Tampa: University of South Florida. Available at http://rtckids.fmhi.usf.edu/rtcpubs/study04/index.htm

Lambert, N. M., Bower, E. M., Caplan, G., et al. (1964). *The protection and promotion of mental health in the schools.* Washington, DC: U.S. Government Printing Office.

Leiter, M. P., & Maslach, C. (2000). *Preventing burnout and building engagement: A complete program for organizational renewal.* San Francisco: Jossey-Bass.

Leiter, M. P., & Maslach, C. (2005). *Banishing burnout: Six strategies for improving your relationship with work.* San Francisco: Jossey-Bass.

Lopez, M. E. (2003). *Transforming schools through community organizing: A research review.* Cambridge, MA: Harvard Family Research Project. Retrieved July 1, 2007, from http://www.gse.harvard.edu/hfrp/projects/fine/resources/research/lopez.html

Lyon, G. R. (2002). *Testimony before the subcommittee on educational reform.* U.S. Senate.

Mahony, P., & Hextall, I. (2000). *Reconstructing teaching: Standards, performance, and accountability.* New York: Routledge Falmer.

Martinez, R. S., & Nellis, L. M. (2008). Response to intervention: A school-wide approach for promoting academic wellness for all students. In B. Doll & J. A. Cummings (Eds.), *Transforming school mental health services.* Thousand Oaks, CA: Corwin.

Marx, E., & Wooley, S. with Northrop, D. (Eds.). (1998). *Health is academic: A guide to coordinated school health programs.* New York: Teachers College Press.

Maser, J. D., Norman, S. B., Zisook, S., Everall, I. P., Stein, M. B., Schettler, P. J., & Judd, L. L. (2009). Psychiatric nosology is ready for a paradigm shift in DSM-V. *Clinical Psychology: Science and Practice, 16,* 24–40.

Maslach, C., Schaufeli, W. B., & Leiter, M. P. (2001). Job burnout. *Annual Review of Psychology, 52,* 397–422.

Mason, J., Benjamin, M. P., & Lewis, S. A. (1996). The cultural competence model. In C. A. Heflinger & C. T. Nixon (Eds.), *Families and the mental health system for children and adolescence.* Thousand Oaks, CA: Sage.

Mazza, J. J., & Reynolds, W. M. (2008). Schoolwide approaches to prevention and intervention of depression and suicidal behaviors. In B. Doll & J. A. Cummings (Eds.), *Transforming school mental health services.* Thousand Oaks, CA: Corwin.

Melaville, A., & Blank, M. J. (1998). *Learning together: The developing field of school-community initiatives.* Flint, MI: Mott Foundation.

Merrill, K. W., Gueldner, B. A., & Tran, O. K. (2008). Social and emotional learning: A schoolwide approach to intervention for socialization, friendship problems, and more. In B. Doll & J. A. Cummings (Eds.), *Transforming school mental health services.* Thousand Oaks, CA: Corwin.

Merseth, K. K. (1999). *The case for cases in teacher education.* Washington, DC: American Association of Colleges for Teacher Education.

Millstein, S. (1988). *The potential of school-linked centers to promote adolescent health and development.* Washington, DC: Carnegie Council on Adolescent Development.

Monk, D. H., Pijanowski, J. C., & Hussain, S. (1997). How and where the education dollar is spent. *The Future of Children, 7,* 51–62.

Moos, R. H. (1979). *Evaluating educational environments.* San Francisco: Jossey-Bass.

National Association of State Mental Health Program Directors and the Policymaker Partnership for Implementing IDEA at the National Association of State Directors of Special Education. (2002). *Mental health, schools and families working together for all children and youth: Toward a shared agenda.* Available at http://www.nasdse.org/sharedagenda.pdf

National Center for Educational Statistics. (2008). *Revenues and expenditures for public elementary and secondary education school year 2005–06 (Fiscal Year 2006).* Washington, DC: Institute of Education Sciences (IES). Available at http://nces.ed.gov/pubs2008/expenditures/index.asp

National Center for Education in Maternal and Child Health. (2002). *Bright futures in practice: Mental health.* Arlington, VA: Author. Available at http://www.brightfutures.org/mentalhealth/

National Coalition of Advocates for Students. (2000). *Capacity building for Southeast Asian family-school partnerships.* Harvard Family Research Project. Available at http://www.hfrp.org

National Commission on Teaching and America's Future. (2007). *High teacher turnover drains school and district resources.* Washington, DC: Author. Available at http://www.nctaf.org/resources/demonstration_projects/turnover/TeacherTurnoverCostStudy.htm

National Comprehensive Center for Teacher Quality. (2007). *America's challenge: Effective teachers for at-risk schools and students.* Washington, DC: Author. Retrieved July 17, 2008, at http://www.tqsource.org/publications/NCCTQBiennialReport.php

National Implementation Research Network. (2009). Web site at the Frank Porter Graham Child Development Institute at the University of North Carolina at Chapel Hill. Available at http://www.fpg.unc.edu/~nirn/

National Institute of Mental Health. (1993). *The prevention of mental disorders: A national research agenda.* Bethesda, MD: Author.

National Institute of Mental Health. (1998). *Priorities for prevention research.* NIH Publication No. 98–4321. Bethesda, MD: Author.

National Research Council and the Institute of Medicine. (2004). *Engaging schools: Fostering high school students' motivation to learn.* Washington, DC: National Academies Press.

Neville, K. S., Sherman, R. H., & Cohen, C. E. (2005). *Preparing and training professionals: Comparing education to six other fields.* Washington, DC: The Finance Project. Retrieved July 17, 2008, from http://www.financeproject.org/Publications/preparingprofessionals.pdf

O'Connell, M. E., Boat, T., & Warner, K. (Eds.). (2009). *Preventing mental, emotional, and behavioral disorders among young people: Progress and possibilities.* Washington, DC: National Academies Press.

Payne, C. M. (2008). *So much reform, so little change: The persistence of failure of urban schools.* Cambridge, MA: Harvard Education Press.

Payton, J., Weissberg, R. P., Durlak, J. A., Dymnicki, A. B., Taylor, R. D., Schellinger, K. B., & Pachan, M. (2008). *The positive impact of social and emotional learning for kindergarten to eighth-grade students: Findings from three scientific reviews.* Chicago: Collaborative for Academic, Social, and Emotional Learning.

Peth-Pierce, R. (Ed.). (2000). *A good beginning: Sending America's children to school with the social and emotional competence they need to succeed.* Bethesda, MD: The Child Mental Health Foundations and Agencies Network.

Policy Leadership Cadre for Mental Health in Schools. (2001). *Mental health in schools: Guidelines, models, resources, & policy considerations.* Los Angeles: Center for Mental Health in Schools at UCLA. Available at http://smhp.psych.ucla.edu/pdfdocs/policymakers/cadreguidelines.pdf

Power, T. J., DuPaul, G. J., Shapiro, E. S., & Kazak, A. E. (2003). *Promoting children's health: Integrating school, family, and community.* New York: Guilford Press.

President's New Freedom Commission on Mental Health. (2003). *Final report to the president.* Washington, DC: Author. Available at http://www.mentalhealthcommission.gov/reports/reports.htm

President's New Freedom Initiative. (2007). *The 2007 progress report.* Washington, DC: White House. Available at http://www.mentalhealthcommission.gov/reports/reports.htm

Price, R. H. (1997). In praise of a cumulative prevention science. *American Journal of Community Psychology, 25*(2), 169–176.

Pynoos, R., & Nader, L. (1988). Psychological first aid and treatment approach to children exposed to community violence. *Journal of Traumatic Stress, 1,* 445–473.

Rappaport, N., Osher, D., Garrison, E., Anderson-Ketchmark, C., & Dwyer, K. (2003). Enhancing collaboration within and across disciplines to advance mental health programs in schools. In M. D. Weist, S. W. Evans, & N. A. Lever (Eds.), *Handbook of school mental health: Advancing practice and research.* New York: Kluwer Academic/Plenum Publishers.

Reyes, P., Scribner, J. D., & Scribner, A. P. (Eds.). (1999). *Lessons from high-performing Hispanic schools: Creating learning communities.* New York: Teachers College Press.

Riger, S. (1993). What's wrong with empowerment. *American Journal of Community Psychology, 21,* 278–292.

Romer, D., & McIntosh, M. (2005). The roles and perspectives of school mental health professionals in promoting adolescent mental health. In D. L. Evans, E. B. Foa, R. E. Gur, H. Hendin, C. P. O'Brien, M. E. P. Seligman, & T. B. Walsh (Eds.), *Treating and preventing adolescent mental health disorders.* New York: Oxford University Press.

Rossi, P. H., & Freeman, H. E. (1989). *Evaluation: A systematic approach* (4th ed.). Newbury Park, CA: Sage.

Rossi, P. H., Freeman, H. E., & Wright, S. (1979). *Evaluation: A systemaric approach* (4th ed.). Beverly Hills, CA: Sage.

Samuels, C. (2008, January 23). Response to intervention sparks interest, questions. *Education Week.* Available at http://www.edweek.org/ew/articles/2008/01/23/20rtireact.h27.html

Sarason, S. B. (1971). *The culture of school and the problem of change.* Boston: Allyn & Bacon. (This book was updated in 1996 as *Revisiting "the culture of school and the problem of change."* New York: Teachers College Press.)

Scales, P. C., & Leffert, N. (1999). *Developmental assets.* Minneapolis, MN: Search Institute.

Schorr, L. B. (1997). *Common purpose: Strengthening families and neighborhoods to rebuild America.* New York: Anchor Press.

Section 504 of the 1973 Rehabilitation Act. (1993, September 26). Public Law 93–112, 93rd Congress, H.R. 8070. Available at www.dotcr.ost.dot.gov/Documents/ycr/REHABACT.HTM

Simpson, G. A., Cohen, R. A., Pastor, P. N., & Reuben, C. A. (2006). *U.S. children 4–17 years of age who received treatment for emotional or behavioral difficulties: Preliminary data from the 2005 National Health Interview Survey.* Health E-stats. National Center for Health Statistics.

Smith, P. L., & Moss, S. B. (2009). Psychologist impairment: What is it, how can it be prevented, and what can be done to address it? *Clinical Psychology: Science and Practice, 16,* 1–15.

Southwest Educational Development Laboratory. (2001). *Emerging issues in school, family, & community connections: Annual synthesis.* Austin, TX: Author.

Sprague, J. (2006). RTI and positive behavior support. *The Special Edge, 19,* 11–13.

Stake, R. E. (1967). The countenance of educational evaluation. *Teachers College Record, 68,* 523–540.

Stake, R. E. (1976). *Evaluating educational programs: The need and the response.* Paris: Organization for Economic Cooperation and Development.

Steiner, G. (1976). *The children's cause.* Washington, DC: Brookings Institution.

Stewart-Brown, S. (2006). *What is the evidence on school health promotion in improving health or preventing disease and specifically, what is the effectiveness of the health promoting schools approach?* WHO Regional Office for Europe's Health Evidence Network. Health Evidence Network Report. Available at www.euro.who.int/document/e88185.pdf

Stroul, B. A., & Friedman, R. M. (1986). *A system of care for seriously emotionally disturbed children and youth.* Washington, DC: Georgetown University Child Development Center.

Substance Abuse and Mental Health Services Administration, Office of Applied Studies. (2008, September 25). *Mental health service use among youths aged 12 to 17: 2005 and 2006.* Rockville, MD: Author.

Swearer, S. M., Espelage, D. L., Loe, K. B., & Kingsbury, W. (2008). Schoolwide approaches to intervention for school aggression and bullying. In B. Doll & J. A. Cummings (Eds.), *Transforming school mental health services.* Thousand Oaks, CA: Corwin.

Taylor, L., & Adelman, H. S. (1996). Mental health in the schools: Promising directions for practice. *Adolescent Medicine: State of the Art Reviews, 7,* 303–317.

Taylor, L., & Adelman, H. S. (1999). Personalizing classroom instruction to account for motivational and developmental differences. *Reading & Writing Quarterly, 15,* 255–276.

Taylor, L., & Adelman, H. S. (2000). Toward ending the marginalization of mental health in schools. *Journal of School Health, 70,* 210–215.

Taylor, L., & Adelman, H. S. (2002). Lessons learned from working with a district's mental health unit. *Childhood Education, 78,* 295–300.

Taylor, L., & Adelman, H. S. (2004). Advancing mental health in schools: Guiding frameworks and strategic approaches. In K. Robinson (Ed.), *Advances in school-based mental health.* Kingston, NJ: Civic Research Institute, Inc.

Taylor, L., Nelson, P., & Adelman, H. S. (1999). Scaling-up reforms across a school district. *Reading & Writing Quarterly, 15,* 303–326.

Teich, J. L., Robinson, G., & Weist, M. D. (2007). What kinds of mental health services do public schools in the United States provide. *Advances in School Mental Health Promotion, 1,* 13–20.

Thomas, R. M. (2002). *Overcoming inertia in school reform: How to successfully implement change.* Thousand Oaks, CA: Corwin.

Trickett, E. J. (2002). Context, culture, and collaboration in AIDS interventions: Ecological ideas for enhancing community impact. *The Journal of Primary Prevention, 23,* 157–174.

Tyack, D. (1992). Health and social services in public schools: Historical perspectives. *The Future of Children, 2,* 19–31.

U.S. Department of Education, Office of Special Education and Rehabilitative Services, Office of Special Education Programs. (2005). *Twenty-fifth annual (2003) report to Congress on the implementation of the Individuals with Disabilities Education Act* (Vol. 1), Washington, DC.

U.S. Department of Health and Human Services. (1994). *A guide to enhancing the cultural competence of runaway and homeless youth programs,* Washington, DC: Administration for Children and Families, Administration on Children, Youth, and Families, Families and Youth Services Bureau.

U.S. Department of Health and Human Services. (1999). *Mental health: A report of the surgeon general—Executive summary.* Rockville, MD: U.S. Department of Health and Human Services, Substance Abuse and Mental Health Services Administration, Center for Mental Health Services, National Institutes of Health, National Institute of Mental Health.

U.S. Department of Health and Human Services. (2001). *Report of the surgeon general's conference on children's mental health: A national action agenda.* Washington, DC: Author. Available at http://www.surgeongeneral.gov/cmh/childreport.htm

Vandenberghe, R., & Huberman, A. M. (Eds.). (1999). *Understanding and preventing teacher burnout: A sourcebook of international research and practice.* New York: Cambridge University Press.

Vander Ark, T. (2002). The case for small schools. *Educational Leadership, 59,* 55–59.

Vansteenkiste, M., Lens, W., & Deci, E. (2006). Intrinsic versus extrinsic goal contents in Self-Determination Theory: Another look at the quality of academic motivation. *Educational Psychologist, 4,* 19–31.

Warren, M. R. (2005). Communities and schools: A new view of urban education reform. *Harvard Educational Review, 75,* 133–173.

Weare, K. (2000). *Promoting mental, emotional, and social health: A whole-school approach.* London: Routledge.

Weist, M. D., & Murray, M. (2007). Advancing school mental health globally. *Advances in School Mental Health Promotion, 1,* 2–12.

Wentzel, K. R., & Wigfield, A. (2007). Motivational interventions that work: Themes and remaining issues. *Educational Psychologist, 42,* 261–271.

Whitley, D. M., White, K. R., Kelly, S. J., & Yorke, B. (1999). Strengths-based case management: The application to grandparents raising grandchildren. *Families in Society, 80,* 110–119.

Willis, S., & Mann, L. (2000, Winter). Differentiating instruction: Finding manageable ways to meet individual needs. *Curriculum Update.* Retrieved August 21, 2009, from http://www.ascd.org/publications/curriculum_update/winter2000/Differentiating_Instruction.aspx

Winter, G. (2003, May 17). Study finds no sign that testing deters students' drug use. *New York Times.* Available at http://www.nytimes.com/2003/05/17/national/17DRUG.html?pagewanted=print

Wolfgang, C. H., & Glickman, C. D. (1986). *Solving discipline problems: Strategies for classroom teachers* (2nd ed.). Boston: Allyn & Bacon.

Wolraich, M, L., Felice, M. E., & Drotar, D. (Eds.). (1996). *The classification of child and adolescent mental diagnoses in primary care: Diagnostic and statistical manual for primary care (DSM-PC). Child and adolescent version.* Elk Grove Village, IL: American Academy of Pediatrics.

World Health Organization. (2004). *Promoting mental health: Concepts, emerging evidence, practice: Summary report.* Geneva: Author, in collaboration with the Victorian Health Promotion Foundation and the University of Melbourne.

Index